P9-EDY-555

THE BOOK OF CATHOLIC PRAYER

THE BOOK OF CATHOLIC PRAYER

Prayers for Every Day and All Occasions

COMPILED BY SEÁN FINNEGAN

Loyola Press

Chicago

Loyola Press

3441 North Ashland Avenue
Chicago, Illinois 60657

Published in 2000 by Loyola Press
© 1998 Seán Finnegan
All rights reserved

First published in 1998 by the Canterbury Press Norwich

Interior design by Rose Design, Carol Sawyer

**Library of Congress
Cataloging-in-Publication Data**

The book of Catholic prayer : prayers for every day and all occasions / compiled by Seán Finnegan. — 1st Loyola Press ed.

     p.   cm.

    Includes bibliographical references and index.

    ISBN 0-8294-1386-3 (hardcover)

    1. Catholic Church Prayer-books and devotions—English.

  I. Finnegan, Sean.

  BX2130.B66 2000

  242'.802—dc21   99-31670

                                    CIP

Printed in the United States of America
00 01 02 03 04 / 10 9 8 7 6 5 4 3 2 1

For my parents, Nancy and Brendan Finnegan,
who taught me to pray

CONTENTS

PRAYERS FOR PARTICULAR NEEDS

DEVOTIONS

Each of the four main sections of *The Book of Catholic Prayer* begins with a detailed table of contents. Consult those tables and the indexes for help in finding specific prayers and prayers for specific occasions.

INTRODUCING CATHOLIC PRAYER

I am convinced that the important thing is not *how* one prays but *that* one prays. Prayer is not the acquisition of a technique. Prayer is above all an exercise of the will, not something to talk about, but something to do. Prayer is also fundamentally simple. One of my mentors in the spiritual life had a saying: "Pray as you can, not as you can't." The lesson seems obvious, yet how many devout people feel that they aren't really praying until they have reached some form of transforming union or ecstasy?

This book is put together by someone perfectly willing to admit that he hasn't got the key to rapture in prayer. I, too, get distracted and sometimes bored when I sit or kneel in church. But I am also utterly convinced of the transforming power of prayer and of the vitally important role that it plays in the daily life of a Christian. In prayer, simplicity is the thing, together with honesty. We pray simply because God is God, and to relate to God is the highest function, glory, and ultimate destiny of any human being. We pray to adore, praise, and thank him, to apologize for our shortcomings, and to ask him to fulfill our needs and those of our neighbors. In these acts the Christian truly becomes the priest, and since prayer is not the practice of a technique, what form a prayer takes is not so important. Neither is enjoyment very important.

Enjoyment may help prayer along and encourage us to pray more often, but it must not be confused with the prayer itself.

The challenge of prayer is to pray in a way that involves the three faculties of the soul—memory, understanding, and will. It is with these faculties that we relate to God, because it is the soul that bears the closest resemblance to God.

One of the best ways of doing this is the use of vocal prayer. Engaging in vocal prayer means following a text—whether read or memorized—making it our own, and using it to focus our devotion. Praying in this way involves all our mental faculties and a few of our physical ones too. I am a great enthusiast for the Christian who "merely" wants to say his or her prayers. Vocal prayer is a far surer path to God than any direct attempt to be a second St. John of the Cross, because vocal prayer involves the crucial virtue of humility. If you want more authority than mine for the transforming power of vocal prayer, look at what St. Teresa of Avila had to say on the subject (you'll find her comments on page 264). Contemplative prayer is the work of God, and nothing we do can bring it on, other than living a holy life, saying our prayers, and being faithful. Leave progress in the hands of the Holy Spirit, the best of all teachers.

I have designed this book to help Christians pray as they can, not as they can't. It is a book to assist you in vocal prayer.

The first part is a Psalter that is loosely based on the form of the Liturgy of the Hours. I have laid out prayers and psalms for a potential day of seven hours, or prayer sessions, on the principle of the psalmist's pledge "Seven times a day will I praise you, O Lord" and following the custom of the Church. Please read "Praying the Psalter" for more information about how the Psalter is put together and how you can adapt it for use in your own particular circumstances.

The second half of this book speaks for itself. I have attempted to assemble a collection of prayers—prayers not necessarily written by Catholics—that Catholics may find useful. The collection as a whole is intended to reflect six hundred fruitful years of vernacular prayers in English. You will find many new prayers and many old ones, especially some of the classics that I want to preserve for another generation's use. Likewise, I have translated some prayers from the Latin that formerly were accessible only to clerics. Use these prayers in the way you find most helpful, either on your own or in groups.

I must add a word about the translations used in this book. I gave some consideration to using a familiar translation of the Scriptures, especially of the Psalms, but then felt that there was an advantage to be gained by using a less familiar one. Since I was aiming for a classical flavor, I gently updated the Douai-Challoner translation. I strove to retain the flavor of the original, which has formed the spirituality of so many generations of English-speaking Catholics, but render it accessible to the modern reader.

These days, some thought must be given to the use of inclusive language. After consultation with the publishers and those who are more experienced than I in these matters, the decision was made not to tamper with existing texts, which would in some cases amount to cultural vandalism. In newly composed texts, I have used inclusive language when referring to humanity, while adhering to traditional masculine pronouns for the Deity.

Finally, I would like to thank the many people who have made this publication possible. To the fathers and brothers of the Oratories in Oxford and London; to Walter Hooper, who so persistently encouraged me to produce this book; to Mhairi Ellis, Brian Brindley, and especially the Reverend William Perry, who each labored generously to prevent many a howler from reaching your eyes. If any remain, it must be my own fault. Also to Christine Smith, for her encouragement, and to Fr. Graham Leonard, who gave me much good advice—all of which I have taken. I would like to thank those who helped me in the collection of material: Sr. Brigid O'Brien (sadly recently deceased), Fr. Jerome Bertram, Fr. Dominic Jacob, Fr. Nicholas Kearney, Peter Ward, Richard and Lepel Kornicki and family, Iestyn Evans, and my own family, from whom I first learned whatever I know of the grace of prayer.

PRAYING THE PSALTER

Christians have prayed a cycle of fixed daily prayers ever since the first followers of Christ gathered together in Jerusalem to begin and end each day with prayers of praise, thanksgiving, and intercession. Early in the life of the Church, psalms, hymns, Scripture readings, and other prayers were gathered together into a pattern that became known as the Liturgy of the Hours. For many centuries this method of prayer was followed primarily by monastic communities and ordained clergy. But the Liturgy of the Hours has always been the prayer of the Church—the whole Church—and in recent years great numbers of laypeople have been praying this prayer as well.

The first part of *The Book of Catholic Prayer* is for lay Christians who seek a flexible, contemporary pattern of daily prayer. It is an adaptation of the traditional prayer of the Church—a way to praise God, sanctify the day, and make intercession in a fashion suited to the circumstances of busy people with a full schedule of responsibilities at work, in their homes, and in their communities.

An important purpose of the Liturgy of the Hours is to "pray without ceasing," as Paul put it in 1 Thessalonians. It permeates the day with prayer by calling Christians to pause and pray at seven specified times each day. These are the "hours" that give the Liturgy of the Hours its name. The two principal hours are morning prayer *(lauds)* and evening prayer *(vespers)*. The others are *terce, sext,* and *none* during the working day; *compline,* upon retiring to bed; and *vigils,* or *matins,* traditionally prayed in the early hours of the morning. These prayers link the natural rhythm of the day to the paschal mystery of Christ. The sun appears at dawn, rises in the sky, sets, and disappears; we rise from our beds, work, and rest. We pray throughout this daily cycle, lifting our thoughts to God, praising him for his goodness and mercy, interceding for our needs, and joining our prayers to those of countless other Christians throughout the world who seek to follow Christ.

WHAT THE HOURS MEAN

The Psalter in this book is a shortened and simplified version of the Liturgy of the Hours, but it preserves the traditional character of each hour. At the heart of every hour lie the psalms. In some versions of the Liturgy of the Hours, the entire Psalter of 150 psalms is prayed over the course of one or three weeks. This book's version includes a much smaller selection of psalms, but psalms are still prayed at every hour. Indeed, this version of the Church's daily prayer is called the Psalter, reflecting the importance of the psalms in daily worship.

The hours also include canticles from the Old and New Testaments, readings from Scripture, times for spiritual reading, and intercessions. Certain canticles and themes are associated with certain hours and certain days of the week. The following is an explanation of what the hours mean and how the compiler adapted traditional themes and reflections in this Psalter:

Vigils. Traditionally called matins, these prayers were said during the night. Since the reform of the liturgy in 1971, vigils can be prayed at any time during the day, although some monastic communities still gather to pray it in the predawn hours. Vigils consists of a call to prayer, a psalm, and two readings: one from Scripture and another from a spiritual book. The theme of vigils is watchfulness and expectant hope, in anticipation of the dawn.

Lauds. The morning prayer, marking the beginning of the new day, is the first of the two principal hours of the Liturgy of the Hours. The other is vespers, the evening prayer. Lauds, from the Latin word for "praise," rejoices in the new day and recalls the resurrection of Jesus, the true Light, who comes with the dawn. It opens with a call to prayer and a hymn and includes a psalm, a reading, intercessions, and the Lord's Prayer. At the center of each day's lauds is the canticle of Zechariah (Luke 1:68–79), Zechariah's great hymn of praise upon the birth of his son, John the Baptist.

Terce. From the Latin word for "three," terce is traditionally said at the third hour after sunrise, or about 9 A.M. if sunrise is at 6 A.M. Terce, also known as midmorning prayer, consists of a hymn to the Holy Spirit, a psalm, a short reading, and a prayer. Terce, along with the other daytime prayers sext and none, has traditionally been associated with meditation on Christ's passion.

Sext. From the Latin for "six," sext is prayed at the sixth hour of the day, or around noon. Also known as midday prayer, sext consists of a short hymn, a psalm, a reading, and a prayer.

None. From the Latin for "nine," none is prayed at the ninth hour, or around 3 P.M. Also known as midafternoon prayer, none consists of a short hymn, a psalm, a reading, and a prayer.

Vespers. The evening prayer is one of the two principal hours of the Church's daily prayer. The heart of vespers is the Magnificat (Luke 1:46–55), prayed by Mary after she was greeted by her cousin Elizabeth. Vespers opens with a hymn and a psalm and includes a Scripture reading and intercessions.

Compline. The Liturgy of the Hours is concluded with compline, which is said upon retiring for the night. It begins with an examination of conscience, includes a psalm and a reading, and concludes with an antiphon in honor of Mary. Compline also includes the Nunc Dimittis, Simeon's canticle of thanksgiving upon seeing Jesus in the temple (Luke 2:29–32).

DAYS OF THE WEEK AND THE CHURCH CALENDAR

Special themes for meditation and prayer are associated with several days of the week. Monday is a day of prayer for the afflicted, Thursday is a day of reflection on the sacraments, Friday commemorates Jesus' passion and death, and Saturday is a day of honor for Mary. It is also customary to pray the Saturday hours on many feasts of Mary and the Sunday hours on other solemn feasts.

Two special sets of hours—an Office of the Dead and an Office of Saints—are substituted for the ordinary hours on particular days and feasts. Pray the Office of the Dead on All Souls' Day, on the anniversary of a loved one's death, or at other times when it is appropriate. Pray the Office of Saints on the feasts of great saints and your own favorite saints.

Consult the calendar of saints beginning on page xxi for these substitutions. The calendar also lists popular saints' feast days. You may use the calendar to remember favorite saints, deceased loved ones, and other anniversary dates you wish to note in your daily prayer.

HOW TO USE THE PSALTER

Use this book as you want to. The daily prayer in the Psalter is based on the traditional Liturgy of the Hours, but I have deliberately avoided making it an official prayer of the Church. The purpose of this book is to give you a resource to help you speak to your Creator, to help you find words to express your prayer. Words are, after all, the key to human meaning.

I have organized prayers and psalms for a day of seven hours, but I do not imagine that many people have the leisure to interrupt their day seven times. Some may; for instance, the sick and housebound or those who work at home in their own time may wish to celebrate the entire Psalter. Others may wish simply to keep the hours nearest to whenever they have time to pray, uniting themselves in spirit with those keeping the liturgical hours at that time. In this way, the round of the day itself is sanctified.

Some, wishing to establish a routine each day, may find the unchanging hours each week a little arid. They should not feel constrained to follow the form I have provided but, for example, should instead use the psalm from one of the offices that do not form part of their routine. Or they could interchange offices, praying vigils one week and lauds the next or circulating the three midday offices of terce, sext, and none through three weeks.

In other words, because this is not an official prayer book of the Church, feel free to modify it as you see fit.

A few modifications may be especially desirable. The intercessions given, for instance, would be much better replaced with prayers that have a particular relevance for you, the one who is praying. Use this opportunity to intercede for members of your family or for matters that occupy your concern.

The hours may be prayed individually or in groups. Both these traditions have a lively and long history in the Church. The life of many monastic communities is patterned on the regular observance of all seven hours, but individual Christians have long prayed the hours in the form of the breviary or Divine Office. You might mix the communal and individual approaches, praying some hours privately and others—especially morning and evening prayer (lauds and vespers)—with your spouse, family, companions, or coworkers.

The hours are opened and closed by a call and response. The call is typically read by the person leading the prayer; the response is read together by others in the group. If you are praying the hours alone, you may read both the call and response yourself.

The sign ☩ signifies a sign of the cross, made customarily at the start of each hour and at the beginning of the Gospel canticles: the Benedictus at lauds, the Magnificat at vespers, and the Nunc Dimittis at compline. It is customary to stand while reciting these canticles.

SCRIPTURE AND SPIRITUAL READINGS

Spiritual reading is often considered the food of the spiritual life, essential for any Christian who wishes to make progress in prayer. Hence, I have provided in the hour of vigils an opportunity, modeled on the Office of Readings in the official Liturgy of the Hours, for you to benefit from this practice. Concerning what you might read, pride of place must, of course, go to the Scriptures. It is quite easy to obtain schemata, and even whole printed Bibles, laid out in such a way as to cover the entire Bible during the course of a year. Alternatively, you might consider simply reading one book of the Bible at a time. I would not advise reading the Bible directly from Genesis to Revelation; most people who try this seem to get bogged down in Leviticus and Deuteronomy! I recommend reading a Gospel, then an Old Testament book, then a letter from the New Testament, and so forth.

Spiritual reading is not so easy to define. You may ask what you should read. I recommend that you read a page or two of any spiritual book that helps you in your devotion. For preference, read the classics. I have provided a list of books that ought to be easily obtained from a bookstore (see pp. 595–96).

When reading, if something strikes you, don't think you have to struggle on to the end. Pause and consider. Also, if you have time, close your eyes for five minutes after each reading and reflect on what you have read before saying the response.

CALENDAR OF SAINTS

You can use this calendar in deciding which office to say. Days of particular importance are marked in bold type. On those days it is especially recommended that you use the office indicated. Saints that have particular relevance to you—for instance, patrons of your country, diocese, or town—could be honored with a special office. Other saints could be commemorated simply by using the collect in their honor from your daily missal or by adding the collect prayer from the ends of the Office of Saints to the end of the normal daily office. If any of the saints pique your curiosity, there are several good dictionaries of saints available that you can consult. You may also wish to write in the margin of this calendar the anniversaries of your deceased friends and family, a reminder to offer the Office of the Dead on those occasions.

JANUARY

1. **Mary, Mother of God** *Saturday Office*
2. Sts. Basil and Gregory
3.
4. St. Elizabeth Ann Seton (U.S.)
5. St. John Neumann (U.S.)
6. **The Epiphany of the Lord** *Sunday Office*
7. St. Raymond of Peñafort
8.
9.
10.
11.
12.

13. St. Hilary of Poitiers also St. Kentigern (Scotland)
14.
15.
16.
17. St. Anthony of Egypt
18.
19.
20. Sts. Fabian and Sebastian
21. St. Agnes
22. St. Vincent
23.
24. St. Francis de Sales
25. **The Conversion of St. Paul** *Office of Saints*
26. Sts. Timothy and Titus
27. St. Angela Merici
28. St. Thomas Aquinas
29.
30.
31. St. John Bosco

FEBRUARY
1. St. Brigid (Ireland)
2. **The Presentation** *Sunday Office*
3. St. Blaise also St. Ansgar
4.
5. St. Agatha
6. St. Paul Miki and companions
7.
8. St. Jerome Emiliani
9.
10. St. Scholastica
11. Our Lady of Lourdes *Saturday Office if desired*
12.
13.

14. Sts. Cyril and Methodius
15.
16.
17. Seven Founders of the Order of Servites
18.
19.
20.
21. St. Peter Damian
22. **The Chair of St. Peter** *Office of Saints*
23. St. Polycarp
24.
25.
26.
27.
28.
(29.)

MARCH
1. St. David (Wales) *Office of Saints*
2.
3.
4. St. Casimir
5.
6.
7. Sts. Perpetua and Felicity
8. St. John of God
9. St. Frances of Rome
10. St. John Ogilvie (Scotland)
11.
12.
13.
14.
15.
16.

17. St. Patrick (Ireland) *Office of Saints*
18. St. Cyril of Jerusalem
19. **St. Joseph** *Office of Saints*
20.
21.
22.
23. St. Turibius of Mogrovejo
24.
25. **The Annunciation** *Sunday Office*
26.
27.
28.
29.
30.
31.

APRIL

1.
2. St. Francis of Paola
3.
4. St. Isidore of Seville
5. St. Vincent Ferrer
6.
7. St. John Baptist de la Salle
8.
9.
10.
11. St. Stanislaus
12.
13. St. Martin I
14.
15.
16.
17.

18.
19.
20.
21. St. Anselm
22.
23. St. George (England) *Office of Saints*
24. St. Fidelis of Sigmaringen
25. **St. Mark** *Office of Saints*
26.
27.
28. St. Peter Chanel
29. St. Catherine of Siena
30. St. Pius V

MAY

1. Feast of St. Joseph the Worker
2. St. Athanasius
3. **Sts. Philip and James** *Office of Saints*
4.
5.
6.
7.
8.
9.
10.
11.
12. Sts. Nereus and Achilleus also St. Pancras
13.
14. **St. Matthias** *Office of Saints*
15. St. Isidore the Farmer
16.
17.
18. St. John I
19.

20. St. Bernadine of Siena
21.
22.
23.
24. Our Lady Help of Christians (Australia)
    Saturday Office
25. St. Bede the Venerable also St. Gregory VII
26. St. Philip Neri
27. St. Augustine of Canterbury (England) *Office of Saints*
28.
29.
30.
31. **The Visitation of the Blessed Virgin Mary**
    Saturday Office

JUNE

1. St. Justin
2. Sts. Marcellinus and Peter
3. St. Charles Lwanga and companions
4.
5. St. Boniface
6. St. Norbert
7.
8.
9. St. Ephraem of Syria also St. Columba
10.
11. St. Barnabas
12.
13. St. Anthony of Padua
14.
15.
16.
17.

18.
19. St. Romuald
20. St. Alban (England) *Office of Saints*
21. St. Aloysius Gonzaga
22. Sts. John Fisher and Thomas More (England) *Office of Saints* also St. Paulinus of Nola
23.
24. **The Birth of St. John the Baptist** *Office of Saints*
25.
26.
27. St. Cyril of Alexandria
28. St. Irenaeus
29. **Sts. Peter and Paul** *Office of Saints*
30. First martyrs of Rome

JULY
1. St. Oliver Plunket (Ireland)
2.
3. **St. Thomas** *Office of Saints*
4. St. Elizabeth of Portugal
5. St. Anthony Zaccaria
6. St. Maria Goretti
7.
8.
9.
10.
11. St. Benedict
12.
13. St. Henry
14. St. Camillus of Lellis
15. St. Bonaventure
16. Our Lady of Mount Carmel *Saturday Office if desired*

17.
18.
19.
20.
21. St. Lawrence of Brindisi
22. St. Mary Magdalene
23. St. Bridget
24.
25. **St. James** *Office of Saints*
26. Sts. Joachim and Anne (parents of our Lady)
27.
28.
29. St. Martha
30. St. Peter Chrysologus
31. St. Ignatius of Loyola

AUGUST
1. St. Alphonsus Liguori
2. St. Eusebius of Vercelli
3. St. Peter Eymard
4. St. John Vianney (Curé d'Ars)
5. Dedication of the Basilica of St. Mary Major
   Saturday Office if desired
6. **The Transfiguration** *Sunday Office*
7. St. Sixtus II and companions also St. Cajetan
8. St. Dominic
9.
10. St. Lawrence
11. St. Clare
12.
13. Sts. Pontian and Hippolytus
14. St. Maximilian Kolbe
15. **The Assumption of Our Lady** *Saturday Office*
16. St. Stephen of Hungary

17.
18. St. Jane Frances de Chantal
19. St. John Eudes
20. St. Bernard
21. St. Pius X
22. Our Lady, Queen and Mother *Saturday Office if desired*
23. St. Rose of Lima
24. **St. Bartholomew** *Office of Saints*
25. St. Louise also St. Joseph of Calasanz
26. Bl. Dominic Barberi (England)
27. St. Monica
28. St. Augustine
29. **The Death of St. John Baptist** *Office of Saints*
30.
31.

SEPTEMBER

1.
2.
3. St. Gregory the Great (England) *Office of Saints*
4.
5.
6.
7.
8. **The Birthday of Our Lady** *Saturday Office*
9. St. Peter Claver
10.
11.
12.
13. St. John Chrysostom
14. **The Triumph of the Cross** *Sunday Office*
15. Our Lady of Sorrows *Saturday Office if desired*
16. Sts. Cornelius and Cyprian

17. St. Robert Bellarmine
18.
19. St. Januarius
20. Sts. Andrew Kim Taegon, Paul Chong Hasang, and companions
21. **St. Matthew** *Office of Saints*
22.
23.
24. Our Lady of Ransom (England) *Saturday Office*
25.
26. Sts. Cosmas and Damian
27. St. Vincent de Paul
28. St. Wenceslaus also St. Lawrence Ruiz and companions
29. **The Holy Archangels** *Office of Saints or Sunday Office*
30. St. Jerome

OCTOBER
1. St. Thérèse of the Child Jesus (of Lisieux)
2. The Guardian Angels
3.
4. St. Francis of Assisi
5.
6. St. Bruno
7. Our Lady of the Rosary *Saturday Office if desired*
8.
9. St. Denis and companions also St. John Leonardi
10. St. Paulinus
11.
12.
13. St. Edward the Confessor (England) *Office of Saints*
14. St. Callistus I

15. St. Teresa of Jesus (of Avila)
16. St. Margaret Mary Alacoque also St. Hedwig
17. St. Ignatius of Antioch
18. **St. Luke** *Office of Saints*
19. Sts. John de Brébeuf, Isaac Jogues, and companions
20.
21.
22.
23. St. John Capistrano
24. St. Anthony Mary Claret
25. Forty martyrs of England and Wales (England and Wales) *Office of Saints*
26.
27.
28. **Sts. Simon and Jude** *Office of Saints*
29.
30.
31.

NOVEMBER
1. **All Saints** *Office of Saints*
2. **All Souls** *Office of the Dead*
3. St. Martin de Porres
4. St. Charles Borromeo
5.
6. All Saints of Ireland (Ireland)
7.
8.
9. Dedication of the Lateran Basilica *Sunday Office*
10. St. Leo the Great
11. St. Martin of Tours
12. St. Josaphat
13. St. Frances Xavier Cabrini (U.S.)

14.
15. St. Albert the Great
16. St. Margaret of Scotland (Scotland) *Office of Saints* also St. Gertrude the Great
17. St. Elizabeth of Hungary
18. Dedication of the Basilicas of Sts. Peter and Paul
19.
20.
21. The Presentation of Our Lady *Saturday Office*
22. St. Cecilia
23. St. Clement I also St. Columbanus
24. St. Andrew Dung-Lac and companions
25.
26.
27.
28.
29.
30. **St. Andrew** *Office of Saints*

DECEMBER
1.
2.
3. St. Francis Xavier
4. St. John Damascene
5.
6. St. Nicholas
7. St. Ambrose
8. **The Immaculate Conception of Our Lady** *Saturday Office*
9.
10.
11. St. Damasus I
12. Our Lady of Guadalupe (U.S.) *Saturday Office*
13. St. Lucy

14. St. John of the Cross
15.
16.
17.
18.
19.
20.
21. St. Peter Canisius
22.
23.
24.
25. **Christmas Day** *Sunday Office*
26. St. Stephen (first martyr)
27. **St. John** *Office of Saints*
28. The Holy Innocents
29. St. Thomas Becket
30.
31. St. Sylvester I

MOVABLE FEASTS

Sunday after January 6: **The Baptism of the Lord**

First Sunday after Pentecost: **Trinity Sunday**

Thursday after Trinity Sunday: **Corpus Christi** *Sunday Office*

Friday after second Sunday after Pentecost: **The Sacred Heart of Jesus** *Sunday Office*

The next day: **The Immaculate Heart of Mary** *Saturday Office*

The last Sunday of the liturgical year: **Christ the King**

PART ONE

PRAYERS FOR EVERY DAY

THE PSALTER

Seven times a day
will I praise you, O Lord.

Psalm 119:164

THE PSALTER

CONTENTS

SUNDAY
And feasts of the Lord

VIGILS
The night office

CALL: O Lord, ✠ open my lips.

RESPONSE: And my mouth shall declare your praise.

ANTIPHON: I shall see your glory when I awake, O Lord.

O God, my God, for you I watch at break of day;
for you my soul is thirsting.
My flesh longs for you!
as in a desert land without way or water.
Thus in the sanctuary have I come before you
to see your power and your glory.

For your loving-kindness is better than many lives:
my lips will declare your praise.

7

Thus I will bless you all my life long,
and in your name I will lift up my hands.
Let my soul be filled as with marrow and fat,
and my mouth shall praise you with joyful lips.

I have remembered you upon my bed.
On you I meditated in the morning

for you have been my helper;
and I will rejoice under the cover of your wings.
My soul clings close to you;
your right arm holds me tight.

PSALM 63:1–8

Glory be to the Father, and to the Son,
and to the Holy Spirit.
As it was in the beginning, is now and ever shall be,
world without end. Amen.

ANTIPHON: I shall see your glory when I awake,
O Lord.

CALL: O Lord, open the Scriptures to me.
RESPONSE: May my heart burn within me as you
teach me.

FIRST READING
Read one chapter from the Scriptures, ideally the Sunday Gospel.

RESPONSE TO THE READING

CALL: May my footsteps be firm, O Lord,
RESPONSE: In obeying your word.
CALL: May I be pleasing to you, O Lord,
RESPONSE: In obeying your word.

SECOND READING
Choose a spiritual reading.

TE DEUM

We praise you, O God!
We acknowledge you as Lord.
Everlasting Father: the whole world worships you.
The angels and the heavenly powers,
The cherubim and seraphim,
With endless voices cry:
Holy! Holy! Holy!
The Lord, the God of might!
The heavens and the earth are filled
With the splendor of your glorious reign!
The glorious apostolic choir,
And the prophets numberless do cry
The white robed martyrs' army sings,
And the holy Church throughout the world
Acclaims you as the Holy One:
The Father, limitlessly great;
His worshipful and only Son
And Holy Spirit, Paraclete.

O Christ! You are the glorious king!
You are the Father's only Son
Who, that you might rescue sinful man,
Did not despise the Virgin's womb.
Death's sting you boldly overthrew
And opened heaven's mighty gates
For your believers to pass inside.
Now you are throned at God's right hand
And share the glory of the Father.
We wait for you to come as judge.

So guide your servants here below,
For whom you shed your precious blood,
And give them glory with your saints.

Save your people, Lord, we pray,
And bless your own inheritance.
Forever rule us, raise us up.

For every day we bless your name,
We praise you to eternity,
Forever and forevermore.
O grant us, Lord, this very day
To pass without a stain of sin
Have mercy on us, Lord, we pray.

Your mercy, Lord, we here implore
For see, Lord, we have hoped in you.

In you, O Lord, I put my trust—
Never, then, abandon me!

Let us pray.

O God, our teacher, by your mighty Word made flesh, keep us, we pray, always attentive to your teaching and true in proclaiming your Word, Jesus Christ our Lord. Amen.

> *CALL:* Let us bless the Lord.
> **RESPONSE:** Thanks be to God.

LAUDS
Morning prayer

CALL: O God, ✝ come to my assistance.
RESPONSE: O Lord, be swift to my aid.
CALL: Glory be to the Father, and to the Son,
              and to the Holy Spirit.
RESPONSE: As it was in the beginning, is now and
              ever shall be, world without end. Amen.

Eternal maker of all things
Who rules the nighttime and the day,
Grant us the changing season's round
Our fickle mortal minds to cheer.

Now daytime's herald sends to rest
That watcher through the deepest night,
Whose beams, to nighttime travelers' eyes
Do cleave the dark from dark with light.

And thus awakened, scattering dark,
Light's bearer rises over all;
And leaving all their evil ways,
The wicked flee the deadly paths.

The mariner finds courage fresh,
The angry seas leave off their fret,
And at this hour flowed Peter's tears,
Blessed water flowing from the Rock!

Look on us sinners, Jesu, Lord,
Reprove us with one kindly glance;
For in thy sight our sins do melt,
And tears anoint the wounds of guilt.

And be a light unto our sense
And drive dull sleep far from our minds,
That, praising thee at break of day,
We may perform our duties well.

All praise, O Christ, all praise to thee,
And to the Father glory be,
And likewise to the Holy Ghost
Both now and for eternity. Amen.

> **ANTIPHON:**   O let all the works of the Lord bless
> the Lord; praise and exalt him forever.

CANTICLE OF THE THREE CHILDREN

Bless the Lord, you angels of the Lord,
    All you heavens, bless the Lord.
Bless the Lord, you waters over the heavens,
    All you stars of the heavens, bless the Lord.

Bless the Lord, you showers and dew,
    All spirits of God, bless the Lord.
Bless the Lord, fire and heat,

Cold and heat, bless the Lord.
Bless the Lord, you dews and frosts,
　　Ice and cold, bless the Lord.
Bless the Lord, ice and snow,
　　Night and day, bless the Lord.
Bless the Lord, light and darkness,
　　Lightning and clouds, bless the Lord.

Bless the Lord, O earth: praise and exalt him forever.

Bless the Lord, mountains and hills,
　　All things that grow on earth, bless the Lord.
Bless the Lord, O you springs,
　　Seas and rivers, bless the Lord.
Bless the Lord, you whales and fishes,
　　Beasts and cattle, bless the Lord.

Bless the Lord, you children of men.
Bless the Lord, O Israel: praise and exalt him forever.

Bless the Lord, O you his priests,
　　Servants of the Lord, bless the Lord.
Bless the Lord, just spirits and souls,
　　Holy hearts and humble, bless the Lord.

Bless the Lord, Ananias, Azarias, and Misael:
　　praise and exalt him forever.

Let us bless the Father, Son and the Holy Spirit:
　　praise and exalt him forever.
You are blessed, O Lord, in the vault of heaven,
　　to be praised and exalted forever.

DANIEL 3:59–90

The Glory Be is not said.

ANTIPHON:　　O let all the works of the Lord bless the
　　　　　　Lord; praise and exalt him forever.

SHORT READING

Salvation to our God who sits upon the throne, and to the Lamb! . . . Benediction and glory and wisdom and thanksgiving, honor and power and strength to our God forever and ever. Amen.

REVELATION 7:10–12

THE BENEDICTUS

The Gospel canticle is the heart of the hour. Jesus Christ is the promised day that will dawn on us from on high, so the Church greets every morning with this canticle from the first chapter of St. Luke's Gospel: Zechariah's great hymn of praise at the birth of his son, John the Baptist.

Blessed ✠ be the Lord, the God of Israel,
    who has visited and redeemed his people,
and has lifted up a horn of salvation for us
    in the family of his servant David.
For this he swore through the mouths of holy men,
    those who were prophets, from the beginning:
There would be salvation from our foes,
    and from the hand of all those who hate us;
to comfort our fathers,
    and to honor his holy covenant,
which oath once he swore to Abraham, our father,
    that he would grant us,
that freed from the hand of our enemies,
    and without fear, we may serve him,
    in holiness and justice in his very presence
      all our days.
And you, my son, will be named Prophet of the
  Most High;
    for you will go before the presence of the Lord
    to prepare his way,
to teach knowledge of salvation to his people
    that their sins may be forgiven,

through the merciful heart of our God,
when the Daystar shall visit us from on high
to enlighten those who sit in darkness
and in the shadow of death,
and guide our feet to the way of peace.

LUKE 1:68–79

Glory be . . .

INTERCESSIONS

Offer these intercessions, or pray for other needs.

CALL: Lord, bless our parish. *(Pause for prayer.)*
RESPONSE: Hear us, we pray.
CALL: Lord, bless our clergy and fill them
with wisdom. *(Pause.)*
RESPONSE: Hear us, we pray.
CALL: Lord, bless our young people and fill
them with faith. *(Pause.)*
RESPONSE: Hear us, we pray.
CALL: Lord, bless our sick and infirm. *(Pause.)*
RESPONSE: Hear us, we pray.
CALL: Lord, bless those we find difficult, and
give us patience with them. *(Pause.)*
RESPONSE: Hear us, we pray.
CALL: Lord, bless our parish catechists,
ministers, and all who generously give
their time and energy to your Church.
(Pause.)
RESPONSE: Hear us, we pray.
CALL: Lord, bless all our people. *(Pause.)*
RESPONSE: Hear us, we pray.

Lord, have mercy.
Christ, have mercy.
Lord, have mercy.

Our Father . . .

Let us pray.

Lord, God Almighty, since you have brought us safely to the start of this day, defend us as this day proceeds by your mighty power, so that we do not fall into any sin but that all our words, our thoughts, and our actions may be so governed as to be ever righteous in your sight. Through our Lord Jesus Christ, your Son, who lives and reigns with you in the unity of the Holy Spirit, one God forever and ever. Amen.

CALL: Let us bless the Lord.
RESPONSE: Thanks be to God.

TERCE
Midmorning prayer

CALL:	O God, ✠ come to my assistance.
RESPONSE:	O Lord, be swift to my aid.
CALL:	Glory be to the Father, and to the Son, and to the Holy Spirit.
RESPONSE:	As it was in the beginning, is now and ever shall be, world without end. Amen.

Come, Holy Ghost, with God the Son
And God the Father, ever one;
Shed forth thy grace within our breast
And dwell with us a ready guest.

By every power, by heart and tongue,
By act and deed, thy praise be sung;
Inflame with perfect love each sense
That others' souls may kindle thence.

O Father, that we ask be done,
Through Jesus Christ, thine only Son;
Who, with the Holy Ghost and thee,
Doth live and reign eternally. Amen.

    ANTIPHON: Lord, give us your blessing forever.

Behold how good and how pleasant it is
    for brethren to dwell together in unity!

Like precious ointment upon the head
    that ran down upon the beard,
ran down upon Aaron's beard,
down to the skirt of his robe.
Like the dew of Hermon that descends
    on the mount of Zion.
For there the Lord has commanded his blessing,
    and life forevermore.

PSALM 133

Glory be . . .

    ANTIPHON: Lord, give us your blessing forever.

SHORT READING

We have known and have believed the love that God has toward us. God is love, and he that abides in love abides in God, and God in him.

1 JOHN 4:16

Let us pray.

O God, the protector of those who hope in you, without whom nothing is true, nothing holy, increase your mercy toward us so that with you as our leader and guide, we may so go through the things of temporary value as not to miss the things of eternal worth. Through Christ our Lord. Amen.

CALL: Let us bless the Lord.
RESPONSE: Thanks be to God.

SEXT
Midday prayer

CALL: O God, ✠ come to my assistance.
RESPONSE: O Lord, be swift to my aid.
CALL: Glory be to the Father, and to the Son,
           and to the Holy Spirit.
RESPONSE: As it was in the beginning, is now and
           ever shall be, world without end. Amen.

O God of truth, O Lord of might,
Who orderest time and change aright,
And send'st the early morning ray,
And light'st the glow of perfect day:

Extinguish thou each sinful fire,
And banish every ill desire;
And while thou keep'st the body whole,
Shed forth thy peace upon the soul.

O Father, that we ask be done,

Through Jesus Christ, thine only Son;
Who, with the Holy Ghost and thee,
Doth live and reign eternally. Amen.

ANTIPHON: Lord, how I love your law.

Blessed are the undefiled in the way,
    who walk in the law of the Lord.
Blessed are they that keep his testimonies,
    that seek him with their whole hearts.
For those who commit iniquities
    have not walked in his ways.
You have commanded your commandments
    to be kept most diligently.
O that my ways may be directed
    to keep your statutes.
Then I shall not be confounded,
    as I examine all your commandments.
I will praise you with uprightness of heart
    when I have learned your just decrees.
I will keep your statutes:
    O do not utterly forsake me!

PSALM 119:1–8

Glory be . . .

ANTIPHON: Lord, how I love your law.

SHORT READING

He that sows according to the flesh will from the flesh reap
corruption; but he who sows according to the Spirit will
reap from the Spirit everlasting life. So let us not fail in
doing good, for in due time we shall reap, if we do not fail.
Therefore, while we have time, let us do good to all, but
especially to those who are of the household of the faith.

GALATIANS 6:8–10

Let us pray.

O God, you who have prepared good things for those who love you, pour your love into our hearts that we may love you in all and above all and that we may come to what you have promised: that which surpasses all our desires. Through Christ our Lord. Amen.

CALL: Let us bless the Lord.
RESPONSE: Thanks be to God.

NONE
Midafternoon prayer

CALL:	O God, ✝ come to my assistance.
RESPONSE:	O Lord, be swift to my aid.
CALL:	Glory be to the Father, and to the Son, and to the Holy Spirit.
RESPONSE:	As it was in the beginning, is now and ever shall be, world without end. Amen.

O God, Creation's secret force,
Thyself unmoved, all motion's source,
Who from the morn till evening ray
Through all its changes guid'st the day:

Grant us, when this short life is past,
The glorious evening that shall last;
That, by a holy death attained,
Eternal glory may be gained.

O Father, that we ask be done,
Through Jesus Christ, thine only Son;
Who, with the Holy Ghost and thee,
Doth live and reign eternally. Amen.

ANTIPHON: O Lord, I seek you with all my heart.

How shall the young correct his way?
By obeying your words.
With my whole heart I have sought after you;
let me not stray from your commandments.
Your words I have hidden in my heart,
that I may not sin against you.
Blessed are you, O Lord:
teach me your commandments.
With my lips I have pronounced
all the judgments you have made.
I delight in the way of your testimonies
as if in all riches.
I will meditate on your commandments;
and I will consider your ways.
I will delight in your commandments;
Never will I forget your words.

PSALM 119:9–16

Glory be . . .

ANTIPHON: O Lord, I seek you with all my heart.

SHORT READING

We know that everything created groans and travails in pain until now; and not only the creation, but also ourselves, who have the firstfruits of the Spirit, even we groan within ourselves as we wait for our adoption as sons of God, the redemption of our bodies. For we are saved in this hope.

ROMANS 8:22–24

Let us pray.

Grant, Lord, that the world may be governed according to your order and that the Church may rejoice in tranquil devotion. Through Christ our Lord. Amen.

> *CALL:* Let us bless the Lord.
> *RESPONSE:* Thanks be to God.

VESPERS
Evening prayer

CALL: O God, ✝ come to my assistance.

RESPONSE: O Lord, be swift to my aid.

CALL: Glory be to the Father, and to the Son, and to the Holy Spirit.

RESPONSE: As it was in the beginning, is now and ever shall be, world without end. Amen.

O wondrous maker of the light,
Who brought forth light to bless the day,
And with new light did glorify
Creation's first ecstatic dawn;

Who, morning unto evening joined,
Decreed that day should be its name,
Now that this day declines to eve
Hear all our heartfelt prayers and psalms:

That all our minds be free from fault,

Free from the weight of reckless sin,
That sin which, self-entangling, drowns,
Forgetting your eternal love.

We knock at heaven's secret place
That we may win the prize of life;
Now let us flee all evil thoughts
And cast away unholiness.

Grant this, most holy Father blessed,
And Jesus with the Father one,
And Holy Spirit, Paraclete
While everlasting ages run. Amen.

ANTIPHON: The Lord will send forth his scepter of power, and his dominion will be forever.

The Lord said to my Lord:
"Sit at my right hand:
your foes I will make your footstool."

The Lord will send forth your scepter of power
from Zion:
    rule in the midst of all your enemies!

Dominion is yours in the day of your strength
    in the splendor of the saints;
from the womb before the daystar I begot you.

The Lord has sworn and he will not retract:
    "You are a priest forever,
according to the order of Melchizedek."

The Lord standing at your right hand
    has broken kings in the day of his wrath.

He shall judge among nations, heap high the bodies;
    he shall break heads in many lands.

He shall drink of the brook by the way
    and therefore shall he lift up his head.

PSALM 110

Glory be . . .

    ANTIPHON: The Lord will send forth his scepter
    of power, and his dominion will be
    forever.

SHORT READING

Blessed be the God and Father of our Lord Jesus Christ,
who according to his great mercy has regenerated us to a
living hope by the resurrection of Jesus Christ from the
dead, and to an inheritance that is incorruptible and undefiled and that cannot fade, reserved in heaven for you, who
by the power of God are kept by faith for salvation, which
is ready to be revealed in the last time.

1 PETER 1:3–5

THE MAGNIFICAT

The Gospel canticle is the heart of the hour. This is the great hymn of Mary,
uttered, according to St. Luke's Gospel, just after Elizabeth, Mary's cousin and
mother of John the Baptist, greeted our Lady.

My ✠ soul magnifies the Lord,
    my spirit rejoices in God who is my Savior,
    who has looked upon the humility of his
      handmaiden.
Behold, all generations from now
    will acknowledge me blessed,
For the mighty one has done great things for me:
    Holy is his name!
His mercy is from one generation to the next on those
    who fear him.
    Mighty is his arm!

He has scattered the proud in the imagination of
 their hearts,
      and has put down the powerful from their thrones,
      exalting those of humble degree.
The hungry he has filled with good things,
      but the rich he has dismissed with nothing.
Remembering his mercy, he has helped his servant Israel,
      as he promised to our fathers,
      to Abraham and to his posterity forevermore.

Luke 1:46–55

Glory be . . .

INTERCESSIONS
Offer these intercessions, or pray for other needs.

CALL:	Lord, bless and give wisdom to [N.] our pope. *(Pause for prayer.)*
RESPONSE:	Hear us, O Lord.
CALL:	Lord, bless and give wisdom to [N.] our bishop. *(Pause.)*
RESPONSE:	Hear us, O Lord.
CALL:	Lord, bless and give wisdom to our country's leaders. *(Pause.)*
RESPONSE:	Hear us, O Lord.
CALL:	Lord, bless and give wisdom to our local government. *(Pause.)*
RESPONSE:	Hear us, O Lord.
CALL:	Lord, grant rest to the dead. *(Pause.)*
RESPONSE:	Hear us, O Lord.

Lord, have mercy.
Christ, have mercy.
Lord, have mercy.

Our Father . . .

Let us pray.

Lord, as we have celebrated today the mystery of your Son's resurrection from the dead, grant that this celebration may bear fruit in our lives, that we too may one day rise with him to eternal life. Through the same Jesus Christ, your Son, who lives and reigns with you and the Holy Spirit, one God, world without end. Amen.

> *CALL:*   Let us bless the Lord.
> **RESPONSE:** Thanks be to God.

COMPLINE
Night prayer

CALL: O God, ✠ come to my assistance.
RESPONSE: O Lord, be swift to my aid.
CALL: Glory be to the Father, and to the Son, and to the Holy Spirit.
RESPONSE: As it was in the beginning, is now and ever shall be, world without end.
Amen.

It is fitting to make an examination of conscience, followed by an act of penance, such as the Confiteor as at Mass, or an act of contrition (see pp. 360–62).

Before the ending of the day,
Creator of the world, we pray
That with thy wonted favor thou
Wouldst be our guard and keeper now.

From all ill dreams defend our eyes,
From nightly fears and fantasies;
Tread underfoot our ghostly foe,
That no pollution we may know.

O Father, that we ask be done,
Through Jesus Christ, thine only Son;
Who, with the Holy Ghost and thee,
Doth live and reign eternally. Amen.

> **ANTIPHON:**   Bless the Lord throughout the night.

Behold, bless the Lord,
    all you servants of the Lord,
who stand in the house of the Lord,
    in the courts of the house of our God by night.

Lift up your hands to the holy places,
    and bless the Lord.

May the Lord bless you out of Zion,
    he that made both heaven and earth.

PSALM 134

Glory be . . .

> **ANTIPHON:**   Bless the Lord throughout the night.

SHORT READING

They shall see God's face, and his name shall be on their foreheads. And night shall be no more; they shall not need the light of the lamp nor the light of the sun, because the Lord God shall enlighten them, and they shall reign forever and ever.

REVELATION 22:4–5

THE NUNC DIMITTIS
This Gospel canticle uses the words of Simeon, who gave thanks to God when he first set eyes on the Messiah.

ANTIPHON: Save us, O Lord, while we wake, and watch over us as we sleep, that we may pass the night with Christ and rest in peace.

Lord, ✠ now let your servant depart in peace,
     according to your promise;
for my eyes have seen your salvation,
     which you have prepared in the presence of
       all peoples,
a light for revelation to the Gentiles,
     and for glory to your people Israel.

LUKE 2:29–32

Glory be . . .

ANTIPHON: Save us, O Lord, while we wake, and watch over us as we sleep, that we may pass the night with Christ and rest in peace.

Let us pray.

Visit this house, O Lord, we pray, and drive far from it the deadly power of the enemy. May your holy angels dwell here instead, that we may be preserved in peace with your blessing on us always. Through Christ our Lord. Amen.

The day is traditionally closed with an antiphon in honor of our Lady, varied according to the liturgical season (see pp. 577–82). At any season of the year, the following may be said instead:

We fly to thy patronage, holy mother of God.
Despise not our petitions in our necessities
But deliver us from every evil,
O glorious and blessed Virgin!

MONDAY
A day of prayer for the afflicted

VIGILS
The night office

CALL: O Lord, ☩ open my lips.

RESPONSE: And my mouth shall declare
your praise.

ANTIPHON: The Lord remembers the cry
of the poor.

The Lord is a refuge for the poor,
> a timely helper in tribulation.

Let those who know your name trust you:
>> for, Lord, you will never forsake those who
>> seek you.

Sing to the Lord who dwells in Zion,
>> Declare his mighty ways among the Gentiles;

34

for he who seeks recompense for blood has
  remembered them,
    he has not forgotten the cry of the poor.

Have mercy on me, O Lord, see my humiliation,
    you who lift me up from the gates of death;
that I may declare all your praises
    at the gates of the daughter of Zion,
    and rejoice in your salvation.

The Gentiles have stuck fast in the trap that they made,
    their foot caught in the very snare they hid.
The Lord shall be known when he executes judgment.
    The sinner is snared in the works of his own hands.

Let the wicked go down into hell,
    all the nations that forget God.
For the needy shall never be forgotten,
    nor the patience of the poor perish forever.

PSALM 9:9–18

Glory be . . .

ANTIPHON: The Lord remembers the cry
              of the poor.

CALL: O Lord, inflame my heart,
RESPONSE: And I will teach your way to the poor.

FIRST READING
Read one chapter from the Scriptures.

RESPONSE TO THE READING
  CALL: Let me know your will, O Lord,
  RESPONSE: And do it with all my heart.
  CALL: May I proclaim your word with
          my lips,
  RESPONSE: And do it with all my heart.

SECOND READING
Choose a spiritual reading.

RESPONSE TO THE READING

CALL: I shall proclaim your decrees to the mighty,

RESPONSE: For your word is my delight.

CALL: All night, O Lord, I have remembered your name,

RESPONSE: For your word is my delight.

Let us pray.

Almighty God, by whose just decrees we are governed, grant that all people may recognize your word and come to live by it. Through Christ our Lord. Amen.

CALL: Let us bless the Lord.

RESPONSE: Thanks be to God.

LAUDS
Morning prayer

CALL: O God, ✞ come to my assistance.
RESPONSE: O Lord, be swift to my aid.
CALL: Glory be to the Father, and to the Son,
and to the Holy Spirit.
RESPONSE: As it was in the beginning, is now and
ever shall be, world without end. Amen.

Splendor of the Father's glory,
Radiance from eternal light,
Light of lights and fount of radiance,
Day that art the light of days,

Truest Sun that flows upon us,
Shining beam, eternal light:
Now command the Holy Spirit
Our dull senses to illume.

Let us also ask the Father:

He who sends most powerful grace,
He of everlasting glory:
Cast away all dangerous sin.

Now inspire us to do battle,
Blunt the teeth of tempter's power,
Be the downfall of our brashness,
Be the giver of thy grace.

Guide and rule our wayward spirits,
Make our bodies pure and true,
Stir our faith into a fire lest
Poisoned error us molest.

And may Christ our finest food be,
Give true faith to quench our thirst.
Joyfully we drink that sober
Spirit that inebriates.

May this joyful day so flourish,
Pure as dawn then may we be,
So that faith may shine like noonday
And no setting ever know.

As the dawn brings on the daylight,
So may dawn bring now to us
In the Father, all the Sonhood,
All the Father in the Word. Amen.

    ANTIPHON: Bless the righteous, O Lord.

Give ear to my words, O Lord,
    understand my cry.
Hearken to the voice of my prayer,
    O my king and my God.

It is you to whom I pray, O Lord.
    In the morning you will hear my voice;

in the morning I will stand before you,
and I will wait and watch.

You are no God who wills iniquity;
neither can the sinner dwell near you.
The unjust shall not abide before your face.
You hate all who work iniquity:
you destroy all who speak lies.
The deceitful and bloody man
the Lord abhors.

But as for me, through the multitude of your mercies
I will come into your house.
I will worship in your holy temple,
filled with reverence.

Conduct me, Lord, in your justice,
because of my enemies;
direct my way in your sight.
For there is no truth in their mouth,
their heart is all vanity,
their throat an open sepulchre,
their tongues all deceit.

Judge them, O God.
Let them fall from their devices.
Cast them out for their multitude of wickednesses;
for they have provoked you, O Lord.

But let all those who hope in you be glad:
for you shall dwell within them,
and those who love your name shall glory in you.

For you will bless the just, O Lord:
You have crowned us,
as with a shield of your good will.

PSALM 5

Glory be . . .

ANTIPHON: Bless the righteous, O Lord.

SHORT READING

Now is the hour for us to rise from sleep. For now our salvation is nearer to us than when we first believed. The night is passed, the day is at hand. Let us therefore cast off the works of darkness and put on the armor of light; let us walk honestly as in the day.

ROMANS 13:11–13

THE BENEDICTUS

Blessed ✠ be the Lord, the God of Israel,
    who has visited and redeemed his people,
and has lifted up a horn of salvation for us
    in the family of his servant David.
For this he swore through the mouths of holy men,
    those who were prophets, from the beginning:
There would be salvation from our foes,
    and from the hand of all those who hate us;
to comfort our fathers,
    and to honor his holy covenant,
which oath once he swore to Abraham, our father,
    that he would grant us,
that freed from the hand of our enemies,
    and without fear, we may serve him,
    in holiness and justice in his very presence
    all our days.
And you, my son, will be named Prophet of the
  Most High;
        for you will go before the presence of the Lord
        to prepare his way,
to teach knowledge of salvation to his people

that their sins may be forgiven,
through the merciful heart of our God,
when the Daystar shall visit us from on high
to enlighten those who sit in darkness
and in the shadow of death,
and guide our feet to the way of peace.

LUKE 1:68–79

Glory be . . .

INTERCESSIONS

Offer these intercessions, or pray for other needs.

CALL: Lord, strengthen those who give food
to the hungry. *(Pause for prayer.)*

RESPONSE: Hear us, Father.

CALL: Lord, strengthen those who give drink
to the thirsty. *(Pause.)*

RESPONSE: Hear us, Father.

CALL: Lord, strengthen those who give
clothing to the naked. *(Pause.)*

RESPONSE: Hear us, Father.

CALL: Lord, strengthen those who give shelter
to the homeless. *(Pause.)*

RESPONSE: Hear us, Father.

CALL: Lord, strengthen those who care for
the sick. *(Pause.)*

RESPONSE: Hear us, Father.

CALL: Lord, strengthen those who visit and
help the imprisoned. *(Pause.)*

RESPONSE: Hear us, Father.

Lord, have mercy.
Christ, have mercy.
Lord, have mercy.

Our Father . . .

Let us pray.

God of righteousness, grant us the sight to see what needs to be done and the courage to do it. Through our Lord Jesus Christ, your Son, who lives and reigns with you in the unity of the Holy Spirit, one God forever and ever. Amen.

CALL: Let us bless the Lord.
RESPONSE: Thanks be to God.

TERCE
Midmorning prayer

CALL:	O God, ✝ come to my assistance.
RESPONSE:	O Lord, be swift to my aid.
CALL:	Glory be to the Father, and to the Son, and to the Holy Spirit.
RESPONSE:	As it was in the beginning, is now and ever shall be, world without end. Amen.

Come, Holy Ghost, with God the Son
And God the Father, ever one;
Shed forth thy grace within our breast
And dwell with us a ready guest.

By every power, by heart and tongue,
By act and deed, thy praise be sung;
Inflame with perfect love each sense
That others' souls may kindle thence.

O Father, that we ask be done,
Through Jesus Christ, thine only Son;
Who, with the Holy Ghost and thee,
Doth live and reign eternally. Amen.

> **ANTIPHON:** Lord, your testimonies are
> my meditation.

Deal generously with your servant:
> enliven me and I shall keep your word.
Open my eyes that I may consider
> the wondrous things of your law.
I am a sojourner on the earth;
> hide not your commands from me.
My soul is ever longing for
> and coveting your decrees.
You have rebuked the proud; they are cursed
> who turn away from your commands.
Remove from me reproach and contempt
> for I have sought after your will.
For princes sat and spoke against me,
> but your servant was studying your statutes.
Your will is my meditation;
> your statutes are my counsel.

PSALM 119:17–24

Glory be . . .

> **ANTIPHON:** Lord, your testimonies are
> my meditation.

SHORT READING

Seek good, and not evil, that you may live; and the Lord
God of hosts will be with you. Hate evil, and love good,
and establish just judgment in the gate; it may be that the

Lord, the God of hosts, will have mercy on the remnant of Joseph.

AMOS 5:14–15

Let us pray.

O God, delighting in virtue and despising evil, make us strong in the same virtue, and grant us the grace to be ever ready to run according to your commands. Through Christ our Lord. Amen.

CALL: Let us bless the Lord.
RESPONSE: Thanks be to God.

SEXT
Midday prayer

CALL: O God, ✠ come to my assistance.
RESPONSE: O Lord, be swift to my aid.
CALL: Glory be to the Father, and to the Son,
and to the Holy Spirit.
RESPONSE: As it was in the beginning, is now and
ever shall be, world without end. Amen.

O God of truth, O Lord of might,
Who orderest time and change aright,
And send'st the early morning ray,
And light'st the glow of perfect day:

Extinguish thou each sinful fire,
And banish every ill desire;
And while thou keep'st the body whole,
Shed forth thy peace upon the soul.

O Father, that we ask be done,
Through Jesus Christ, thine only Son;
Who, with the Holy Ghost and thee,
Doth live and reign eternally. Amen.

ANTIPHON: Lord, revive me according to
your word.

My soul cleaves to the dust;
    by your word give me life.
I have declared my ways and you have heard me:
    teach me your commands.
Make me understand the way of your statutes,
    and I will consider your wondrous works.
My soul is heavy with sorrow;
    by your word strengthen me.
Remove me from the way of iniquity,
    and by reason of your law, have mercy on me.
I have chosen the way of truth;
    I put to myself your judgments.
I have bound myself to your testimonies;
    Lord, do not put me to shame.
I have run the way of your commands;
    you have given joy to my heart.

PSALM 119:25–32

Glory be . . .

ANTIPHON: Lord, revive me according to
your word.

SHORT READING
Is not this, rather, the fast that I have chosen? Loose the
bonds of wickedness, undo the oppressive burdens, let the
broken go free, and break asunder every yoke! Give your
bread to the hungry, and bring the needy and homeless

into your house. When you see someone naked, cover him, and do not despise your own flesh. Then shall your light break forth like the morning, and your healing shall speedily arise; your justice shall go before your face, and the glory of the Lord shall gather you up. Then you shall call, and the Lord will hear; you shall cry, and he will say, Here I am. If you take away the chain from the midst of you, the pointing of the finger, and speaking what does no good, if you pour out your soul for the hungry and satisfy the soul of the afflicted, then shall your light rise up in darkness and your darkness shall be as the noonday. And the Lord will give you rest continually, and will fill your soul with brightness, and rescue your bones, and you shall be like a watered garden, and like a fountain of water, whose waters shall not fail.

ISAIAH 58:6–11

Let us pray.

Lord, pour your love into our hearts that we may love you above all things, and our neighbor as ourselves. Through Christ our Lord. Amen.

CALL: Let us bless the Lord.
RESPONSE: Thanks be to God.

NONE
Midafternoon prayer

CALL:	O God, ✛ come to my assistance.
RESPONSE:	O Lord, be swift to my aid.
CALL:	Glory be to the Father, and to the Son, and to the Holy Spirit.
RESPONSE:	As it was in the beginning, is now and ever shall be, world without end. Amen.

O God, Creation's secret force,
Thyself unmoved, all motion's source,
Who from the morn till evening ray
Through all its changes guid'st the day:

Grant us, when this short life is past,
The glorious evening that shall last;
That, by a holy death attained,
Eternal glory may be gained.

O Father, that we ask be done,
Through Jesus Christ, thine only Son;
Who, with the Holy Ghost and thee,
Doth live and reign eternally. Amen.

ANTIPHON: Lead me in the path of your
commandments.

Set before me the way of your statutes, O Lord,
and I will always seek after them.
Give me understanding, and I will search your law
and I will keep it with my whole heart.
Lead me in the path of your commandments;
for this I have desired.
Incline my heart to your testimonies,
and not to covetousness.
Turn away my eyes from vanities:
give me life in your way.
Fulfill the word you have spoken
to the servant who stands in your fear.
Turn away from the reproach I dread,
for your judgments are delightful.
Behold, I have longed after your precepts:
give me life in your justice.

PSALM 119:33–40

Glory be . . .

ANTIPHON: Lead me in the path of your
commandments.

SHORT READING
The Lord raises up the needy from the dust; he lifts the
poor from the dunghill, that they may sit with princes and
hold a throne of glory.

1 SAMUEL 2:8

Let us pray.

Take away, Lord, our heart of stone, and give us a heart of tenderness for you and our neighbors. Through Christ our Lord. Amen.

CALL: Let us bless the Lord.

RESPONSE: Thanks be to God.

VESPERS
Evening prayer

CALL: O God, ✢ come to my assistance.
RESPONSE: O Lord, be swift to my aid.
CALL: Glory be to the Father, and to the Son,
and to the Holy Spirit.
RESPONSE: As it was in the beginning, is now and
ever shall be, world without end. Amen.

O blessed Creator of the earthly sphere,
Who 'stablished dry land firm upon its base,
In separating land from land you toiled,
And driving fretful waters to their place;

Who from that soil brought seeds of various kinds,
Bright flowers to beautify both hill and vale,
Abundant fruits that hang from many a bough,
Delightful food supplying without fail:

Cleanse with the freshness of your grace the wounds
That mar the beauty of our sin-seared minds
And wash away with tears our evil deeds,
Grind down whatever sin unto us binds.

Now let our souls obey your just commands,
And let no evil thing to us draw nigh,
That filled with good, we may in you rejoice,
And come at last to eternal life on high.

Eternal Father, hear our earnest prayer,
And you, O equal, sole-begotten Son,
Who with the Holy Spirit reigns supreme,
One only God, while endless ages run. Amen.

ANTIPHON: The Lord of hosts is with us: the God
of Jacob is our stronghold.

Our God is for us a refuge and strength,
    a helper in troubles that have hit us hard:
Therefore we shall not fear
    though the earth should be troubled,
    and the mountains collapse into the heart of the sea;
Though its waters roar and are troubled,
    though mountains are shaken by its strength.

The Lord of hosts is with us:
    the God of Jacob is our stronghold.

The stream of a river makes joyful God's city,
    the tabernacle made holy by the Most
        High's dwelling.
God is in its midst, it shall not be moved;
    God will help it at the break of day.
Nations were troubled, kingdoms were humbled:
    he uttered his voice; the earth trembled.

The Lord of hosts is with us:
>   the God of Jacob is our stronghold.

Come and behold the works of the Lord
>   the wonderful things he has done upon earth
>   making wars to cease to the ends of the world;
He shall destroy the bow and break the weapons;
>   the shields he shall burn in the fire.
"Be still and see that I am God,
>   I will be exalted among the nations,
>   I will be exalted on the earth!"

The Lord of hosts is with us:
>   the God of Jacob is our stronghold.

PSALM 46

Glory be . . .

ANTIPHON: The Lord of hosts is with us: the God
of Jacob is our stronghold.

SHORT READING
Blessed be the God and Father of our Lord Jesus Christ,
the Father of mercies and the God of all comfort, who
comforts us in all our tribulation, so that we also may be
able to comfort those who are in any distress, with the
comfort with which we ourselves are comforted by God.

2 CORINTHIANS 1:3–4

THE MAGNIFICAT
My ✠ soul magnifies the Lord,
>   my spirit rejoices in God who is my Savior,
>   who has looked upon the humility of his
>   handmaiden.
Behold, all generations from now
>   will acknowledge me blessed,

For the mighty one has done great things for me:
Holy is his name!
His mercy is from one generation to the next on those
who fear him.
Mighty is his arm!
He has scattered the proud in the imagination of
their hearts,
and has put down the powerful from their thrones,
exalting those of humble degree.
The hungry he has filled with good things,
but the rich he has dismissed with nothing.
Remembering his mercy, he has helped his servant Israel,
as he promised to our fathers,
to Abraham and to his posterity forevermore.

LUKE 1:46–55

Glory be . . .

INTERCESSIONS
Offer these intercessions, or pray for other needs.

CALL:	For those unjustly deprived of freedom, *(Pause for prayer.)*
RESPONSE:	Hear us, O Lord.
CALL:	For those who lack the necessities of life, *(Pause.)*
RESPONSE:	Hear us, O Lord.
CALL:	For those who fight evil with good, *(Pause.)*
RESPONSE:	Hear us, O Lord.
CALL:	For an end to famine and war, *(Pause.)*
RESPONSE:	Hear us, O Lord.
CALL:	Grant rest to those who have given their lives for justice or truth. *(Pause.)*
RESPONSE:	Hear us, O Lord.

Lord, have mercy.
Christ, have mercy.
Lord, have mercy.

Our Father . . .

Let us pray.

Lord, grant us the gift to be always contemplating what is right, and make us well disposed to putting it into action, that we who can do nothing without you may be worthy to live as you wish. Through our Lord Jesus Christ, your Son, who lives and reigns with you and the Holy Spirit, one God, world without end. Amen.

CALL: Let us bless the Lord.
RESPONSE: Thanks be to God.

COMPLINE
Night prayer

CALL:	O God, ✠ come to my assistance.
RESPONSE:	O Lord, be swift to my aid.
CALL:	Glory be to the Father, and to the Son, and to the Holy Spirit.
RESPONSE:	As it was in the beginning, is now and ever shall be, world without end. Amen.

Make an examination of conscience, and perform an act of penance.

Before the ending of the day,
Creator of the world, we pray
That with thy wonted favor thou
Wouldst be our guard and keeper now.

From all ill dreams defend our eyes,
From nightly fears and fantasies;

Tread underfoot our ghostly foe,
That no pollution we may know.

O Father, that we ask be done,
Through Jesus Christ, thine only Son;
Who, with the Holy Ghost and thee,
Doth live and reign eternally. Amen.

ANTIPHON: The Lord is with us in tribulation.

He that dwells in the help of the Most High
    shall abide in the protection of the Almighty.
He shall say to the Lord: You are my protector,
    and my refuge: my God in whom I will trust!

For he has delivered me from the snare
    of the hunter, and from the barbed word;
he will shelter you with his shoulders
    and under the protection of his wings you will flee.

His truth shall compass you as with a shield:
    you will not be afraid of the terror in the night,
Nor the arrow that flies in the day,
    nor the scourge that stalks in the darkness
    nor the destroying noonday devil.

A thousand may fall by your side,
    and ten thousand at your right hand,
    never shall it come nigh to you.

Open your eyes and consider,
    and you will see the reward of the wicked.
You, O Lord, are my hope:
    and have made your refuge on high.

There shall no evil come upon you,
    nor shall the scourge come near your dwelling.

For he has given his angels charge over you,
    to keep you in all your ways.

In their hands they shall bear you up,
    lest you dash your foot against a stone.
You shall walk upon the asp and the basilisk
    and trample underfoot the lion and the dragon.

Because he hoped in me, I will deliver him;
    I will protect him for he has known my name.
He shall cry to me, and I will hear him:
    I am with him in tribulation and I will glorify him.

With length of days I will fill him;
    and I will show him my salvation.

PSALM 91

Glory be . . .

ANTIPHON: The Lord is with us in tribulation.

SHORT READING

For God has not destined us for wrath, but to purchase salvation by means of our Lord Jesus Christ, who died for us so that whether we watch or sleep we might live together with him. Because of this, encourage one another and edify one another, as you are doing already.

1 THESSALONIANS 5:9–11

THE NUNC DIMITTIS

ANTIPHON: Save us, O Lord, while we wake, and
                watch over us as we sleep, that we
                may pass the night with Christ and
                rest in peace.

Lord, ✛ now let your servant depart in peace,
    according to your promise;

for my eyes have seen your salvation,
  which you have prepared in the presence of
  all peoples,
a light for revelation to the Gentiles,
  and for glory to your people Israel.

LUKE 2:29–32

Glory be . . .

ANTIPHON: Save us, O Lord, while we wake, and
watch over us as we sleep, that we
may pass the night with Christ and
rest in peace.

Let us pray.

Visit this house, O Lord, we pray, and drive far from it the
deadly power of the enemy. May your holy angels dwell
here instead, that we may be preserved in peace with your
blessing on us always. Through Christ our Lord. Amen.

*Say the antiphon in honor of our Lady (see pp. 577–82), or use
the following:*

We fly to thy patronage, holy mother of God.
Despise not our petitions in our necessities
But deliver us from every evil,
O glorious and blessed Virgin!

TUESDAY

VIGILS
The night office

CALL: O Lord, ✝ open my lips.
RESPONSE: And my mouth shall declare
your praise.

ANTIPHON: Come, let us worship the Lord.

Come, let us praise the Lord with joy;
let us joyfully sing to God our Savior.
Let us come before his presence with thanksgiving,
and make a joyful noise to him with psalms.

For the Lord is a great God,
and a great king above all gods.
For in his hand are all the depths of the earth;
and the heights of the mountains are his.
For the sea is his, and it was he that made it
and his hands formed the dry land.

Come, let us adore and fall down;
    let us kneel before the Lord who made us,
for he is the Lord our God,
        and we are the people of his pasture,
        and the sheep fed by his hand.

If only today you would hear his voice!
    Harden not your hearts
as at the provocation,
        as on that day of temptation in the desert
        when your fathers tempted me;
        when they proved me and saw my works.

Forty years long I was offended with that generation
        and I said: "These always err in their hearts,
        these men have not known my ways."
So I swore in my wrath
        that they shall not enter into my rest.

PSALM 95

Glory be . . .

ANTIPHON: Come, let us worship the Lord.

CALL: Keep my eyes from what is false.
RESPONSE: By your word give me life.

FIRST READING
Read one chapter from the Scriptures.

RESPONSE TO THE READING

CALL: This is my comfort in sorrow,
RESPONSE: That your promise gives me life.
CALL: And I shall answer those who
        taunt me,
RESPONSE: That your promise gives me life.

SECOND READING
Choose a spiritual reading.

RESPONSE TO THE READING

CALL: Keep me from the way of error;
RESPONSE: Teach me your law.
CALL: I have chosen the way of truth;
RESPONSE: Teach me your law.

Let us pray.

Almighty God, grant us greater faith, hope, and charity, and that we might come to what you promise, make us to love what you command. Through Christ our Lord. Amen.

CALL: Let us bless the Lord.
RESPONSE: Thanks be to God.

LAUDS
Morning prayer

CALL: O God, ✠ come to my assistance.
RESPONSE: O Lord, be swift to my aid.
CALL: Glory be to the Father, and to the Son,
             and to the Holy Spirit.
RESPONSE: As it was in the beginning, is now and
             ever shall be, world without end. Amen.

The fair-winged chorus of the dawn
Proclaims the coming of the light,
And Christ, the soul's awakener,
Bids us arise now into life.

Now cast away, he cries, your beds,
You drowsy captives of your sleep!
Be upright, sober, pure, alert,
And for my coming vigil keep.

To Jesus lift our voices loud,
Now clamor, praying without sleep;
For prayer directly from the heart
That heart from slumbering will keep.

So, Christ, dispel our lazy sleep,
And break the chains of slothful night,
And break the power of sins long past,
And fill us with the grace of light.

To God the Father glory be
And to his only Son, our Lord,
Who with the Holy Spirit, three
Yet one eternal is adored. Amen.

ANTIPHON: Sing to the Lord; praise his
glorious name.

Praise the Lord, for praising him is good;
It is joyful and comely to sing his praise!

The Lord builds up Jerusalem
he will gather together the dispersal of Israel.
It is he who heals the brokenhearted,
he binds up all their bruises.
He can tell the number of the stars,
and calls each one by its name.

Great is our Lord, and great is his power;
the acts of his wisdom are numberless.
The Lord lifts up the meek;
and brings the wicked down to the dust.
Sing to the Lord with praise:
sing to our God upon the harp!

It is he who covers the heavens with clouds;
and prepares rain for the earth,

making grass to grow on the mountains
     and herbs for the service of men.

He gives the beasts their food
     and feeds the young ravens that call upon him.
His delight is not in the power of the horse,
     nor his pleasure in the strength of a man's legs.
But the Lord takes pleasure in those who fear him,
     and in those who hope in his mercy.

PSALM 147:1–11

Glory be . . .

ANTIPHON: Sing to the Lord; praise his
                 glorious name.

SHORT READING

But you, brethren, are not in darkness, that day should over-
take you like a thief. For you are all children of light and
children of the day; we are not of the night nor of darkness.

1 THESSALONIANS 5:4–5

THE BENEDICTUS

Blessed ✛ be the Lord, the God of Israel,
     who has visited and redeemed his people,
and has lifted up a horn of salvation for us
     in the family of his servant David.
For this he swore through the mouths of holy men,
     those who were prophets, from the beginning:
There would be salvation from our foes,
     and from the hand of all those who hate us;
to comfort our fathers,
     and to honor his holy covenant,
which oath once he swore to Abraham, our father,
     that he would grant us,
that freed from the hand of our enemies,

and without fear, we may serve him,
in holiness and justice in his very presence
all our days.
And you, my son, will be named Prophet of the
Most High;
for you will go before the presence of the Lord
to prepare his way,
to teach knowledge of salvation to his people
that their sins may be forgiven,
through the merciful heart of our God,
when the Daystar shall visit us from on high
to enlighten those who sit in darkness
and in the shadow of death,
and guide our feet to the way of peace.

LUKE 1:68–79

Glory be . . .

INTERCESSIONS

Offer these intercessions, or pray for other needs.

CALL: Lord, bless all teachers and educators.
(Pause for prayer.)
RESPONSE: Lord, have mercy.
CALL: Lord, bless all those who care for
the sick. *(Pause.)*
RESPONSE: Lord, have mercy.
CALL: Lord, bless all those who labor to
make you better known. *(Pause.)*
RESPONSE: Lord, have mercy.
CALL: Lord, strengthen the vocation of nuns
and sisters. *(Pause.)*
RESPONSE: Lord, have mercy.
CALL: Lord, strengthen the vocation of
brothers and priests. *(Pause.)*

RESPONSE: Lord, have mercy.
CALL: Lord, strengthen the vocation of all
            married people. *(Pause.)*
RESPONSE: Lord, have mercy.

Lord, have mercy.
Christ, have mercy.
Lord, have mercy.

Our Father . . .

Let us pray.

God of mercy and goodness, in whose gift it is that we should serve you worthily and well, grant that we may run toward the fulfillment of your promises without offence and with alacrity. Through our Lord Jesus Christ, your Son, who lives and reigns with you in the unity of the Holy Spirit, one God forever and ever. Amen.

CALL: Let us bless the Lord.
RESPONSE: Thanks be to God.

TERCE
Midmorning prayer

CALL: O God, ✝ come to my assistance.
RESPONSE: O Lord, be swift to my aid.
CALL: Glory be to the Father, and to the Son,
             and to the Holy Spirit.
RESPONSE: As it was in the beginning, is now and
             ever shall be, world without end. Amen.

Come, Holy Ghost, with God the Son
And God the Father, ever one;
Shed forth thy grace within our breast
And dwell with us a ready guest.

By every power, by heart and tongue,
By act and deed, thy praise be sung;
Inflame with perfect love each sense
That others' souls may kindle thence.

O Father, that we ask be done,
Through Jesus Christ, thine only Son;
Who, with the Holy Ghost and thee,
Doth live and reign eternally. Amen.

ANTIPHON: I shall always keep your law
forever and ever.

Let your mercy come upon me, O Lord,
    your salvation according to your word.
So shall I answer those who reproach me,
    that I have trusted in your word.
Do not take the word of truth utterly out of my mouth
    for in your word I have greatly hoped.
So shall I always keep your law
    forever and ever.
I shall walk in freedom,
    for I have sought your commandments.
I have spoken of your will before kings
    and I was not ashamed.
I delighted also in your commandments:
    which I have loved.
And I lifted up my hands to your decrees, which I love,
    and I contemplate your judgments.

PSALM 119:41–48

Glory be . . .

ANTIPHON: I shall always keep your law
forever and ever.

SHORT READING

For my thoughts are not your thoughts, nor your ways my
ways, says the Lord. For as the heavens are exalted above
the earth, so are my ways exalted above your ways and my
thoughts above your thoughts. And as the rain and the

snow come down from heaven, and return there no more but soak the earth, and water it, and make it spring up, and give seed to the sower and bread to the eater, so shall my word be, which goes forth from my mouth; it shall not return to me empty, but it shall do whatsoever I please, and shall prosper in the things for which I sent it.

ISAIAH 55:8–11

Let us pray.

O God of truth, send us the Holy Spirit to be our advocate and guide, according to your promise. Through Christ our Lord. Amen.

CALL: Let us bless the Lord.
RESPONSE: Thanks be to God.

SEXT
Midday prayer

CALL:　　　O God, ✟ come to my assistance.
RESPONSE:　O Lord, be swift to my aid.
CALL:　　　Glory be to the Father, and to the Son,
　　　　　　and to the Holy Spirit.
RESPONSE:　As it was in the beginning, is now and
　　　　　　ever shall be, world without end. Amen.

O God of truth, O Lord of might,
Who orderest time and change aright,
And send'st the early morning ray,
And light'st the glow of perfect day:

Extinguish thou each sinful fire,
And banish every ill desire;
And while thou keep'st the body whole,
Shed forth thy peace upon the soul.

O Father, that we ask be done,
Through Jesus Christ, thine only Son;
Who, with the Holy Ghost and thee,
Doth live and reign eternally. Amen.

> **ANTIPHON:**   This has been my reward,
>   the keeping of your law.

Be mindful of your word to your servant;
    in which you gave me hope.
This has comforted me in humiliation,
    that your word has given me life.

Though the proud have greatly despised me,
    I have not left your law.
I remembered, O Lord, your judgments of old,
    and these are my comfort.
I am seized with indignation
    at the wicked who forsake your law.
Your commandments have become my song
    in the place of my wanderings.
In the night I remember your name, O Lord,
    and I have kept your law.
This is what has been my reward:
    because I have sought the keeping of your law.

PSALM 119:49–56

Glory be . . .

> **ANTIPHON:**   This has been my reward,
>   the keeping of your law.

SHORT READING

The Lord sees not as man sees; for man sees those things
that are merely apparent, but the Lord sees the heart.

1 SAMUEL 16:7

Let us pray.

Lord, help us to rise above petty hypocrisy and self-seeking. May our outward appearance show a true heart within. Through Christ our Lord. Amen.

CALL: Let us bless the Lord.
RESPONSE: Thanks be to God.

NONE
Midafternoon prayer

CALL: O God, ✛ come to my assistance.
RESPONSE: O Lord, be swift to my aid.
CALL: Glory be to the Father, and to the Son, and to the Holy Spirit.
RESPONSE: As it was in the beginning, is now and ever shall be, world without end. Amen.

O God, Creation's secret force,
Thyself unmoved, all motion's source,
Who from the morn till evening ray
Through all its changes guid'st the day:

Grant us, when this short life is past,
The glorious evening that shall last;
That, by a holy death attained,
Eternal glory may be gained.

O Father, that we ask be done,
Through Jesus Christ, thine only Son;
Who, with the Holy Ghost and thee,
Doth live and reign eternally. Amen.

>**ANTIPHON:** Lord, your mercy fills the earth;
>teach me your statutes.

My portion is the Lord;
 I have said: I will keep your law.
With all my heart I implore your kindness;
 have mercy on me according to your word.
I have thought on my ways
 and turned my feet to do your will.
I am ready and am not troubled
 to obey your commandments.
The cords of the wicked encompassed me,
 but I have not forgotten your law.
I rose at midnight to give you praise
 for your just judgments.
I am friend to all those who fear you,
 and who keep your commandments.
The earth, O Lord, is full of your mercy:
 teach me your statutes.

PSALM 119:57–64

Glory be . . .

>**ANTIPHON:** Lord, your mercy fills the earth;
>teach me your statutes.

SHORT READING

But the fruit of the Spirit is charity, joy, peace, patience, benignity, goodness, longanimity, mildness, faith, modesty, continence, chastity; against such there is no law. And those who are Christ's have crucified their flesh with its vices and desires. If we live in the Spirit, let us also walk in the Spirit.

GALATIANS 5:22–25

Let us pray.

Send us, Lord, the gifts of your Holy Spirit in abundance, that we may reap the fruits in our lives and walk by the same Spirit. Through Christ our Lord. Amen.

CALL: Let us bless the Lord.
RESPONSE: Thanks be to God.

VESPERS
Evening prayer

CALL: O God, ✢ come to my assistance.
RESPONSE: O Lord, be swift to my aid.
CALL: Glory be to the Father, and to the Son,
and to the Holy Spirit.
RESPONSE: As it was in the beginning, is now and
ever shall be, world without end. Amen.

Glory to thee, my God, this night,
For all the blessings of the light;
Keep me, O keep me, King of Kings,
Beneath thy own almighty wings.

Forgive me, Lord, for thy dear Son
The ill that I this day have done,
That with the world, myself, and thee,
I, ere I sleep, at peace may be.

Teach me to live, that I may dread
The grave as little as my bed;
Teach me to die, that so I may
Rise glorious at the awful day.

O may my soul on thee repose
And with sweet sleep mine eyelids close,
Sleep that may me more vigorous make
To serve my God when I awake.

Praise God, from whom all blessings flow,
Praise him, all creatures here below,
Praise him above, ye heavenly host,
Praise Father, Son and Holy Ghost. Amen.

THOMAS KEN

ANTIPHON: May we be blessed by the Lord,
who made heaven and earth.

When Israel came out of Egypt,
the house of Jacob from a barbarous people,
Judah was made his sanctuary,
Israel his dominion.
The sea looked and fled:
even the Jordan turned back;
the mountains skipped like rams,
and the hills like the lambs of the flock.

Why was it, O sea, that you fled,
that you were turned back, O Jordan?
You mountains, that you skipped like rams,
and you hills, like lambs of the flock?

At the presence of the Lord the earth quaked,
at the presence of the God of Jacob,
who turned the rock into pools of water
and the stony hill into fountains of waters.

Not to us, O Lord, not to us,
    but to your name give glory,
for your mercy and your truth's sake,
    lest the Gentiles say: "Where is their God?"

But our God is in heaven;
    he does all things as he wills.
The idols of the Gentiles are silver and gold,
    the work of the hands of men.

They have mouths yet cannot speak;
    they have eyes yet cannot see;
they have ears yet cannot hear;
    they have nostrils yet cannot smell.
They have hands yet cannot feel;
    they have feet yet cannot walk.
Nor can they cry out through their throats.

Let those who make them become like them,
    and all such who trust in them.

The house of Israel hopes in the Lord;
    he is their helper and their protector.
The house of Aaron hopes in the Lord;
    he is their helper and their protector.
Those who fear him hope in the Lord;
    he is their helper and their protector.
The Lord remembers us,
    and has blessed us;
He has blessed the sons of Israel.
    He has blessed the sons of Aaron.
He has blessed all those who fear him,
    both the little and the great.

May the Lord add blessings upon you,
    upon you and upon your children.

May you be blessed by the Lord,
> he who has made heaven and earth.

The heaven of heavens is the Lord's
> but the earth he has given to the children of men.

The dead shall not praise you, O Lord,
> nor any of those who go down into hell.

But we that live bless the Lord
> from this time, now and forever.

PSALMS 114–115

Glory be . . .

ANTIPHON: May we be blessed by the Lord,
who made heaven and earth.

SHORT READING

But we ought to give thanks to God always for you, brethren, beloved of God, because God has chosen you as firstfruits of salvation, through sanctification by the Spirit and faith in the truth. To which he has called you by our gospel, so that you may obtain the glory of our Lord Jesus Christ. Therefore, brethren, stand fast and hold to the traditions that you have learned either by word or by our letter. Now may our Lord Jesus Christ himself, and God our Father, who has loved us and has given us everlasting consolation and good hope in grace, comfort your hearts and confirm you in every good work and word.

2 THESSALONIANS 2:13–17

THE MAGNIFICAT

My ✝ soul magnifies the Lord,
> my spirit rejoices in God who is my Savior,
> who has looked upon the humility of his
> handmaiden.

Behold, all generations from now
   will acknowledge me blessed,
For the mighty one has done great things for me:
   Holy is his name!
His mercy is from one generation to the next on those
who fear him.
   Mighty is his arm!
He has scattered the proud in the imagination of
their hearts,
   and has put down the powerful from their thrones,
   exalting those of humble degree.
The hungry he has filled with good things,
   but the rich he has dismissed with nothing.
Remembering his mercy, he has helped his servant Israel,
   as he promised to our fathers,
   to Abraham and to his posterity forevermore.

LUKE 1:46–55

Glory be . . .

INTERCESSIONS
Offer these intercessions, or pray for other needs.

CALL:	Keep us firm in your faith, O Lord. *(Pause for prayer.)*
RESPONSE:	Grant our prayer, we beg.
CALL:	Sanctify us: make us saints, O Lord. *(Pause.)*
RESPONSE:	Grant our prayer, we beg.
CALL:	Give us courage to do good and avoid evil. *(Pause.)*
RESPONSE:	Grant our prayer, we beg.
CALL:	Overcome our wayward dispositions. *(Pause.)*
RESPONSE:	Grant our prayer, we beg.

CALL: Lord, grant rest to those of our friends who have died. *(Pause.)*
RESPONSE: Grant our prayer, we beg.

Lord, have mercy.
Christ, have mercy.
Lord, have mercy.

Our Father . . .

Let us pray.

O God, our refuge and strength, heed the devout prayers of your Church, and grant that what we beg in faith may truly come to pass. Through our Lord Jesus Christ, your Son, who lives and reigns with you and the Holy Spirit, one God, world without end. Amen.

CALL: Let us bless the Lord.
RESPONSE: Thanks be to God.

COMPLINE
Night prayer

CALL: O God, ✠ come to my assistance.

RESPONSE: O Lord, be swift to my aid.

CALL: Glory be to the Father, and to the Son,
             and to the Holy Spirit.

RESPONSE: As it was in the beginning, is now and
             ever shall be, world without end. Amen.

Make an examination of conscience, and perform an act of penance.

Before the ending of the day,
Creator of the world, we pray
That with thy wonted favor thou
Wouldst be our guard and keeper now.

From all ill dreams defend our eyes,
From nightly fears and fantasies;
Tread underfoot our ghostly foe,
That no pollution we may know.

O Father, that we ask be done,
Through Jesus Christ, thine only Son;
Who, with the Holy Ghost and thee,
Doth live and reign eternally. Amen.

ANTIPHON: Into your hands I commend
my spirit, Lord.

In you, O Lord, I have hoped.
Let me never be confounded.
In your justice, deliver me:
Bow your ear; make haste to rescue me.

Be to me a God, a protector,
and a house of refuge to save me,
for you are my strength and my stronghold,
and for your name's sake, lead me and nourish me.

Bring me out of this snare
which they have hidden for me:
for you are my protector, Lord.
Into your hands I commend my spirit:
It is you who will redeem me, O Lord,
God of truth.

You hate those who have empty regard for vanities,
but I have hoped in the Lord:
I will be glad and rejoice in your mercy,
for you have looked upon my humiliation,
and have saved my soul out of distress:
you have not placed me in the hands of the enemy,
but set my feet in a spacious place.

PSALM 31:1-8

Glory be . . .

ANTIPHON: Into your hands I commend
my spirit, Lord.

SHORT READING

Be angry (if you must) but do not sin; do not let the sun go down upon your anger, and give no place to the devil.

EPHESIANS 4:26–27

THE NUNC DIMITTIS

ANTIPHON: Save us, O Lord, while we wake, and watch over us as we sleep, that we may pass the night with Christ and rest in peace.

Lord, ✛ now let your servant depart in peace,
    according to your promise;
for my eyes have seen your salvation,
    which you have prepared in the presence of
    all peoples,
a light for revelation to the Gentiles,
    and for glory to your people Israel.

LUKE 2:29–32

Glory be . . .

ANTIPHON: Save us, O Lord, while we wake, and watch over us as we sleep, that we may pass the night with Christ and rest in peace.

Let us pray.

Visit this house, O Lord, we pray, and drive far from it the deadly power of the enemy. May your holy angels dwell here instead, that we may be preserved in peace with your blessing on us always. Through Christ our Lord. Amen.

Say the antiphon in honor of our Lady (see pp. 577–82), or use the following:

We fly to thy patronage, holy mother of God.
Despise not our petitions in our necessities
But deliver us from every evil,
O glorious and blessed Virgin!

WEDNESDAY

VIGILS
The night office

CALL: O Lord, ✠ open my lips.
RESPONSE: And my mouth shall declare
           your praise.

ANTIPHON: In your decrees I find
           instruction, Lord.

The heavens show forth the glory of God
    and the firmament declares the work of his hands.
Day unto day tells the tale
    and night unto night shows forth knowledge.

There are no speeches, no languages,
    where their voices are not understood.
Their sound goes forth through all the earth,
    and their words to the very ends of the world.

Among them he has pitched his tent of the sun:
    coming forth like a bridegroom from the
      bridal chamber,
    rejoicing like a giant to run the way.
His going out is from the end of heaven,
    and its circuit to the other end of the same.
    Nothing can be hidden from his heat.

The law of the Lord is immaculate,
    converting the soul.
The rule of the Lord is faithful,
    giving wisdom to little ones.

The commands of the Lord are right,
    rejoicing hearts.
The rule of the Lord is lightsome,
    enlightening the eyes.

The fear of the Lord is pure,
    enduring forever and ever.
The judgments of the Lord are true
    and righteous altogether.

They are more to be desired than gold,
    and many precious stones,
sweeter also than honey,
    than honey from the honeycomb.

Furthermore, in them your servant finds teaching;
    in keeping them is great reward.
But who, then, can understand sins?
    From secret sins cleanse me.

From the sin of presumption keep your servant
    lest it rule me.
Then shall I be without spot,
    cleansed from gravest sin.

And may the words of my mouth,
   the meditations of my heart,
be pleasing in your sight, O Lord,
   my helper, my Redeemer!

PSALM 19

Glory be . . .

ANTIPHON: In your decrees I find
   instruction, Lord.

CALL: I trust in you, O Lord.
RESPONSE: It is you who are my God.

FIRST READING
Read one chapter from the Scriptures.

RESPONSE TO THE READING

CALL: Your word is a lamp for my steps,
RESPONSE: Joy to the heart, light for the eyes.
CALL: I shall walk in the way of your
   commands,
RESPONSE: Joy to the heart, light for the eyes.

SECOND READING
Choose a spiritual reading.

RESPONSE TO THE READING

CALL: The vaults of the heavens
RESPONSE: Cry out your praise, O Lord.
CALL: The saints and the angelic hosts
RESPONSE: Cry out your praise, O Lord.

Let us pray.

Almighty and eternal God, look upon our feebleness with pity, and stretch out your mighty arm to protect us. Through Christ our Lord. Amen.

CALL: Let us bless the Lord.
RESPONSE: Thanks be to God.

LAUDS
Morning prayer

CALL:	O God, ✠ come to my assistance.
RESPONSE:	O Lord, be swift to my aid.
CALL:	Glory be to the Father, and to the Son, and to the Holy Spirit.
RESPONSE:	As it was in the beginning, is now and ever shall be, world without end. Amen.

Now that daylight fills the sky,
We lift our hearts to Christ on high,
That he, in all we do or say,
Would keep us free from harm today.

Would guard our hearts and tongues from strife;
From anger's din would hide our life;
From all ill sights would turn our eyes;
Would close our ears from vanities:

Would keep our inmost conscience pure;
Our souls from folly would secure;
Would bid us check the pride of sense
With due and holy abstinence.

So we, when this new day is gone,
And night in turn is drawing on,
With conscience by the world unstained
Shall praise his name for victory gained.

All laud to God the Father be;
All praise, eternal Son, to thee;
All glory, as is ever meet,
To God the holy Paraclete. Amen.

ANTIPHON: Praise the name of the Lord, for he
alone is exalted.

Praise the Lord from the heavens,
    praise him in the high places.
Praise him, all his angels,
    praise him, all his hosts.
Praise him, O sun and moon,
    praise him all you stars and light.
Praise him, heaven of heavens
    and you waters above the heavens.
Praise the name of the Lord.

For he spoke and they were made:
    he commanded and they were created.
He established them forever,
    he made a decree that shall not pass away.

Praise the Lord from the earth,
    you dragons and all deeps,
fire, hail, snow, ice,
    stormy winds that fulfill his word;

Mountains and all hills,
>fruitful trees and all cedars,
Beasts, and all cattle,
>serpents and feathered fowls;
Kings of the earth and all people:
>princes and all judges of the earth;
Young men and maidens,
>the old with the younger:
Praise the name of the Lord
>for his name alone is exalted.
The praise of his name
>is exalted above heaven and earth.

He exalts the horn of his people.
>He is the praise of all his saints,
of the children of Israel,
>of the people who draw near him.

PSALM 148

Glory be . . .

ANTIPHON: Praise the name of the Lord, for he
alone is exalted.

SHORT READING
God loves no one so much as the one who dwells with
wisdom. For she is more beautiful than the sun, and above
all the order of the stars. Compared with the light she is
found to be surpassing, for light is succeeded by the night,
but no evil can overcome wisdom.

WISDOM 7:28–30

THE BENEDICTUS
Blessed ✠ be the Lord, the God of Israel,
>who has visited and redeemed his people,
and has lifted up a horn of salvation for us

in the family of his servant David.
For this he swore through the mouths of holy men,
   those who were prophets, from the beginning:
There would be salvation from our foes,
   and from the hand of all those who hate us;
to comfort our fathers,
   and to honor his holy covenant,
which oath once he swore to Abraham, our father,
   that he would grant us,
that freed from the hand of our enemies,
   and without fear, we may serve him,
   in holiness and justice in his very presence
   all our days.
And you, my son, will be named Prophet of the
  Most High;
   for you will go before the presence of the Lord
   to prepare his way,
to teach knowledge of salvation to his people
   that their sins may be forgiven,
   through the merciful heart of our God,
when the Daystar shall visit us from on high
   to enlighten those who sit in darkness
   and in the shadow of death,
   and guide our feet to the way of peace.

LUKE 1:68–79

Glory be . . .

INTERCESSIONS
Offer these intercessions, or pray for other needs.

CALL: Lord, protect all those who travel,
           and those who protect them.
           (Pause for prayer.)
RESPONSE: Guard us and save us, Lord.

CALL: Lord, protect those in our armed
forces, and end all wars. *(Pause.)*

RESPONSE: Guard us and save us, Lord.

CALL: Lord, protect our police, and preserve
their sense of justice. *(Pause.)*

RESPONSE: Guard us and save us, Lord.

CALL: Lord, protect our judges and lawyers,
and grant them wisdom. *(Pause.)*

RESPONSE: Guard us and save us, Lord.

CALL: Lord, protect our own sense of
justice, and help us always to do
what is right. *(Pause.)*

RESPONSE: Guard us and save us, Lord.

Lord, have mercy.
Christ, have mercy.
Lord, have mercy.

Our Father . . .

Let us pray.

God of mercy and goodness, in whose gift it is that we
should serve you worthily and well, grant that we may run
toward the fulfillment of your promises without offense
and with alacrity. Through our Lord Jesus Christ, your
Son, who lives and reigns with you in the unity of the
Holy Spirit, one God forever and ever. Amen.

CALL: Let us bless the Lord.

RESPONSE: Thanks be to God.

TERCE
Midmorning prayer

CALL: O God, ✛ come to my assistance.
RESPONSE: O Lord, be swift to my aid.
CALL: Glory be to the Father, and to the Son,
and to the Holy Spirit.
RESPONSE: As it was in the beginning, is now and
ever shall be, world without end. Amen.

Come, Holy Ghost, with God the Son
And God the Father, ever one;
Shed forth thy grace within our breast
And dwell with us a ready guest.

By every power, by heart and tongue,
By act and deed, thy praise be sung;
Inflame with perfect love each sense
That others' souls may kindle thence.

O Father, that we ask be done,
Through Jesus Christ, thine only Son;
Who, with the Holy Ghost and thee,
Doth live and reign eternally. Amen.

ANTIPHON: The law from your mouth is
good to me.

Lord, you have dealt well with your servant,
according to your word.
Teach me goodness, discipline, and knowledge:
I have believed your commandments.
Before I was humbled, I went wrong,
but now I keep your word.
You are good, and in your goodness
teach me your statutes.
The proud have conceived lies about me
but with all my heart will I keep your commands.
Their minds are curdled like milk,
but your law is my delight.
It was good for me to have been humbled,
that I may learn your commandments.
The law from your mouth is good to me;
dearer than thousands in silver or gold.

PSALM 119:65–72

Glory be . . .

ANTIPHON: The law from your mouth is
good to me.

SHORT READING

Now there are diversities of graces, but the same Spirit;
and there are diversities of ministries, but the same Lord;
and there are diversities of operation, but it is the same

God who works all in all. And the manifestation of the Spirit is given to everyone for profit.

1 CORINTHIANS 12:4–7

Let us pray.

O God, who at the third hour poured your Holy Spirit upon our Lady and the apostles: renew your gift of the same Spirit within us at this time, that we may perfectly serve you and come to our eternal reward. Through Christ our Lord. Amen.

> CALL: Let us bless the Lord.
> RESPONSE: Thanks be to God.

SEXT
Midday prayer

CALL: O God, ✝ come to my assistance.
RESPONSE: O Lord, be swift to my aid.
CALL: Glory be to the Father, and to the Son,
           and to the Holy Spirit.
RESPONSE: As it was in the beginning, is now and
           ever shall be, world without end. Amen.

O God of truth, O Lord of might,
Who orderest time and change aright,
And send'st the early morning ray,
And light'st the glow of perfect day:

Extinguish thou each sinful fire,
And banish every ill desire;
And while thou keep'st the body whole,
Shed forth thy peace upon the soul.

O Father, that we ask be done,
Through Jesus Christ, thine only Son;
Who, with the Holy Ghost and thee,
Doth live and reign eternally. Amen.

ANTIPHON: Let my heart be undefiled in your
commandments, O Lord.

Your hands made me and formed me:
give me understanding to learn your commands.
Those who fear you will see me and be glad,
for I greatly hope in your word.
I know, O Lord, that your judgments are right
and that you were right to have humbled me.
O let your mercy be now for my comfort,
according to your promise unto your servant.
Let your tender mercies come to me and I shall live,
for your law is my delight.
Let the proud be ashamed who have been unjust to me,
but I will contemplate your precepts.
Let those who fear you turn to me,
and those who know your decrees.
Let my heart be undefiled in your commandments,
that I may not be confounded.

PSALM 119:73–80

Glory be . . .

ANTIPHON: Let my heart be undefiled in your
commandments, O Lord.

SHORT READING

For as the body is one and has many members, and all the
members of the body, though they are many, yet are one
body, so also is Christ. For in one Spirit we were all baptized

into one body—Jews or Gentiles, slaves or free—and of one Spirit we have all been made to drink.

1 CORINTHIANS 12:12–13

Let us pray.

Set aside, Lord, our envies and our selfish jealousies; help us to realize the true value of each person in building up the Church, the body of Christ, that your kingdom may come and your will be done. Through the same Christ our Lord. Amen.

CALL: Let us bless the Lord.
RESPONSE: Thanks be to God.

NONE
Midafternoon prayer

CALL:	O God, ✢ come to my assistance.
RESPONSE:	O Lord, be swift to my aid.
CALL:	Glory be to the Father, and to the Son, and to the Holy Spirit.
RESPONSE:	As it was in the beginning, is now and ever shall be, world without end. Amen.

O God, Creation's secret force,
Thyself unmoved, all motion's source,
Who from the morn till evening ray
Through all its changes guid'st the day:

Grant us, when this short life is past,
The glorious evening that shall last;
That, by a holy death attained,
Eternal glory may be gained.

O Father, that we ask be done,
Through Jesus Christ, thine only Son;
Who, with the Holy Ghost and thee,
Doth live and reign eternally. Amen.

> **ANTIPHON:** Lord, because of your love, give me life.

My soul longs after your salvation:
    and in your word I strongly hope.
My eyes strain to see your word fulfilled.
    Saying: O when will you comfort me?
I have become like a bottle in the smoke;
    I have not forgotten your statutes.
How many days must your servant endure?
    When will you avenge me on my foes?
The wicked have dug pitfalls for me,
    which are against your law.
All your commandments are true;
    be my help when they persecute me unjustly.
They almost made an end of me on earth,
    but I have not forsaken your commandments.
Give me life according to your mercy
    and I will keep the commands of your mouth.

PSALM 119:81–88

Glory be . . .

> **ANTIPHON:** Lord, because of your love, give me life.

SHORT READING

God has so tempered the body together, that there may be no schism in the body, but that the members might be mutually caring, one for another. So if one member should suffer, all the members suffer with it; or if one member is glorified, all the members rejoice with it.

1 CORINTHIANS 12:24–26

Let us pray.

Almighty God, as you have made the Church the mystical body of your Son, give all its members care for each other, that the Church may be extended throughout the world. Through Christ our Lord. Amen.

CALL: Let us bless the Lord.
RESPONSE: Thanks be to God.

VESPERS
Evening prayer

CALL: O God, ✠ come to my assistance.
RESPONSE: O Lord, be swift to my aid.
CALL: Glory be to the Father, and to the Son,
               and to the Holy Spirit.
RESPONSE: As it was in the beginning, is now and
               ever shall be, world without end. Amen.

O heavenly maker of mankind,
Alone who gave each thing its place,
By whose command the earth brought forth
Both reptiles and the feral race.

And ordered that those mighty beasts
Who live their lives at your behest
Be subject to your servants' word,
Who are of your creation best.

Then drive away those passions bold
That trouble your poor servants here,
And sins ingrained by habit old
Of thought, or word, or deed, or fear.

Grant us reward of heavenly joy
O grant us gifts of heavenly grace!
And break the chains of strife, that peace
May lead us all to see your face.

Grant this, O loving Father God,
And Jesus Christ, your only Son,
Who with the Holy Spirit blessed
Reign ever three and ever one. Amen.

ANTIPHON: Your throne, O God, shall
endure forever.

My heart has uttered noble words.
To the king I must speak of what I have done;
my tongue like the pen of a swift scribe.

You are beautiful above all the children of men;
grace is poured upon your lips:
therefore God has blessed you forever.

O most mighty one, gird your sword upon your thigh,
With your comeliness and beauty
begin, prosper, and reign!
Because of truth and kindness and justice,
your own right hand shall keep you safe.

Your arrows are sharp: peoples will fall beneath you,
even in the midst of the king's enemies.

Your throne, O God, is forever and ever:
The scepter of uprightness is the scepter
of your kingdom.

You have loved justice and have hated iniquity.
    Therefore God, your God, has anointed you
    with the oil of gladness above your fellows:
Your garments are perfumed with myrrh, aloes,
  and cassia;
    from the ivory palace music shall delight you.

The daughters of kings are among your attendants.
    On your right stands the queen
    in garments of gold of Ophir.

Hearken, O daughter, and see: give ear to my words:
    forget your people and your father's house.
And the king will greatly desire your beauty.
    He is your lord; then adore him.

And the daughters of Tyre shall entreat with gifts,
    all the rich of the people shall beg your favor.
The glory of the daughter of the king is in golden
  borders,
    clothed round about with varieties.

She is conducted to the king with her virgin
  companions.
    They are brought with gladness and rejoicing;
    they enter within the temple of the king.

Instead of your fathers you shall have sons:
    you shall make them princes over all the earth.

They shall remember your name throughout all
  generations.
    Therefore shall people praise you forever
    and forever.

PSALM 45

Glory be . . .

ANTIPHON: Your throne, O God, shall
endure forever.

SHORT READING

Therefore we also thank God without ceasing, because when you received the word of God that you heard from us, you received it not as the word of men but (as it is indeed) the word of God, who is at work in you who have believed.

1 THESSALONIANS 2:13

THE MAGNIFICAT

My ✠ soul magnifies the Lord,
 my spirit rejoices in God who is my Savior,
 who has looked upon the humility of his
 handmaiden.
Behold, all generations from now
 will acknowledge me blessed,
For the mighty one has done great things for me:
 Holy is his name!
His mercy is from one generation to the next on those
 who fear him.
 Mighty is his arm!
He has scattered the proud in the imagination of
 their hearts,
 and has put down the powerful from their thrones,
 exalting those of humble degree.
The hungry he has filled with good things,
 but the rich he has dismissed with nothing.
Remembering his mercy, he has helped his servant Israel,
 as he promised to our fathers,
 to Abraham and to his posterity forevermore.

LUKE 1:46–55

Glory be . . .

INTERCESSIONS

Offer these intercessions, or pray for other needs.

> *CALL:* Grant us faith in its fullness, O Lord. *(Pause for prayer.)*
> *RESPONSE:* Kyrie eleison.
> *CALL:* Grant us hope for our salvation. *(Pause.)*
> *RESPONSE:* Kyrie eleison.
> *CALL:* Give us charity in abundance. *(Pause.)*
> *RESPONSE:* Kyrie eleison.
> *CALL:* Make us perfect in your sight, O Lord. *(Pause.)*
> *RESPONSE:* Kyrie eleison.
> *CALL:* Lord, grant rest to the dead in purgatory. *(Pause.)*
> *RESPONSE:* Kyrie eleison.

Lord, have mercy.
Christ, have mercy.
Lord, have mercy.

Our Father . . .

Let us pray.

Almighty God, our heavenly Father, hear the prayers of your children, and grant that what we ask in faith may be according to your holy will. Through our Lord Jesus Christ, your Son, who lives and reigns with you and the Holy Spirit, one God, world without end. Amen.

> *CALL:* Let us bless the Lord.
> *RESPONSE:* Thanks be to God.

COMPLINE
Night prayer

CALL:	O God, ✠ come to my assistance.
RESPONSE:	O Lord, be swift to my aid.
CALL:	Glory be to the Father, and to the Son, and to the Holy Spirit.
RESPONSE:	As it was in the beginning, is now and ever shall be, world without end. Amen.

Make an examination of conscience, and perform an act of penance.

Before the ending of the day,
Creator of the world, we pray
That with thy wonted favor thou
Wouldst be our guard and keeper now.

From all ill dreams defend our eyes,
From nightly fears and fantasies;

Tread underfoot our ghostly foe,
That no pollution we may know.

O Father, that we ask be done,
Through Jesus Christ, thine only Son;
Who, with the Holy Ghost and thee,
Doth live and reign eternally. Amen.

> **ANTIPHON:**   I will bless the Lord, who even at
> night directs my heart.

Preserve me, God, I put my trust in you.
I say to the Lord: You are my God.
All I have is nothing without you.

He has placed in me a wonderful love
for the saints, great men, who are in the land.
Those who run after other gods shall have great trouble.
I will not offer their offerings of blood.
I will not mention their name with my lips.

The Lord is my portion and my cup;
it is you who will restore my inheritance to me.
My lines have fallen in pleasant places:
welcome is my heritage to me.

I will bless the Lord who gives me understanding,
even at night he advises my heart.
I set the Lord always in my sight:
because he is at my right hand, I shall not fall.

Therefore my heart is glad, my tongue rejoices;
even my flesh shall rest in hope.
For you will not leave my soul in hell,
nor let your holy one know corruption.

You have made known to me the way of life,
you will fill me with joy when I see your face,

at your right hand are delights forevermore.

PSALM 16

Glory be . . .

ANTIPHON: I will bless the Lord, who even at
night directs my heart.

SHORT READING

May the God of peace himself sanctify you in all things:
that your whole spirit and soul and body may be preserved blameless at the coming of our Lord Jesus Christ.
He who has called you is faithful, and he will do it.

1 THESSALONIANS 5:23–24

THE NUNC DIMITTIS

ANTIPHON: Save us, O Lord, while we wake, and
watch over us as we sleep, that we
may pass the night with Christ and
rest in peace.

Lord, ✛ now let your servant depart in peace,
according to your promise;
for my eyes have seen your salvation,
which you have prepared in the presence of
all peoples,
a light for revelation to the Gentiles,
and for glory to your people Israel.

LUKE 2:29–32

Glory be . . .

ANTIPHON: Save us, O Lord, while we wake, and
watch over us as we sleep, that we
may pass the night with Christ and
rest in peace.

Let us pray.

Visit this house, O Lord, we pray, and drive far from it the deadly power of the enemy. May your holy angels dwell here instead, that we may be preserved in peace with your blessing on us always. Through Christ our Lord. Amen.

Say the antiphon in honor of our Lady (see pp. 577–82), or use the following:

We fly to thy patronage, holy mother of God.
Despise not our petitions in our necessities
But deliver us from every evil,
O glorious and blessed Virgin!

THURSDAY

VIGILS
The night office

CALL: O Lord, ✝ open my lips.

RESPONSE: And my mouth shall declare
your praise.

ANTIPHON: My soul is thirsting for God, the God
of my life.

Like the hart that pants after fountains of water,
    so my soul is yearning after you, O my God.
My soul is thirsting for God, the living God;
      when can I come and appear before the face
      of God?

My tears have become my bread day and night,
    as I hear it said to me daily: Where is your God?

115

These things I remembered, and poured out my soul:
　　how I would go with the rejoicing multitude
　　even into the house of God,
amid loud cries of joy and thanksgiving,
　　the crowd keeping joyful festival.

Why so sad, my soul, why so troubled within me?
　　Hope in God; I will still give him praise,
　　my salvation and my God.

My soul is troubled within me, therefore I will think
　of you,
　　　from the land of Jordan and Hermon, from the Hill
　　　of Mizar.
Deep is calling on deep, in the roar of your cataracts:
　　your heights and all your billows have passed
　　over me.

In the daytime the Lord has granted his loving-kindness;
　　and at night I sang of him: a prayer to the God
　　of my life.
I sing to God: my Redeemer, why have you
　forgotten me?
　　　Why must I go mourning while my enemy
　　　afflicts me?

While my bones are broken, my enemies reproach me,
　　saying to me day after day: Where is your God?
Why so sad, my soul, why so troubled within me?
　　Hope in God; I will still give him praise,
　　my salvation and my God.

PSALM 42

Glory be . . .

ANTIPHON:　My soul is thirsting for God, the God
　　　　　　of my life.

CALL: You shall ask, and you shall receive,
RESPONSE: A spring of living water inside you.

FIRST READING
Read one chapter from the Scriptures.

RESPONSE TO THE READING
CALL: Go, then, and teach all nations:
RESPONSE: Baptize them in the name of the Father, and of the Son, and of the Holy Spirit.
CALL: Let the little children come to me: do not stop them.
RESPONSE: Baptize them in the name of the Father, and of the Son, and of the Holy Spirit.

SECOND READING
Choose a spiritual reading.

RESPONSE TO THE READING
CALL: From his wounded side flowed blood and water.
RESPONSE: Christ comes to us in water and in blood.
CALL: There are three witnesses, the Spirit, the water, and the blood; and these three agree.
RESPONSE: Christ comes to us in water and in blood.

Let us pray.

Almighty God, whose Son gave himself as the sacrifice for our salvation, and from whose wounded side flowed blood and water, the fountain of sacramental life in the Church, renew within us the grace of the sacraments, first received in our baptism. Through the same Christ our Lord. Amen.

CALL: Let us bless the Lord.
RESPONSE: Thanks be to God.

LAUDS
Morning prayer

CALL: O God, ✝ come to my assistance.
RESPONSE: O Lord, be swift to my aid.
CALL: Glory be to the Father, and to the Son,
             and to the Holy Spirit.
RESPONSE: As it was in the beginning, is now and
             ever shall be, world without end. Amen.

Lord, enthroned in heavenly splendor,
First-begotten from the dead,
Thou alone, our strong defender,
Liftest up thy people's head.
    Alleluia, Alleluia,
Jesu, true and living Bread!

Paschal Lamb, thine offering, finished
Once for all when thou wast slain,
In its fullness undiminished

Shall forevermore remain.
    Alleluia, Alleluia,
Cleansing souls from every stain.

Life-imparting, heavenly Manna,
Stricken Rock with streaming side,
Heaven and earth with loud hosanna
Worship thee, the Lamb who died,
    Alleluia, Alleluia,
Risen, ascended, glorified!

G. H. BOURNE

ANTIPHON: I will go in to the altar of God,
                the God of my joy.

Defend me, O God, and distinguish my cause
    from that of an unholy nation.
From unjust and deceitful men
    deliver me, O God.

For you, O God, are my strength,
    why have you cast me off?
Why do I go sorrowful
    and afflicted by the foe?

Send forth your light and your truth;
    these have directed me,
and brought me unto your holy mountain
    and into your tabernacles.

And I will go in to the altar of God,
    the God of my gladness and joy.
Upon the harp I will give you thanks,
    O God, my God.

Why so sad, my soul,
    why so troubled within me?

Hope in God; I will still give him praise,
    my salvation and my God.

PSALM 43

Glory be . . .

ANTIPHON: I will go in to the altar of God,
            the God of my joy.

SHORT READING

For I received from the Lord that which I also delivered to you, that the Lord Jesus the same night in which he was betrayed took bread and, giving thanks, broke it and said, "Take and eat: this is my body, which shall be delivered for you. Do this in commemoration of me." In the same way also the chalice, after he had eaten, saying, "This chalice is the new testament in my blood. Do this, as often as you drink it, for the commemoration of me." For as often as you shall eat this bread and drink the chalice, you shall show the Lord's death until he comes.

1 CORINTHIANS 11:23–26

THE BENEDICTUS

Blessed ✠ be the Lord, the God of Israel,
    who has visited and redeemed his people,
and has lifted up a horn of salvation for us
    in the family of his servant David.
For this he swore through the mouths of holy men,
    those who were prophets, from the beginning:
There would be salvation from our foes,
    and from the hand of all those who hate us;
to comfort our fathers,
    and to honor his holy covenant,
which oath once he swore to Abraham, our father,
    that he would grant us,

that freed from the hand of our enemies,
    and without fear, we may serve him,
    in holiness and justice in his very presence
      all our days.
And you, my son, will be named Prophet of the
  Most High;
    for you will go before the presence of the Lord
    to prepare his way,
to teach knowledge of salvation to his people
    that their sins may be forgiven,
    through the merciful heart of our God,
when the Daystar shall visit us from on high
    to enlighten those who sit in darkness
    and in the shadow of death,
    and guide our feet to the way of peace.

LUKE 1:68–79

Glory be . . .

INTERCESSIONS

Offer these intercessions, or pray for other needs.

CALL:	Lord Jesus, deepen our faith in your real presence in the Eucharist. *(Pause for prayer.)*
RESPONSE:	You, Lord, have the words of eternal life.
CALL:	Grant us the grace to receive communion worthily. *(Pause.)*
RESPONSE:	You, Lord, have the words of eternal life.
CALL:	Help all our priests to offer your sacrifice reverently and well. *(Pause.)*
RESPONSE:	You, Lord, have the words of eternal life.

CALL: Strengthen with your grace those deprived of the Eucharist. *(Pause.)*

RESPONSE: You, Lord, have the words of eternal life.

CALL: Deepen the reverence and faith of those who bring communion to the sick. *(Pause.)*

RESPONSE: You, Lord, have the words of eternal life.

Lord, have mercy,
Christ, have mercy,
Lord, have mercy.

Our Father . . .

Let us pray.

God, who has given us in this wonderful sacrament a memorial of your passion, grant, we beg, that we may so honor it in this life that the redemption which it signifies may be ours in the life to come. Through our Lord Jesus Christ, your Son, who lives and reigns with you in the unity of the Holy Spirit, one God forever and ever. Amen.

CALL: Let us bless the Lord.

RESPONSE: Thanks be to God.

TERCE
Midmorning prayer

CALL: O God, ✚ come to my assistance.
RESPONSE: O Lord, be swift to my aid.
CALL: Glory be to the Father, and to the Son,
           and to the Holy Spirit.
RESPONSE: As it was in the beginning, is now and
           ever shall be, world without end. Amen.

Come, Holy Ghost, with God the Son
And God the Father, ever one;
Shed forth thy grace within our breast
And dwell with us a ready guest.

By every power, by heart and tongue,
By act and deed, thy praise be sung;
Inflame with perfect love each sense
That others' souls may kindle thence.

O Father, that we ask be done,
Through Jesus Christ, thine only Son;
Who, with the Holy Ghost and thee,
Doth live and reign eternally. Amen.

> **ANTIPHON:** O Lord, how wonderful is the work
> of your Spirit in us.

Forever, O Lord, your word
    stands firm in heaven.
Your truth lasts unto all generations,
    as the earth that you created:
Which, by your ordinance, endures to this day;
    for all things serve you.
Unless your law had been my meditation
    I might have perished in my abjection.
Your precepts I will never forget,
    for by them you have given me life.
I am yours: save me,
    for I have sought your statutes.
Though the wicked have waited to destroy me,
    still I meditate on your will.
I have seen that all perfection has its limits,
    but broad indeed is your command.

PSALM 119:89–96

Glory be . . .

> **ANTIPHON:** O Lord, how wonderful is the work
> of your Spirit in us.

SHORT READING

For in one Spirit we were all baptized into one body—
Jews or Gentiles, slaves or free—and of one Spirit we
have all been made to drink.

1 CORINTHIANS 12:13

Let us pray.

O God, the lover of truth and the source of every blessing, grant, through the Holy Spirit dwelling within us, that we may be confirmed in truth and truly blessed. Through Christ our Lord. Amen.

> CALL: Let us bless the Lord.
> RESPONSE: Thanks be to God.

SEXT
Midday prayer

CALL: O God, ✝ come to my assistance.
RESPONSE: O Lord, be swift to my aid.
CALL: Glory be to the Father, and to the Son,
and to the Holy Spirit.
RESPONSE: As it was in the beginning, is now and
ever shall be, world without end. Amen.

O God of truth, O Lord of might,
Who orderest time and change aright,
And send'st the early morning ray,
And light'st the glow of perfect day:

Extinguish thou each sinful fire,
And banish every ill desire;
And while thou keep'st the body whole,
Shed forth thy peace upon the soul.

O Father, that we ask be done,
Through Jesus Christ, thine only Son;
Who, with the Holy Ghost and thee,
Doth live and reign eternally. Amen.

ANTIPHON: Lord, restrain my feet from evil ways.

O how have I loved your law!
    It is ever in my mind.
Your command makes me wiser than my foes;
    for it is mine forever.
I have understood more than all my teachers
    because your testimonies are my meditation.

I have understanding above the ancients
    because I have sought your commandments.
I have restrained my feet from every evil way
    that I may keep your word.
I have not turned away from your judgments,
    because you have taught me your law.
How sweet are your words to my palate!
    more than honey in my mouth.
By your commandments I gain understanding,
    and so I hate every way of iniquity.

PSALM 119:97–104

Glory be . . .

ANTIPHON: Lord, restrain my feet from evil ways.

SHORT READING

Blessed be the God and Father of our Lord Jesus Christ,
who has blessed us with spiritual blessings in the heavenly
places in Christ, as he chose us in him before the foundation of the world, that we should be holy and unspotted
before him in love. He predestined us to be his own adopt-
ed children through Jesus Christ, according to the purpose

of his will, to the praise of the glory of his grace with which he graced us in his beloved Son. In him we have redemption through his blood, the remission of sins, according to the riches of his grace that he lavished upon us in all wisdom and prudence.

EPHESIANS 1:3–8

Let us pray.

Almighty Father, whose own dear Son died on the cross for our forgiveness, overcome our bashfulness, give us a true sense of shame for our sins, and help us to seek your pardon in the sacrament of penance. Through the same Christ our Lord. Amen.

CALL: Let us bless the Lord.
RESPONSE: Thanks be to God.

NONE
Midafternoon prayer

CALL:	O God, ✛ come to my assistance.
RESPONSE:	O Lord, be swift to my aid.
CALL:	Glory be to the Father, and to the Son, and to the Holy Spirit.
RESPONSE:	As it was in the beginning, is now and ever shall be, world without end. Amen.

O God, Creation's secret force,
Thyself unmoved, all motion's source,
Who from the morn till evening ray
Through all its changes guid'st the day:

Grant us, when this short life is past,
The glorious evening that shall last;
That, by a holy death attained,
Eternal glory may be gained.

O Father, that we ask be done,
Through Jesus Christ, thine only Son;
Who, with the Holy Ghost and thee,
Doth live and reign eternally. Amen.

ANTIPHON: Your laws are the joy of my heart,
O Lord.

Your word is a lamp to my feet
and a light to my paths.
I have sworn and am determined
to keep the judgments of your justice.
Lord, I have been humbled exceedingly:
give me life according to your word.
Accept, O Lord, the free offering of my mouth
and teach me your judgments.
My soul is continually in my hands,
yet I have not forgotten your law.
Sinners have laid a snare for me:
but I have not erred from your precepts.
I have your laws as an eternal inheritance,
because they are the joy of my heart.
I have inclined my heart to do your will forever,
and this is my reward forevermore.

PSALM 119:105–112

Glory be . . .

ANTIPHON: Your laws are the joy of my heart,
O Lord.

SHORT READING

The spirit of the Lord is upon me, because the Lord has
anointed me: he has sent me to preach to the meek; to heal
the contrite of heart, to preach release to the captives, and
deliverance to those who are imprisoned; to proclaim the

acceptable year of the Lord, and the day of vengeance of our God; to comfort all who mourn.

ISAIAH 61:1-2

Let us pray.

Protect with your grace, Lord, those whom you have called to share your sacred ministry by the laying on of hands. May they be gentle but ardent servants of the gospel, seeking not to be served but to serve and to do your will in all things. Through Christ our Lord. Amen.

CALL: Let us bless the Lord.

RESPONSE: Thanks be to God.

VESPERS
Evening prayer

CALL:	O God, ✠ come to my assistance.
RESPONSE:	O Lord, be swift to my aid.
CALL:	Glory be to the Father, and to the Son, and to the Holy Spirit.
RESPONSE:	As it was in the beginning, is now and ever shall be, world without end. Amen.

Love Divine, all loves excelling,
Joy of Heaven, to earth come down,
Fix in us thy humble dwelling,
All thy faithful mercies crown.

Jesu, thou art all compassion,
Pure unbounded love thou art;
Visit us with thy salvation,
Enter every trembling heart.

Come, almighty to deliver,
Let us all thy life receive;
Suddenly return and never,
Never more thy temples leave.

Thee we would be always blessing,
Serve thee as thy hosts above,
Pray, and praise thee without ceasing,
Glory in thy perfect love.

Finish then thy new creation,
Pure and spotless let us be;
Let us see thy great salvation,
Perfectly restored in thee.

Changed from glory into glory,
Till in Heaven we take our place,
Till we cast our crowns before thee
Lost in wonder, love and praise!

C. WESLEY

ANTIPHON:　You are beautiful, my love, comely
as Jerusalem.

O blessed are all that fear the Lord,
that walk in his ways!

You shall eat the fruit of the labor of your hands.
You will be blessed: it shall be well with you;
Your wife like a fruitful vine
that grows on the wall of your house;
your children like olive plants,
round about your table.

Behold, thus shall the one be blessed
that fears the Lord.
May the Lord bless you out of Zion:

and may you see the good things of Jerusalem
all the days of your life.
May you live to see your children's children.
Peace upon Israel!

PSALM 128

Glory be . . .

ANTIPHON: You are beautiful, my love, comely
as Jerusalem.

SHORT READING
Many waters cannot quench love; neither can the floods
drown it. If a man should give all the substance of his house
for love, it would be despised as nothing.

SONG OF SONGS 8:7

THE MAGNIFICAT
My ✠ soul magnifies the Lord,
my spirit rejoices in God who is my Savior,
who has looked upon the humility of his
handmaiden.
Behold, all generations from now
will acknowledge me blessed,
For the mighty one has done great things for me:
Holy is his name!
His mercy is from one generation to the next on those
who fear him.
Mighty is his arm!
He has scattered the proud in the imagination of
their hearts,
and has put down the powerful from their thrones,
exalting those of humble degree.
The hungry he has filled with good things,
but the rich he has dismissed with nothing.

Remembering his mercy, he has helped his servant Israel,
  as he promised to our fathers,
  to Abraham and to his posterity forevermore.

LUKE 1:46–55

Glory be . . .

INTERCESSIONS

Offer these intercessions, or pray for other needs.

CALL:	Let us pray for all those who are married. *(Pause for prayer.)*
RESPONSE:	May your love be upon us, O Lord.
CALL:	For those who are preparing for marriage. *(Pause.)*
RESPONSE:	May your love be upon us, O Lord.
CALL:	For those whose marriage is a source of pain. *(Pause.)*
RESPONSE:	May your love be upon us, O Lord.
CALL:	For the gift of understanding between married people. *(Pause.)*
RESPONSE:	May your love be upon us, O Lord.
CALL:	Lord, give comfort to those who have been widowed. *(Pause.)*
RESPONSE:	May your love be upon us, O Lord.

Lord, have mercy.
Christ, have mercy.
Lord, have mercy.

Our Father . . .

Let us pray.

Lord, you who do not wish that human beings should be alone, renew the grace of the sacrament of marriage within those whom you have called to this state, and enable them to bear the difficulties with fortitude, and the joys with gratitude. Through our Lord Jesus Christ, your Son, who lives and reigns with you and the Holy Spirit, one God, world without end. Amen.

CALL: Let us bless the Lord.
RESPONSE: Thanks be to God.

COMPLINE
Night prayer

CALL: O God, ✠ come to my assistance.

RESPONSE: O Lord, be swift to my aid.

CALL: Glory be to the Father, and to the Son, and to the Holy Spirit.

RESPONSE: As it was in the beginning, is now and ever shall be, world without end.

Amen.

Make an examination of conscience, and perform an act of penance.

Before the ending of the day,
Creator of the world, we pray
That with thy wonted favor thou
Wouldst be our guard and keeper now.

From all ill dreams defend our eyes,
From nightly fears and fantasies;

Tread underfoot our ghostly foe,
That no pollution we may know.

O Father, that we ask be done,
Through Jesus Christ, thine only Son;
Who, with the Holy Ghost and thee,
Doth live and reign eternally. Amen.

> **ANTIPHON:** Your mercy, Lord, will follow me all
> the days of my life.

The Lord is my shepherd; so I shall need nothing.
     He has set me in a place of pasture.
He has led me by the waters of tranquillity;
     he has restored my soul.
He has led me on the paths of justice,
     for his own name's sake.
For if I should walk in the midst of the shadow of death
     I will fear no evils, for you are there with me.
Your rod and your staff:
     these have comforted me.
You have prepared a table before me
     in the sight of those that afflict me.
You have anointed my head with oil;
     and my cup is overflowing.
And so your mercy will follow me
     all the days of my life.
And I shall dwell in the house of the Lord
     unto length of days.

PSALM 23

Glory be . . .

> **ANTIPHON:** Your mercy, Lord, will follow me all
> the days of my life.

SHORT READING

Is anyone sick among you? Let him bring in the priests of the church, and let them pray over him, anointing him with oil in the name of the Lord; and the prayer of faith shall save the sick man, and the Lord will raise him up; and should he be in sins, they shall be forgiven.

JAMES 5:14–15

THE NUNC DIMITTIS

ANTIPHON: Save us, O Lord, while we wake, and watch over us as we sleep, that we may pass the night with Christ and rest in peace.

Lord, ✠ now let your servant depart in peace,
   according to your promise;
for my eyes have seen your salvation,
   which you have prepared in the presence of
   all peoples,
a light for revelation to the Gentiles,
   and for glory to your people Israel.

LUKE 2:29–32

Glory be . . .

ANTIPHON: Save us, O Lord, while we wake, and watch over us as we sleep, that we may pass the night with Christ and rest in peace.

Let us pray.

Visit this house, O Lord, we pray, and drive far from it the deadly power of the enemy. May your holy angels dwell here instead, that we may be preserved in peace with your blessing on us always. Through Christ our Lord. Amen.

Say the antiphon in honor of our Lady (see pp. 577–82), or use the following:

We fly to thy patronage, holy mother of God.
Despise not our petitions in our necessities
But deliver us from every evil,
O glorious and blessed Virgin!

FRIDAY
Remembering the passion of the Lord

VIGILS
The night office

CALL: O Lord, ✠ open my lips.
RESPONSE: And my mouth shall declare your praise.

ANTIPHON: They tear holes in my hands and my feet.

O God, my God, why have you forsaken me?
Why so far from my salvation;
Why so far from the cries of my affliction?

O my God, I cry by day, and you will not listen,
I cry by night and I find no comfort.

Yet you, O God, are holy,
dwelling in the praise of Israel.

In you our fathers hoped;
　　they hoped, and you delivered them.
They cried to you, and they were saved;
　　they trusted in you and were not confounded.

But I am a worm and no man,
　　the reproach of men, and the outcast of the people.
All who see me laugh me to scorn.
　　They turn their lips, they shake their heads.
"He hoped in the Lord, let him deliver him;
　　let him save him, seeing he delighted in him."

For you are the one who drew me out of the womb,
　　my hope from my mother's breast.
I was cast upon you from the womb,
　　from my mother's womb you are my God.
Do not leave me; for tribulation is very near,
　　for there is no one else to help me.

Many young bulls have surrounded me,
　　fat bulls have besieged me.
They open wide their mouths against me,
　　as a lion, ravening and roaring.

I am poured out like water,
　　and all my bones are scattered.
My heart is become like wax,
　　melting in the midst of my body.
My strength is dried up like a potsherd,
　　and my tongue cleaves to my jaws;
　　　you have brought me down into the dust of death.

For many dogs have encompassed me,
　　the council of the malignant besieges me.
They have dug holes in my hands and my feet;
　　I can count all my bones.

And they have looked and stared upon me;
    they parted my garments among them.
    And upon my vesture they cast lots.

But you, O Lord, do not keep away!
    My strength, look to my defense!
Deliver, O God, my soul from the sword,
    all I have from the grip of the dog.
Save me from the lion's mouth,
    my humble soul from the horns of the unicorns.

I will declare your name to my brethren
    and in the midst of the assembly will I praise you.
You who fear the Lord, praise him;
    all the children of Jacob, glorify him.
Let all the children of Israel fear him,
    for he has not slighted or despised
    the supplication of the poor man.
From him he has not hidden his face,
    but he heard him when he cried.

You are my praise in the great congregation.
    I will pay my vows in the sight of those who
    fear him.
The poor shall eat and shall be filled.
    They shall praise the Lord, that seek him.
    Their hearts shall live forever and ever!

All the ends of the earth shall remember
    and shall be converted to the Lord.
All the families of the Gentiles shall adore in his sight.
    For the kingdom is the Lord's;
    and he shall have dominion over the nations.
All those who sleep in the earth shall worship him alone,
    all who go down to the dust shall fall down
    before him.

And my soul shall live for him,
    and my descendants shall serve him.
A generation to come shall be declared to the Lord,
    and they shall show forth his justice
    to a people yet unborn:
These things the Lord has done.

PSALM 22

Glory be . . .

ANTIPHON: They tear holes in my hands and
    my feet.

CALL: Lord, remember me,
RESPONSE: When you come into your kingdom.

FIRST READING
Read one chapter from the Scriptures.

RESPONSE TO THE READING

CALL: We adore you, O Christ,
RESPONSE: Because by your holy cross you have
    redeemed the world.
CALL: And we bless you,
RESPONSE: Because by your holy cross you have
    redeemed the world.

SECOND READING
Choose a spiritual reading.

RESPONSE TO THE READING

CALL: Christ was obedient even to accepting
    death on a cross,
RESPONSE: So God has raised him high.
CALL: Let every knee bend at the name
    of Jesus,
RESPONSE: For God has raised him high.

Let us pray.

Almighty God, whose Son, Jesus Christ, ascended for us the altar of the cross, grant that we may respond with like generosity to the needs of our neighbors. Through Christ our Lord. Amen.

> CALL: Let us bless the Lord.
> RESPONSE: Thanks be to God.

LAUDS
Morning prayer

CALL: O God, ✝ come to my assistance.
RESPONSE: O Lord, be swift to my aid.
CALL: Glory be to the Father, and to the Son,
and to the Holy Spirit.
RESPONSE: As it was in the beginning, is now and
ever shall be, world without end. Amen.

VIVA! VIVA! GESÙ

Glory be to Jesus,
Who, in bitter pains,
Poured for me the life-blood
From his sacred veins.

Grace and life eternal
In that Blood I find;
Blest be his compassion,
Infinitely kind.

Blest through endless ages
Be that precious stream,
Which from endless torment
Doth the world redeem.

Abel's blood for vengeance
Pleaded to the skies;
But the Blood of Jesus
For our pardon cries.

Oft as it is sprinkled
On our guilty hearts,
Satan in confusion
Terror-struck departs.

Oft as earth, exulting,
Wafts its praise on high,
Hell with terror trembles,
Heaven is filled with joy.

Lift ye then your voices;
Swell the mighty flood;
Louder still and louder
Praise the precious Blood.

ANTIPHON: A contrite and humbled heart, O God,
you will not spurn.

Have mercy on me, O God,
according to your great mercy.
And according to the multitude of your tender mercies
blot out my iniquity.

Wash me yet more from my iniquity
and cleanse me from my sin.
For I know my iniquity;
and my sin is always before me.

Against you only have I sinned;
　　and done evil before you.

That you may be justified in your sentence
　　and may overcome when you are judged:
Behold, I was conceived in iniquities,
　　and in sin did my mother give me life.

For behold, you love truth in the heart;
　　and in secret you have made wisdom known to me.
You shall sprinkle me with hyssop and I shall be
　cleansed;
　　　you shall wash me; I shall be made whiter
　　　　than snow.

You shall make me hear joy and gladness,
　　and the bones that have been humbled shall rejoice.
Turn away your face from my sins
　　and blot out all my iniquities.

Create a clean heart in me, O God,
　　and renew a right spirit within me.
Do not cast me away from your face,
　　nor take away your holy spirit from me.

Give me the joy of your salvation;
　　and strengthen me with a willing spirit.
I will teach the unjust your ways
　　and the wicked shall be converted to you.

Deliver me from blood, O God, the God of my
　salvation,
　　　and my tongue shall extol your justice.
O Lord, you will open my lips
　　and my mouth shall declare your praise.
For if you had desired sacrifice,
　　I would indeed have given it,

but in burnt offerings you would not delight.
A sacrifice to God is an afflicted spirit:
     a contrite and humbled heart O God,
     you will not spurn.

Deal favorably, O Lord in your goodness, with Zion:
     that the walls of Jerusalem may be built up.
Then you will accept the sacrifice of justice,
     oblations and whole burnt offerings:
then they will lay calves upon your altar.

PSALM 51

Glory be . . .

ANTIPHON: A contrite and humbled heart, O God,
          you will not spurn.

SHORT READING
When, in doing well, you suffer for it patiently, this is
praiseworthy before God. For to this you are called,
because Christ also suffered for you, leaving you an example, that you should follow his steps who committed no
sin; neither was guile found in his mouth. Who, when he
was reviled, did not revile in return; when he suffered, he
did not threaten; but he trusted to him who judges justly.
Who himself bore our sins in his body upon the tree, that
we, being dead to sin, should live to righteousness. By his
wounds you have been healed.

1 PETER 2:20–24

THE BENEDICTUS
Blessed ✝ be the Lord, the God of Israel,
     who has visited and redeemed his people,
and has lifted up a horn of salvation for us
     in the family of his servant David.

For this he swore through the mouths of holy men,
    those who were prophets, from the beginning:
There would be salvation from our foes,
    and from the hand of all those who hate us;
to comfort our fathers,
    and to honor his holy covenant,
which oath once he swore to Abraham, our father,
    that he would grant us,
that freed from the hand of our enemies,
    and without fear, we may serve him,
    in holiness and justice in his very presence
    all our days.
And you, my son, will be named Prophet of the
  Most High;
    for you will go before the presence of the Lord
    to prepare his way,
to teach knowledge of salvation to his people
    that their sins may be forgiven,
    through the merciful heart of our God,
when the Daystar shall visit us from on high
    to enlighten those who sit in darkness
    and in the shadow of death,
    and guide our feet to the way of peace.

LUKE 1:68–79

Glory be . . .

INTERCESSIONS
Offer these intercessions, or pray for other needs.

> CALL: Lord, forgive our sins. *(Pause*
>   *for prayer.)*
> **RESPONSE:** Hear us, Father.
> CALL: Lord, deepen our compassion for the
>   sufferings of your Son. *(Pause.)*

RESPONSE: Hear us, Father.

CALL: Lord, strengthen our determination to see the face of your Son in all those who suffer. *(Pause.)*

RESPONSE: Hear us, Father.

CALL: Lord, help us to take up our crosses to follow your Son. *(Pause.)*

RESPONSE: Hear us, Father.

CALL: Lord, help us to make up in our sinful bodies what lacks to the sufferings of Christ. *(Pause.)*

RESPONSE: Hear us, Father.

Lord, have mercy.
Christ, have mercy.
Lord, have mercy.

Our Father . . .

Let us pray.

Look upon your family, Lord, for which our Lord Jesus Christ did not hesitate to give himself into the hands of murderers and undergo the torments of the cross. Through the same Jesus Christ, your Son, who lives and reigns with you in the unity of the Holy Spirit, one God forever and ever. Amen.

CALL: Let us bless the Lord.

RESPONSE: Thanks be to God.

TERCE
Midmorning prayer

CALL: O God, ✠ come to my assistance.

RESPONSE: O Lord, be swift to my aid.

CALL: Glory be to the Father, and to the Son, and to the Holy Spirit.

RESPONSE: As it was in the beginning, is now and ever shall be, world without end. Amen.

Come, Holy Ghost, with God the Son
And God the Father, ever one;
Shed forth thy grace within our breast
And dwell with us a ready guest.

By every power, by heart and tongue,
By act and deed, thy praise be sung;
Inflame with perfect love each sense
That others' souls may kindle thence.

O Father, that we ask be done,
Through Jesus Christ, thine only Son;
Who, with the Holy Ghost and thee,
Doth live and reign eternally. Amen.

> **ANTIPHON:**   Lord, uphold me according to your
> word, and I shall live.

I hate the duplicitous heart:
> but I have loved your law.
You are my helper and my protector;
> and in your word I have greatly hoped.
Depart from me, you malignant people,
> and I will keep God's commandments.
Uphold me according to your word, and I shall live;
> and let me not be confounded in my expectation.
Help me and I shall be saved,
> and I will delight always in your statutes.
You despise all who fall away from your laws;
> for their thoughts are unjust.
I account as fickle all the sinners of the earth:
> therefore I love your commandments.
Pierce my flesh through with your fear;
> for I am afraid of your judgments.

PSALM 119:113–120

Glory be . . .

> **ANTIPHON:**   Lord, uphold me according to your
> word, and I shall live.

SHORT READING
And it was the third hour, when they crucified him. And
the inscription of the charge against him was written over
him: "The King of the Jews." And with him they crucified

two thieves, one on his right hand and the other on his left.

MARK 15:25–27

Let us pray.

Look upon your family, Lord, for which our Lord Jesus Christ did not hesitate to give himself into the hands of murderers and undergo the torments of the cross. Through the same Jesus Christ our Lord. Amen.

CALL: Let us bless the Lord.
RESPONSE: Thanks be to God.

SEXT
Midday prayer

CALL: O God, ✝ come to my assistance.

RESPONSE: O Lord, be swift to my aid.

CALL: Glory be to the Father, and to the Son,
and to the Holy Spirit.

RESPONSE: As it was in the beginning, is now and
ever shall be, world without end. Amen.

O God of truth, O Lord of might,
Who orderest time and change aright,
And send'st the early morning ray,
And light'st the glow of perfect day:

Extinguish thou each sinful fire,
And banish every ill desire;
And while thou keep'st the body whole,
Shed forth thy peace upon the soul.

O Father, that we ask be done,
Through Jesus Christ, thine only Son;
Who, with the Holy Ghost and thee,
Doth live and reign eternally. Amen.

> **ANTIPHON:** Lord, give me understanding, and I will study your law.

I have done justly and rightly:
> do not betray me to my slanderers.
Uphold your servant for his good,
> lest the proud calumniate me.
My eyes faint for your salvation
> and for the word of your justice.
Deal with your servant according to your mercy
> and teach me your commands.
I am your servant, give me understanding:
> that I may know your testimonies.
It is time, O Lord, to act:
> for they have broken your law.
Therefore I love your command
> above gold and the topaz.
Therefore I direct my life to all your precepts:
> I hate all the ways of the liar.

PSALM 119:121–128

Glory be . . .

> **ANTIPHON:** Lord, give me understanding, and I will study your law.

SHORT READING

One of the robbers who were hanged blasphemed Jesus, saying, "If you be the Christ save yourself and us!" But the other answered, saying, "Do you not fear God, since you are under the same condemnation? And we indeed justly;

for we receive the due reward of our deeds; but this man has done no evil." And he said to Jesus, "Lord, remember me when you shall come into your kingdom." And Jesus said to him, "Truly, I say to you, this day you will be with me in paradise." It was almost the sixth hour, and there was darkness over all the earth until the ninth hour.

LUKE 23:39–44

Let us pray.

Look upon your family, Lord, for which our Lord Jesus Christ did not hesitate to give himself into the hands of murderers and undergo the torments of the cross. Through the same Jesus Christ our Lord. Amen.

CALL: Let us bless the Lord.
RESPONSE: Thanks be to God.

NONE
Midafternoon prayer

CALL:	O God, ✚ come to my assistance.
RESPONSE:	O Lord, be swift to my aid.
CALL:	Glory be to the Father, and to the Son, and to the Holy Spirit.
RESPONSE:	As it was in the beginning, is now and ever shall be, world without end. Amen.

O God, Creation's secret force,
Thyself unmoved, all motion's source,
Who from the morn till evening ray
Through all its changes guid'st the day:

Grant us, when this short life is past,
The glorious evening that shall last;
That, by a holy death attained,
Eternal glory may be gained.

O Father, that we ask be done,
Through Jesus Christ, thine only Son;
Who, with the Holy Ghost and thee,
Doth live and reign eternally. Amen.

> **ANTIPHON:** The Lord Jesus was obedient unto
> death on a cross.

Your testimonies are wonderful:
    therefore my soul has sought them.
The declaration of your words gives light
    and understanding to little ones.
I open my mouth and gasp
    because I long for your commandments.
Look upon me and have mercy on me,
    according to the judgment of those that love you.
Direct my steps according to your word;
    and let no iniquity have dominion over me.
Redeem me from the calumnies of men,
    that I may keep your commandments.
Make your face to shine on your servant
    and teach me your laws.
My eyes send forth streams of water
    because your law is not kept.

PSALM 119:129–136

Glory be . . .

> **ANTIPHON:** The Lord Jesus was obedient unto
> death on a cross.

SHORT READING

And at the ninth hour Jesus cried with a loud voice saying: "Eloi, Eloi, lema sabachthani?" Which is, when interpreted, "My God, my God, why have you forsaken me?" And some of the bystanders hearing it said, "Behold, he is calling on Elijah." And one ran and filled a sponge full of vinegar and, putting it on a reed, gave it to him to drink, saying, "Stay, let us see if Elijah will come to take him down." And Jesus having cried with a loud voice, gave up his spirit. And the veil of the temple was rent in two, from the top to the bottom. And the centurion, who stood by him, seeing that he had cried out and given up his spirit, said, "Indeed this man was the Son of God!"

MARK 15:34–39

Let us pray.

Look upon your family, Lord, for which our Lord Jesus Christ did not hesitate to give himself into the hands of murderers and undergo the torments of the cross. Through the same Jesus Christ our Lord. Amen.

CALL: Let us bless the Lord.
RESPONSE: Thanks be to God.

VESPERS
Evening prayer

CALL:	O God, ✛ come to my assistance.
RESPONSE:	O Lord, be swift to my aid.
CALL:	Glory be to the Father, and to the Son, and to the Holy Spirit.
RESPONSE:	As it was in the beginning, is now and ever shall be, world without end. Amen.

When I survey the wondrous cross
On which the Prince of glory died,
My richest gain I count as loss,
And pour contempt on all my pride.

Forbid it, Lord, that I should boast
Save in the death of Christ my God;
All the vain things that charm me most,
I sacrifice them to his blood.

See from his head, his hands, his feet,
Sorrow and love flow mingled down;
Did e'er such love and sorrow meet,
Or thorns compose so rich a crown?

His dying crimson like a robe
Spreads o'er his body on the tree;
Then I am dead to all the globe,
And all the globe is dead to me.

Were the whole realm of nature mine,
It were an offering far too small;
Love so amazing, so divine,
Demands my soul, my life, my all.

ISAAC WATTS

ANTIPHON: Cast your care upon the Lord, and he
will sustain you.

O God, let your ears be open to my prayer,
    do not hide from my supplication,
be attentive to me and hear me.

I am grieved in my prayer,
    I am troubled at the voice of the enemy,
    at the clamor of the sinner;
for they have cast evil upon me,
    and in fury they are set against me.

My heart is troubled within me,
    and the terror of death has fallen upon me,
Fear and trembling have come upon me
    and terror has covered me.

And I said: Who will give me wings like a dove
    that I may fly and be at rest?

So I would go flying far away
    and abide in the wilderness.

I have waited for him who saves me
    from the spirit of cowardice,
    and from the mighty storm.

Cast them down O Lord,
    and divide their tongues;
        for I see iniquity and contention in the city.

Day and night, they go round its walls.
    Inside it is full of trouble and injustice.
    Usury and deceit have not departed its streets.

For if it had been my enemy who reviled me,
    I would truly have borne with it.
If it had been one who hated me who spoke against me,
    I could perhaps have hidden myself from him.

But it was you, a man of my own heart,
    my confidant, my familiar companion!
We used to take sweet counsel together.
    We walked together in the house of God as friends.

Let death come upon them!
    Let them go down alive into hell!
For there is wickedness in their dwellings,
    right in the very midst of them!

But I have cried to God
    and the Lord will save me.
In the evening, morning, and at noon
    I will cry out and pray.

He will redeem my soul in peace
    from those who battle against me:
    for there were many with me.

God will hear
>and the Eternal One will humble them,
for they will not change;
>they will never fear God.

The betrayer has turned his hand
>against those who were at peace with him;
>he has defiled his covenant.
His words are softer than butter,
>while having war in his heart.
His words are smoother than oil,
>but truly they are wicked swords.

Cast your care upon the Lord
>and he will sustain you.
He will never suffer
>the just man to waver.

But you, O God, will bring them down
>into the pit of destruction.
Bloody and deceitful men
>shall not live out half their days.
But I will trust in you, O Lord.

PSALM 55

Glory be . . .

ANTIPHON: Cast your care upon the Lord, and he
will sustain you.

SHORT READING

Christ Jesus, though being in the form of God, did not
think equality with God a thing to be grasped, but emp-
tied himself, taking the form of a servant, being made in
the likeness of men and in habit found as a man. He humbled himself, becoming obedient unto death, even to the
death of the cross. For this, God has also highly exalted

him and given him a name that is above all names, that in the name of Jesus every knee should bow, those in heaven, on earth, and under the earth, and that every tongue should confess that the Lord Jesus Christ is in the glory of God the Father.

PHILIPPIANS 2:6–11

THE MAGNIFICAT

My ✝ soul magnifies the Lord,
>   my spirit rejoices in God who is my Savior,
>   who has looked upon the humility of his
>   handmaiden.

Behold, all generations from now
>   will acknowledge me blessed,

For the mighty one has done great things for me:
>   Holy is his name!

His mercy is from one generation to the next on those who fear him.
>   Mighty is his arm!

He has scattered the proud in the imagination of their hearts,
>   and has put down the powerful from their thrones,
>   exalting those of humble degree.

The hungry he has filled with good things,
>   but the rich he has dismissed with nothing.

Remembering his mercy, he has helped his servant Israel,
>   as he promised to our fathers,
>   to Abraham and to his posterity forevermore.

LUKE 1:46–55

Glory be . . .

INTERCESSIONS
Offer these intercessions, or pray for other needs.

CALL: For those unjustly deprived of freedom,

(Pause for prayer.)

RESPONSE: Hear us, O Lord.

CALL: For those who lack the necessities of life, (Pause.)

RESPONSE: Hear us, O Lord.

CALL: For those who fight evil with good, (Pause.)

RESPONSE: Hear us, O Lord.

CALL: For an end to famine and war, (Pause.)

RESPONSE: Hear us, O Lord.

CALL: Lord, grant rest to those who have given their lives for justice or truth. (Pause.)

RESPONSE: Hear us, O Lord.

Lord, have mercy.
Christ, have mercy.
Lord, have mercy.

Our Father . . .

Let us pray.

Lord, grant us the gift to be always contemplating what is right, and make us well disposed to putting it into action, that we who can do nothing without you may be worthy to live as you wish. Through our Lord Jesus Christ, your Son, who lives and reigns with you and the Holy Spirit, one God, world without end. Amen.

CALL: Let us bless the Lord.

RESPONSE: Thanks be to God.

COMPLINE
Night prayer

CALL: O God, ✠ come to my assistance.
RESPONSE: O Lord, be swift to my aid.
CALL: Glory be to the Father, and to the Son,
            and to the Holy Spirit.
RESPONSE: As it was in the beginning, is now and
            ever shall be, world without end. Amen.

Make an examination of conscience, and perform an act of penance.

Before the ending of the day,
Creator of the world we pray
That with thy wonted favor thou
Wouldst be our guard and keeper now.

From all ill dreams defend our eyes,
From nightly fears and fantasies;
Tread underfoot our ghostly foe,
That no pollution we may know.

O Father, that we ask be done,
Through Jesus Christ, thine only Son;
Who, with the Holy Ghost and thee,
Doth live and reign eternally. Amen.

ANTIPHON: For your name's sake, O Lord,
give me life.

Lord, hear my prayer:
give ear to my supplication in your truth:
hear me in your justice.
And do not enter into judgment with your servant,
for in your sight no one living shall be justified.

For the enemy persecutes my soul;
he has brought down my life to the earth;
he has made me to dwell in darkness
like those who have died long ago.
My spirit is in anguish within me
my heart within me is troubled.

I remember the days of old:
I meditate on all your deeds;
I meditate on the works of your hands.

I stretch forth my hands toward you.
My soul is like waterless earth for you.

Hear me speedily, O Lord;
for my spirit has fainted away.
Do not turn your face away from me,
lest I be like those who go down into the pit.

In the morning let me hear of your mercy,
for in you have I hoped.
Make the way known to me where I should walk:
for I have lifted up my soul to you.

Deliver me from my enemies, O Lord:
>to you I have fled.
Teach me to do your will,
>for you are my God.
Your good spirit shall lead me into the right land.

For your name's sake, O Lord,
>you will give me life in your justice.
You will bring my soul out of trouble
>and in your mercy you will destroy my enemies.
And you will cut off all those who afflict my soul,
>for I am your servant.

PSALM 143

Glory be . . .

ANTIPHON: For your name's sake, O Lord,
give me life.

SHORT READING

Surely he has borne our infirmities and carried our sorrows; yet we thought of him as a leper, one struck by God, and afflicted. But he was wounded for our iniquities, he was bruised for our sins; upon him was the chastisement that gave us peace, and with his bruises we are healed.

ISAIAH 53:4–5

THE NUNC DIMITTIS

ANTIPHON: Save us, O Lord, while we wake, and
watch over us as we sleep, that we
may pass the night with Christ and
rest in peace.

Lord, ✠ now let your servant depart in peace,
>according to your promise;

for my eyes have seen your salvation,
> which you have prepared in the presence of
> > all peoples,
a light for revelation to the Gentiles,
> and for glory to your people Israel.

LUKE 2:29–32

Glory be . . .

> **ANTIPHON:** Save us, O Lord, while we wake, and
> watch over us as we sleep, that we
> may pass the night with Christ and
> rest in peace.

Let us pray.

Visit this house, O Lord, we pray, and drive far from it the deadly power of the enemy. May your holy angels dwell here instead, that we may be preserved in peace with your blessing on us always. Through Christ our Lord. Amen.

Say the antiphon in honor of our Lady (see pp. 577–82), or use the following:

We fly to thy patronage, holy mother of God.
Despise not our petitions in our necessities
But deliver us from every evil,
O glorious and blessed Virgin!

SATURDAY
And feasts of our Lady

VIGILS
The night office

CALL: O Lord, ✛ open my lips.

RESPONSE: And my mouth shall declare
your praise.

ANTIPHON: Blessed are you among women, and
blessed is the fruit of your womb.

Sing to the Lord a new song
    because he has done wonderful things.
His right hand has wrought for him salvation,
    and his arm is holy.

The Lord has made known his salvation:
    he has revealed his justice
    in the sight of the Gentiles.

He has remembered his mercy and his truth
>toward the house of Israel.
All the ends of the earth have seen
>the salvation of our God.

Sing joyfully to God, all the earth;
>make melody, rejoice and sing.
Sing praise to the Lord on the harp,
>on the harp and with the voice of a psalm.

With long trumpets and with the sound of the cornet
>make a joyful noise before the Lord our king.

Let the sea be moved and all its waves,
>the world also, and those that dwell in it.
Let the rivers clap their hands,
>the mountains rejoice together
>at the presence of the Lord.
For he comes to judge the earth.

He shall judge the world with justice,
>and the people with equity.

PSALM 98

Glory be . . .

ANTIPHON: Blessed are you among women, and blessed is the fruit of your womb.

CALL: Grace is poured upon your lips;
RESPONSE: Therefore God has blessed you forever.

FIRST READING
Read one chapter from the Scriptures.

RESPONSE TO THE READING

CALL: Blessed are you, O Virgin Mary, who bore the Lord, the Creator of the world.

RESPONSE: You gave birth to your own Creator, and yet still remain a virgin.

CALL: Hail Mary, full of grace; the Lord is with you.

RESPONSE: You gave birth to your own Creator, and yet still remain a virgin.

SECOND READING
Choose a spiritual reading.

RESPONSE TO THE READING

CALL: How can I praise you, holy and immaculate Virgin?

RESPONSE: For you held him whom even the heavens cannot contain.

CALL: Blessed are you among women, and blessed is the fruit of your womb.

RESPONSE: For you held him whom even the heavens cannot contain.

Let us pray.

Grant, O merciful God, support to our frailty, that we who celebrate the memory of the holy mother of God may, by the help of her intercession, arise from our sins. Through Christ our Lord. Amen.

CALL: Let us bless the Lord.

RESPONSE: Thanks be to God.

LAUDS
Morning prayer

CALL: O God, ✛ come to my assistance.
RESPONSE: O Lord, be swift to my aid.
CALL: Glory be to the Father, and to the Son, and to the Holy Spirit.
RESPONSE: As it was in the beginning, is now and ever shall be, world without end. Amen.

Hail, thou star of ocean,
Portal of the sky;
Ever virgin Mother
Of the Lord most high.
Oh! by Gabriel's Ave
Utter'd long ago,
Eva's name reversing,
'Stablish peace below.

Break the captive's fetters,
Light on blindness pour,
All our ills expelling,
Every bliss implore.
Show thyself a mother;
Offer him our sighs,
Who for us incarnate
Did not thee despise.

Virgin of all virgins,
To thy shelter take us;
Gentlest of the gentle,
Chaste and gentle make us.
Still, as on we journey,
Help our weak endeavor;
Till with thee and Jesus
We rejoice forever.

Through the highest heaven,
To the almighty Three,
Father, Son and Spirit,
One same glory be.

ANTIPHON: The angel Gabriel was sent to Mary,
a virgin espoused to Joseph.

Sing joyfully to God, all the earth.
Serve the Lord with gladness.
Come before his presence with exceeding joy.

Know that the Lord, he is God.
He made us, and we are his,
we are his people, and the sheep of his pasture.

Go within his gates with praise,
into his courts with hymns:
and give glory to him.

Bless his name, for the Lord is sweet,
>his mercy endures forever,
>and his truth from generation to generation.

PSALM 100

Glory be . . .

ANTIPHON: The angel Gabriel was sent to Mary,
a virgin espoused to Joseph.

SHORT READING

There shall come forth a rod out of the root of Jesse, and a flower shall rise up out of his root. And the Spirit of the Lord shall rest upon him, the spirit of wisdom and of understanding, the spirit of counsel and of fortitude, the spirit of knowledge and of godliness.

ISAIAH 11:1–2

THE BENEDICTUS

Blessed ✠ be the Lord, the God of Israel,
>who has visited and redeemed his people,
and has lifted up a horn of salvation for us
>in the family of his servant David.
For this he swore through the mouths of holy men,
>those who were prophets, from the beginning:
There would be salvation from our foes,
>and from the hand of all those who hate us;
to comfort our fathers,
>and to honor his holy covenant,
which oath once he swore to Abraham, our father,
>that he would grant us,
that freed from the hand of our enemies,
>and without fear, we may serve him,
>in holiness and justice in his very presence
>>all our days.

And you, my son, will be named Prophet of the
  Most High;
        for you will go before the presence of the Lord
        to prepare his way,
to teach knowledge of salvation to his people
        that their sins may be forgiven,
        through the merciful heart of our God,
when the Daystar shall visit us from on high
        to enlighten those who sit in darkness
        and in the shadow of death,
        and guide our feet to the way of peace.

LUKE 1:68–79

Glory be . . .

INTERCESSIONS
Offer these intercessions, or pray for other needs.

CALL:	Grant us ever greater love of your Son. *(Pause for prayer.)*
RESPONSE:	Mary, pray for us to God.
CALL:	Grant us the spirit of prayer and penance. *(Pause.)*
RESPONSE:	Mary, pray for us to God.
CALL:	Help us to be better witnesses of your Son. *(Pause.)*
RESPONSE:	Mary, pray for us to God.
CALL:	Cure our sick, and give help to the needy. *(Pause.)*
RESPONSE:	Mary, pray for us to God.
CALL:	Give us grace to imitate your purity. *(Pause.)*
RESPONSE:	Mary, pray for us to God.
CALL:	Help us generously to do God's will, as you did. *(Pause.)*

RESPONSE: Mary, pray for us to God.

CALL: Mary, help us to become saints. *(Pause.)*

Lord, have mercy.
Christ, have mercy.
Lord, have mercy.

Our Father . . .

Let us pray.

Lord God, whose Son was pleased to take flesh in the womb of the Blessed Virgin Mary at the angel's message, grant that, as we venerate her as the mother of God, we may be assisted by her intercession with you. Through the same Lord Jesus Christ, your Son, who lives and reigns with you in the unity of the Holy Spirit, one God forever and ever. Amen.

CALL: Let us bless the Lord.

RESPONSE: Thanks be to God.

TERCE
Midmorning prayer

CALL: O God, ✠ come to my assistance.
RESPONSE: O Lord, be swift to my aid.
CALL: Glory be to the Father, and to the Son,
            and to the Holy Spirit.
RESPONSE: As it was in the beginning, is now and
            ever shall be, world without end. Amen.

Remember, O Creator Lord!
That in the Virgin's sacred womb
Thou wast conceived and of her flesh
Didst our mortality assume.

Mother of grace, O Mary blessed!
To thee, sweet fount of love, we fly:
Shield us through life, and take us hence
To thy dear bosom when we die.

O Jesu, born of Virgin bright!
Immortal glory be to thee;
Praise to the Father infinite,
And Holy Ghost eternally. Amen.

> **ANTIPHON:** Mary said, "Do whatever Jesus
> tells you."

I shall lift up my eyes to the hills.
From whence shall help come to me?
My help is from the Lord,
who made heaven and earth.

May he not let your foot be moved,
nor he who keeps you slumber.
Behold, shall neither slumber nor sleep
he who keeps watch over Israel.

The Lord is your keeper;
the Lord is your protection on your right hand.
The sun shall not burn you by day,
nor the moon by night.

The Lord will keep you from all evil;
may the Lord keep your soul.
The Lord will keep your coming in and your going out
from henceforth, now and forever.

PSALM 121

Glory be . . .

> **ANTIPHON:** Mary said, "Do whatever Jesus
> tells you."

SHORT READING

And on the third day, there was a marriage at Cana of
Galilee and the mother of Jesus was there; Jesus also was
invited with his disciples to the marriage. And when the

wine failed, the mother of Jesus said to him, "They have no wine." And Jesus said to her, "Woman, what is that to do with me and you? My hour is not yet come." His mother said to the servants, "Whatever he says to you, do."

JOHN 2:1–5

Let us pray.

Grant, O merciful God, support to our frailty, that we who celebrate the memory of the holy mother of God may, by the help of her intercession, arise from our sins. Through Christ our Lord. Amen.

CALL: Let us bless the Lord.
RESPONSE: Thanks be to God.

SEXT
Midday prayer

CALL:	O God, ✠ come to my assistance.
RESPONSE:	O Lord, be swift to my aid.
CALL:	Glory be to the Father, and to the Son, and to the Holy Spirit.
RESPONSE:	As it was in the beginning, is now and ever shall be, world without end. Amen.

O queen of all the virgin choir!
Enthroned above the starry sky,
Who with thy bosom's milk didst feed
Thy own Creator, Lord most high:

What man had lost in hapless Eve,
Thy sacred womb to man restores;
Thou to the wretched here beneath
Hast opened heaven's eternal doors.

Hail, O refulgent hall of light!
Hail, gate sublime of heaven's high king,
Through thee redeemed to endless life,
Thy praise let all the nations sing.

O Jesu, born of Virgin bright!
Immortal glory be to thee;
Praise to the Father infinite,
And Holy Ghost eternally. Amen.

> **ANTIPHON:** The Virgin Mary bore the Son of
> the eternal Father.

I rejoiced when they said to me:
    We shall go into the house of the Lord!
Our feet are standing within your courts,
    O Jerusalem!

Jerusalem, built as a city
    that is compact together,
is where the tribes go up,
    the tribes of the Lord,

as was decreed for Israel,
    to praise the name of the Lord.
There were set the seats for judgment,
    seats for the house of David.

O pray for the peace of Jerusalem!
    "Sureness for those who love you!
Peace be within your walls,
    and abundance within your towers!"

For the sake of my brethren and my neighbors,
    I will speak peace within you.
Because of the house of the Lord our God,
    I will seek good things for you.

PSALM 122

Glory be . . .

ANTIPHON: The Virgin Mary bore the Son of the eternal Father.

SHORT READING

The angel Gabriel was sent from God to a virgin espoused to a man whose name was Joseph, of the house of David; and the virgin's name was Mary. And he came in to her and said, "Hail, full of grace, the Lord is with you!" But she, having heard, was greatly troubled at his saying, and thought within herself what manner of greeting this could be. And the angel said to her, "Fear not, Mary, for you have found grace with God. Behold, you will conceive in your womb and bring forth a son, and you shall call his name Jesus." And Mary said, "Behold the handmaid of the Lord; be it done to me according to your word."

LUKE 1:26–31, 38

Let us pray.

Pour forth your grace, we beseech you, Lord, into our hearts, that we who, by the angel's message, have known the incarnation of Christ your Son may, by his passion and cross, be made partakers in his resurrection. Through the same Christ our Lord. Amen.

CALL: Let us bless the Lord.
RESPONSE: Thanks be to God.

NONE
Midafternoon prayer

CALL: O God, ✚ come to my assistance.
RESPONSE: O Lord, be swift to my aid.
CALL: Glory be to the Father, and to the Son, and to the Holy Spirit.
RESPONSE: As it was in the beginning, is now and ever shall be, world without end. Amen.

Under the world-redeeming rood
The most afflicted Mother stood,
Mingling her tears with her Son's blood;
As that streamed down from every part,
Of all his wounds she felt the smart:
What pierced his body pierced her heart.

FROM THE STABAT MATER

ANTIPHON: Our help is in the name of the Lord, who made heaven and earth.

If it had not been that the Lord was with us,
> let Israel now say,
If it had not been that the Lord was with us,
> when men rose up against us,
> perhaps they would have swallowed us up alive.

Our soul has passed through a torrent:
> Our soul has passed
> through the surging waters.

Blessed be the Lord,
> who has not given us to be a prey to their teeth.
Our soul has been delivered
> as a sparrow out of a snare of the fowlers.
> The snare is broken, and we are delivered.

Our help is in the name of the Lord,
> who made heaven and earth.

PSALM 124

Glory be ...

ANTIPHON: Our help is in the name of the Lord,
> who made heaven and earth.

SHORT READING

Now there stood by the cross of Jesus his mother, and his mother's sister, Mary the wife of Cleophas, and Mary Magdalene. When Jesus therefore saw his mother, and the disciple whom he loved standing there, he said to his mother, "Woman, behold your son." After that, he said to the disciple, "Behold your mother." And from that hour the disciple took her as his own.

JOHN 19:25–27

Let us pray.

O Lord Jesus Christ, who out of infinite charity became, for the sake of sinful man, the scorn of men and the out-cast of the people, and who died for us on the cross to obtain our relief from eternal shame: grant us, we beseech, by the merits of your most sorrowful crucifixion and by the glorious intercession of your most tender Mother, who stood beneath your cross, the spirit of perfect contrition for our sins and a holy death. Lord who lives and reigns forever and ever. Amen.

CALL: Let us bless the Lord.
RESPONSE: Thanks be to God.

VESPERS
Evening prayer

CALL: O God, ✠ come to my assistance.

RESPONSE: O Lord, be swift to my aid.

CALL: Glory be to the Father, and to the Son, and to the Holy Spirit.

RESPONSE: As it was in the beginning, is now and ever shall be, world without end. Amen.

O gladsome light, O grace
Of God the Father's face,
The eternal splendor wearing;
Celestial, holy, blessed,
Our Savior Jesus Christ,
Joyful in thine appearing.

Now, ere day fadeth quite,
We see the evening light,
Our wonted hymn outpouring;

Father of might unknown,
Thee, his incarnate Son,
And Holy Spirit adoring.

To thee of right belongs
All praise of holy songs,
O Son of God, Life-giver;
Thee, therefore, O Most High,
The world doth glorify,
And shall exalt forever.

ANTIPHON: In the morning you will see his glory.

Let God arise, and let his enemies be scattered;
  let those that hate him flee from before his face!
As smoke vanishes, so let them vanish away:
  as wax melts before the fire,
   let the wicked perish at the presence of God!
But let the just feast and rejoice before God,
  and be delighted with gladness.

Sing to God, sing a psalm to his name;
  make a way for him who ascends upon the west;
  The Lord is his name.
Father of the orphans and protector of widows
  is God in his holy place.
God gives the homeless a home to dwell in;
  he leads out the bound to prosperity;
  but the rebellious dwell in a parched land.

You have gone up on high,
  you have led captivity captive,
  and received gifts from men,
even among the rebellious,
  that the Lord God may dwell there.

Blessed be the Lord, day be day;

God is our salvation,
and will make our journey prosper.
Our God is a God of salvation;
and to God, the Lord, belongs escape from death.
The Lord said, I will bring them back from Basan,
I will bring them back from the depth of the sea.

They have seen your solemn processions, O God,
the processions of my God, my king,
who goes into the sanctuary.

Princes went before, joined with singers:
in the midst of them, maidens playing on timbrels.
In the assembly, bless God the Lord,
from the fountains of Israel.
There is Benjamin, a youth, in ecstasy,
the princes of Judah are their leaders,
the princes of Zabulon, the princes of Nepthali.

Command your strength, O God;
Confirm, O God, what you have wrought in us.
From your temple in Jerusalem,
kings shall offer gifts to you.

Rebuke the wild beasts that dwell among the reeds,
the herd of bulls with the cattle of the nations.
Trample those who lust after silver,
Scatter the nations who delight in war.
Ambassadors shall come from Egypt;
Ethiopia shall soon stretch out her hands to God.
Sing to God, you kingdoms of the earth;
sing praises to the Lord,

Sing to God who rises above the heaven of heavens,
the eastern heavens;
behold, he gives to his voice the voice of power.

Give glory to God, for the sake of Israel,
> his magnificence and his power is in the clouds.

God is wonderful in his saints:
> the God of Israel is the one

> who will give power and strength to his people.

Blessed be God!

PSALM 68:1–6, 18–20, 22, 24–35

Glory be . . .

ANTIPHON: In the morning you will see his glory.

SHORT READING

But now Christ is risen from the dead, the firstfruits of those who sleep. For as by a man came death, so also by a man has come the resurrection of the dead. For as in Adam all die, so also in Christ all shall be made alive.

1 CORINTHIANS 15:20–22

THE MAGNIFICAT

My ✝ soul magnifies the Lord,
> my spirit rejoices in God who is my Savior,

> who has looked upon the humility of his
> handmaiden.

Behold, all generations from now
> will acknowledge me blessed,

For the mighty one has done great things for me:
> Holy is his name!

His mercy is from one generation to the next on those who fear him.
> Mighty is his arm!

He has scattered the proud in the imagination of their hearts,
> and has put down the powerful from their thrones,

> exalting those of humble degree.

The hungry he has filled with good things,
  but the rich he has dismissed with nothing.
Remembering his mercy, he has helped his servant Israel,
    as he promised to our fathers,
      to Abraham and to his posterity forevermore.

LUKE 1:46–55

Glory be . . .

INTERCESSIONS

Offer these intercessions, or pray for other needs.

CALL: Lord, heal those who are sick in body. *(Pause for prayer.)*
RESPONSE: Hear us, O Lord.
CALL: Lord, heal those who are sick in mind. *(Pause.)*
RESPONSE: Hear us, O Lord.
CALL: Lord, give us greater devotion to your mother. *(Pause.)*
RESPONSE: Hear us, O Lord.
CALL: Lord, grant rest to the dead. *(Pause.)*
RESPONSE: Hear us, O Lord.

Lord, have mercy.
Christ, have mercy.
Lord, have mercy.

Our Father . . .

Let us pray.

O God, as you gave joy to the world through the resurrection of your only Son, Jesus Christ, from the dead, grant that by the prayers of his Virgin Mother we may be freed from all sorrow and come to the fullness of joy in your kingdom. Through the same Jesus Christ, your Son, who lives and reigns with you and the Holy Spirit, one God, world without end. Amen.

CALL: Let us bless the Lord.
RESPONSE: Thanks be to God.

COMPLINE
Night prayer

CALL: O God, ✠ come to my assistance.

RESPONSE: O Lord, be swift to my aid.

CALL: Glory be to the Father, and to the Son, and to the Holy Spirit.

RESPONSE: As it was in the beginning, is now and ever shall be, world without end. Amen.

Make an examination of conscience, and perform an act of penance.

Before the ending of the day,
Creator of the world, we pray
That with thy wonted favor thou
Wouldst be our guard and keeper now.

From all ill dreams defend our eyes,
From nightly fears and fantasies;
Tread underfoot our ghostly foe,
That no pollution we may know.

O Father, that we ask be done,
Through Jesus Christ, thine only Son;
Who, with the Holy Ghost and thee,
Doth live and reign eternally. Amen.

ANTIPHON: Bless the Lord throughout the night.

Lord, my heart is not exalted,
        nor are my eyes lofty;
Neither have I walked in great matters
        nor in wonderful things above me.

But I have calmed and quieted my soul,
        like a child that is weaned by its mother;
        like a child that is quieted is my soul.
Let Israel hope in the Lord
        from henceforth, now, and forever.

PSALM 131

Glory be . . .

ANTIPHON: Bless the Lord throughout the night.

SHORT READING
They shall see God's face, and his name shall be on their
foreheads. And night shall be no more; they shall not need
the light of the lamp nor the light of the sun, because the
Lord God shall enlighten them, and they shall reign forever and ever.

REVELATION 22:4–5

THE NUNC DIMITTIS
ANTIPHON: Save us, O Lord, while we wake, and
                watch over us as we sleep, that we
                may pass the night with Christ and
                rest in peace.

Lord, ✠ now let your servant depart in peace,
    according to your promise;
for my eyes have seen your salvation,
    which you have prepared in the presence of
        all peoples,
a light for revelation to the Gentiles,
    and for glory to your people Israel.

LUKE 2:29–32

Glory be . . .

ANTIPHON: Save us, O Lord, while we wake, and
watch over us as we sleep, that we
may pass the night with Christ and
rest in peace.

Let us pray.

Visit this house, O Lord, we pray, and drive far from it the
deadly power of the enemy. May your holy angels dwell
here instead, that we may be preserved in peace with your
blessing on us always. Through Christ our Lord. Amen.

*Say the antiphon in honor of our Lady (see pp. 577–82), or use
the following:*

We fly to thy patronage, holy mother of God.
Despise not our petitions in our necessities
But deliver us from every evil,
O glorious and blessed Virgin!

OFFICE OF THE DEAD

VIGILS
The night office

CALL: O Lord, ✠ open my lips.

RESPONSE: And my mouth shall declare
your praise.

ANTIPHON: Direct, O Lord God, my way in
your sight.

O Lord, rebuke me not in your indignation,
   nor chastise me in your anger.
Have mercy on me, O Lord, for I am weak:
   heal me, O Lord, for my bones are troubled.
My soul is troubled exceedingly:
   and you, Lord, how long . . . ?

Turn to me, O Lord, and deliver my soul:
　　O save me for your mercy's sake.
For there is no one in death who remembers you
　　and in hell, who shall praise you?

I have labored in my groanings:
　　every night I wash my bed,
　　I water my couch with my tears.
My eye is troubled through grief:
　　I have grown old among my enemies.

Leave me, you workers of iniquity:
　　for the Lord has heard the sound of my weeping.
The Lord has heard my supplication:
The Lord has received my prayer.

So let all my enemies be ashamed
　　and very much troubled.
Let them be turned back,
　　and be ashamed very speedily.

PSALM 6

Eternal rest grant unto them, O Lord,
　　and let perpetual light shine on them.

ANTIPHON: Direct, O Lord God, my way in your sight.

CALL: May the Lord place them with the princes,

RESPONSE: With the princes of his people.

FIRST READING
Read one chapter from the Scriptures.

RESPONSE TO THE READING

CALL: Out of the depths I cry to you, O Lord. Lord, hear my voice.

> *RESPONSE:* Remember me, O Lord, my life is but a breath.
>
> *CALL:* Let your ears be attentive to the voice of my supplication.
>
> *RESPONSE:* Remember me, O Lord, my life is but a breath.

SECOND READING
Choose a spiritual reading.

RESPONSE TO THE READING

> *CALL:* Deliver us, O Lord from eternal death in that mighty day,
>
> *RESPONSE:* When you shall come in fire to judge the world.
>
> *CALL:* Eternal rest grant to them, O Lord, and let perpetual light shine on them,
>
> *RESPONSE:* When you shall come in fire to judge the world.

Use a prayer for special categories of people (see pp. 358–59), or say the following:

Let us pray.

O Lord, whose nature it is to have mercy and spare, we humbly beg your mercy on the souls of the faithful departed, that through your mercy and our feeble prayers they may attain the glory that they have always desired. Through Christ our Lord. Amen.

> *CALL:* Let us bless the Lord.
>
> *RESPONSE:* Thanks be to God.

LAUDS
Morning prayer

CALL: O God, ✟ come to my assistance.
RESPONSE: O Lord, be swift to my aid.
CALL: Glory be to the Father, and to the Son,
          and to the Holy Spirit.
RESPONSE: As it was in the beginning, is now and
          ever shall be, world without end. Amen.

Help, Lord, the souls that thou hast made,
The souls to thee so dear,
In prison for the debt unpaid
Of sins committed here.

Those holy souls, they suffer on,
Resigned in heart and will,
Until thy high behest is done,
And justice has its fill.

For daily falls, for pardoned crime,
They joy to undergo
The shadow of thy cross sublime,
The remnant of thy woe.

O, by their patience of delay,
Their hope amid their pain,
Their sacred zeal to burn away
Disfigurement and stain;

O, by their fire of love, not less
In keenness than the flame,
O, by their very helplessness,
O, by thy own great name,

Good Jesu, help! sweet Jesu, aid
The souls to thee most dear,
In prison for the debt unpaid
Of sins committed here.

J. H. Newman

ANTIPHON:　Lord, do not remember the sins
　　　　　　of my youth.

To you, O Lord, I have lifted up my soul.
　　In you, O Lord, I put my trust: let me not
　　　be ashamed.
Neither permit my enemies to laugh at me:
　　for no one who hopes in you shall be confounded.
But let all those be confounded
　　who do unjustly, without cause.

Show me, Lord, your ways,
　　and teach me your paths.
Direct me in your truth, and teach me:
　　for you are God my Savior:
　　　I have waited for you all the day long.

Remember your compassion, O Lord,
>   and your mercies which have been
>   since the beginning of the world.

Do not remember the sins of my youth, nor my failings:
>   but remember me according to your mercy,
>   for the sake of your goodness, O Lord.

The Lord is sweet and upright:
>   therefore he will lead sinners in the way.
He will guide the mild in judgment,
>   he will teach the meek his ways.

All the ways of the Lord are mercy and truth,
>   to those who keep his covenant and testimonies.
For your name's sake, Lord, pardon my sin:
>   for it is great.
Who is the man who fears the Lord?
>   He will instruct him in the way he has chosen.
His soul shall dwell in good things:
>   and his descendants shall inherit the land.

The Lord is close to those who fear him:
>   and his covenant shall be shown to them.
My eyes are ever on the Lord
>   for it is he who plucks my feet out from the snare.

Look upon me and have mercy on me,
>   for I am alone and poor.
The troubles of my heart have increased:
>   deliver me from my difficulties.
See my abjectness and my labor:
>   and forgive me all my sins.

Look at all my enemies! They are grown greater
>   and hate me with an unjust hatred.
Keep my soul and deliver me:

I shall not be ashamed, for I have hoped in you.
The innocent and the upright have adhered to me,
>because I have waited for you.

Deliver Israel, O Lord,
>from all his tribulations.

PSALM 25

Eternal rest grant unto them, O Lord,
>and let perpetual light shine on them.

> **ANTIPHON:**   Lord, do not remember the sins
> of my youth.

SHORT READING
Who will grant that my words be written? Who will grant me that they be inscribed in a book? Or with an iron pen on a plate of lead, or else be graven in flint? For I know that my Redeemer lives, and on the last day I will rise out of the earth; and I shall be clothed again with my skin, and in my flesh I shall see my God.

JOB 19:23–26

THE BENEDICTUS
Blessed ✛ be the Lord, the God of Israel,
>who has visited and redeemed his people,
and has lifted up a horn of salvation for us
>in the family of his servant David.
For this he swore through the mouths of holy men,
>those who were prophets, from the beginning:
There would be salvation from our foes,
>and from the hand of all those who hate us;
to comfort our fathers,
>and to honor his holy covenant,
which oath once he swore to Abraham, our father,
>that he would grant us,

that freed from the hand of our enemies,
>> and without fear, we may serve him,
>> in holiness and justice in his very presence
>> all our days.
And you, my son, will be named Prophet of the
> Most High;
>> for you will go before the presence of the Lord
>> to prepare his way,
to teach knowledge of salvation to his people
>> that their sins may be forgiven,
>> through the merciful heart of our God,
when the Daystar shall visit us from on high
>> to enlighten those who sit in darkness
>> and in the shadow of death,
>> and guide our feet to the way of peace.

LUKE 1:68–79

Eternal rest grant unto them, O Lord,
>> and let perpetual light shine on them.

INTERCESSIONS

Offer these intercessions, or pray for other needs.

CALL:	Grant rest to those we love who have died. *(Pause for prayer.)*
RESPONSE:	Lord, hear us in your love.
CALL:	Give us greater faith in the resurrection. *(Pause.)*
RESPONSE:	Lord, hear us in your love.
CALL:	Help us to face our own death with courage and faith. *(Pause.)*
RESPONSE:	Lord, hear us in your love.
CALL:	Bless and strengthen those who work with the dying. *(Pause.)*
RESPONSE:	Lord, hear us in your love.

Lord, have mercy.
Christ, have mercy.
Lord, have mercy.

Our Father . . .

Use a prayer for special categories of people (see pp. 358–59), or say the following:

Let us pray.

O Lord, whose nature it is to have mercy and spare, we humbly beg your mercy on the souls of the faithful departed, that through your mercy and our feeble prayers they may attain the glory that they have always desired. Through Christ our Lord. Amen.

CALL: Let us bless the Lord.
RESPONSE: Thanks be to God.

TERCE
Midmorning prayer

CALL: O God, ✠ come to my assistance.

RESPONSE: O Lord, be swift to my aid.

CALL: Glory be to the Father, and to the Son, and to the Holy Spirit.

RESPONSE: As it was in the beginning, is now and ever shall be, world without end. Amen.

Hear what the voice from Heaven proclaims
For all the pious dead:
Sweet is the savor of their names,
And soft their sleeping bed.

Far from this world of toil and strife,
In going to their Lord,
The labors of their mortal life
End in a large reward.

ISAAC WATTS

ANTIPHON: The Lord keeps trust forever.

Praise the Lord, O my soul:
    I will praise the Lord while I yet live,
    I will sing to my God as long as I shall be.

Put not your trust in princes,
    in the children of men,
    in whom there is no salvation.
For when the breath of man goes forth,
    he returns unto the earth;
    and on that day all his thoughts shall perish.

But blessed is the one
    who has the God of Jacob as his helper,
    whose hope is in the Lord his God,
Who made the heavens and the earth,
    the seas and all things that are in them,
Who keeps truth forever,
    who does justly for those that suffer wrong,
    who gives food to the hungry.

The Lord looses those who are fettered;
    the Lord enlightens the blind.
The Lord lifts up those who are cast down,
    the Lord loves the just.

The Lord shelters the strangers,
    he supports the fatherless and the widow,
    but the ways of sinners he will destroy.
The Lord will reign forever:
    your God, O Zion, for generation unto generation.

PSALM 146

Eternal rest grant unto them, O Lord,
    and let perpetual light shine on them.

ANTIPHON: The Lord keeps trust forever.

SHORT READING

And we will not have you ignorant, brethren, concerning those who are asleep, that you may not sorrow as others who have no hope. For if we believe that Jesus died and rose again, so, through Jesus, God will bring with him those who sleep.

1 THESSALONIANS 4:13–14

Use a prayer for special categories of people (see pp. 358–59), or say the following:

Let us pray.

O Lord, whose nature it is to have mercy and spare, we humbly beg your mercy on the souls of the faithful departed, that through your mercy and our feeble prayers they may attain the glory that they have always desired. Through Christ our Lord. Amen.

> *CALL:* Let us bless the Lord.
> **RESPONSE:** Thanks be to God.

SEXT
Midday prayer

CALL:	O God, ✝ come to my assistance.
RESPONSE:	O Lord, be swift to my aid.
CALL:	Glory be to the Father, and to the Son, and to the Holy Spirit.
RESPONSE:	As it was in the beginning, is now and ever shall be, world without end. Amen.

Jesu, Son of Mary,
Fount of life alone
Oft we hail thee present
On thine altar-throne.
Humbly we adore thee,
Lord of endless might,
In the mystic symbols
Veiled from earthly sight.

Think, O Lord, in mercy
On the souls of those
Who, in faith gone from us,
Now in death repose.
Here 'mid stress and conflict
Toils can never cease;
There, the warfare ended,
Bid them rest in peace.

Often were they wounded
In the deadly strife;
Heal them, good Physician,
With the balm of life,
Every taint of evil,
Frailty and decay,
Good and gracious Savior,
Cleanse and purge away.

Rest eternal grant them,
After weary fight;
Shed on them the radiance
Of thy heavenly light.
Lead them onward, upward,
To the holy place,
Where thy saints made perfect
Gaze upon thy face.

ANTIPHON: Lord, you have delivered my soul that
it should not perish.

I said: In the midst of my days
I shall go to the gates of the dead.
I sought for the residue of my years.

I said: After all, I shall not see the Lord God
in the land of the living!

So I shall behold man no more,
    among the inhabitants of the world.

My generation is now at an end,
    and it is rolled away from me,
    as a shepherd's tent.
My life is cut off, as by a weaver:
    while I was yet but beginning he cut me off.
From morning until night
    you will make an end of me.

I hoped until morning,
    but as a lion so has he broken all my bones,
and from morning till night
    you will make an end of me.

I will cry like a young swallow,
    I will groan like a dove:
    my eyes are weakened from looking upward.
Lord, I suffer violently:
    then answer me!

What shall I say, or what can be an answer,
    when he himself has done this?
I will recount to you all my years
    in the bitterness of my soul.

O Lord, if man's life be such,
    and if the life of my spirit be in such things as these,
    you must correct me and make me live.
For behold, when I am at peace
    is my bitterness most bitter.

But you have delivered my soul,
    that it should not perish:
    you have cast all my sins behind your back.

For hell shall not acknowledge you,
neither shall death praise you,
nor shall those who go down to the pit
look for your truth.

The living, the living shall give praise to you,
as I do this day:
the father shall make your truth known
to his children.

O Lord, save me,
and we will sing our psalms all the days of our life
in the house of the Lord.

ISAIAH 38:10–20

Eternal rest grant unto them, O Lord,
and let perpetual light shine on them.

ANTIPHON: Lord, you have delivered my soul that
it should not perish.

SHORT READING

For God has not made death, neither has he any pleasure
in the destruction of the living. For he created all things
that they might be, and he made the nations of the earth
for health; and there is no poison of destruction in them,
nor kingdom of hell upon earth. For justice is perpetual
and immortal.

WISDOM 1:13–15

*Use a prayer for special categories of people (see pp. 358–59), or
say the following:*

Let us pray.

O Lord, whose nature it is to have mercy and spare, we
humbly beg your mercy on the souls of the faithful

departed, that through your mercy and our feeble prayers they may attain the glory that they have always desired. Through Christ our Lord. Amen.

CALL: Let us bless the Lord.
RESPONSE: Thanks be to God.

NONE
Midafternoon prayer

CALL: O God, ✝ come to my assistance.
RESPONSE: O Lord, be swift to my aid.
CALL: Glory be to the Father, and to the Son,
and to the Holy Spirit.
RESPONSE: As it was in the beginning, is now and
ever shall be, world without end. Amen.

O Lord, to whom the spirits live
Of all the faithful passed away,
Upon their path that brightness give
Which shineth to the perfect day.

O Light eternal, Jesu blest,
Shine on them all, and give them rest.

Direct us with thine arm of might
And bring us perfected with them

To dwell within thy city bright,
The heavenly Jerusalem.

O Light eternal, Jesu blest,
Shine on them all, and give them rest.

R. F. LITTLEDALE

ANTIPHON: Turn again, O Lord, and set my
soul free.

O God come to my assistance,
O Lord, make haste to help me.
Let them be confounded and ashamed
that seek my soul.

Let them be turned backward and blush for shame
that desire evils to me.
Let them be directly turned away in confusion
that say to me: It is well, it is well!

Let all that seek you rejoice
and be glad in you;
and let such as love your salvation say always:
The Lord be glorified!

But I am needy and poor:
O God, help me!
You are my helper and my deliverer;
O Lord, make no delay.

PSALM 70

Eternal rest grant unto them, O Lord,
and let perpetual light shine on them.

ANTIPHON: Turn again, O Lord, and set my
soul free.

SHORT READING

And the Lord of hosts will make for all peoples on this mountain a feast of fat things, a feast of wine, of fat things full of marrow, of wine purified from the lees. And he will destroy on this mountain the bond that ties all peoples, the web that is cast over all nations. He will throw down death headlong forever, and the Lord God will wipe away tears from every face, and the reproach of his people he shall take away from off the whole earth; for the Lord has spoken it.

ISAIAH 25:6–8

Use a prayer for special categories of people (see pp. 358–59), or say the following:

Let us pray.

O Lord, whose nature it is to have mercy and spare, we humbly beg your mercy on the souls of the faithful departed, that through your mercy and our feeble prayers they may attain the glory that they have always desired. Through Christ our Lord. Amen.

CALL: Let us bless the Lord.
RESPONSE: Thanks be to God.

VESPERS
Evening prayer

CALL: O God, ✠ come to my assistance.

RESPONSE: O Lord, be swift to my aid.

CALL: Glory be to the Father, and to the Son, and to the Holy Spirit.

RESPONSE: As it was in the beginning, is now and ever shall be, world without end. Amen.

KONTAKION OF THE DEPARTED

Give rest, O Christ,
to thy servants with thy saints:
where sorrow and pain are no more,
neither sighing, but life everlasting.

Thou only art immortal,
the Creator and maker of man,
and we are mortal, formed of the earth
and unto earth shall we return.

For so thou didst ordain
when thou createdst us, saying:
"Dust thou art and unto dust thou shalt return."
All we go down to the dust;
but weeping o'er the grave we make our song:

Alleluia! Alleluia! Alleluia!

ANTIPHON: You will turn, O God, and bring us
to life.

Lord, you have blessed your land,
you have reversed the captivity of Jacob.
You have forgiven the iniquity of your people,
you have covered all their sins.

You have mitigated all your anger,
you have turned away
from the wrath of your indignation.
Convert us, O God our Savior,
and turn away your anger from us.

Will you be angry with us forever:
will you extend your wrath
from generation to generation?
Will you not turn, O God, and bring us to life:
and your people shall rejoice in you.
Show us, O Lord, your mercy,
and grant us your salvation.

I will hear what the Lord has to say to me:
for he will speak peace to his people,
and to his saints,
and to those who are converted in the heart.

Surely, his salvation is near
to those who fear him:
that glory may dwell in our land.

Mercy and truth have met each other:
>justice and peace have kissed.
Truth has sprung out of the earth,
>and justice has looked down from heaven.

For the Lord will bestow goodness,
>and our earth shall yield her fruit.
Justice shall walk before him,
>and shall set his steps on their way.

PSALM 85

Eternal rest grant unto them, O Lord,
>and let perpetual light shine on them.

ANTIPHON:　You will turn, O God, and bring us
>to life.

SHORT READING
But now Christ is risen from the dead, the firstfruits of
those who sleep. For as by a man came death, so by a man
has come the resurrection of the dead. For as in Adam all
die, so also in Christ all shall be made alive.

1 CORINTHIANS 15:20–22

THE MAGNIFICAT
My ✝ soul magnifies the Lord,
>my spirit rejoices in God who is my Savior,
>who has looked upon the humility of his
>handmaiden.
Behold, all generations from now
>will acknowledge me blessed,
For the mighty one has done great things for me:
>Holy is his name!
His mercy is from one generation to the next on those
who fear him.
>Mighty is his arm!

He has scattered the proud in the imagination of
 their hearts,
        and has put down the powerful from their thrones,
        exalting those of humble degree.
The hungry he has filled with good things,
        but the rich he has dismissed with nothing.
Remembering his mercy, he has helped his servant Israel,
        as he promised to our fathers,
        to Abraham and to his posterity forevermore.

LUKE 1:46–55

Eternal rest grant unto them, O Lord,
        and let perpetual light shine on them.

INTERCESSIONS

Offer these intercessions, or pray for other needs.

CALL: Grant resurrection to those who sleep
             in death. *(Pause for prayer.)*
RESPONSE: Lord, bring us to life in your name.
CALL: Give pardon and mercy to the dead in
             purgatory. *(Pause.)*
RESPONSE: Lord, bring us to life in your name.
CALL: Give the gift of faith to those who have
             none. *(Pause.)*
RESPONSE: Lord, bring us to life in your name.
CALL: Grant rest to those we love [N. and N.]
             who have died. *(Pause.)*
RESPONSE: Lord, bring us to life in your name.

Lord, have mercy.
Christ, have mercy.
Lord, have mercy.

Our Father . . .

Use a prayer for special categories of people (see pp. 358–59), or say the following:

Let us pray.

O Lord, whose nature it is to have mercy and spare, we humbly beg your mercy on the souls of the faithful departed, that through your mercy and our feeble prayers they may attain the glory that they have always desired. Through Christ our Lord. Amen.

> CALL: Let us bless the Lord.
> **RESPONSE:** Thanks be to God.

COMPLINE
Night prayer

CALL: O God, ✛ come to my assistance.

RESPONSE: O Lord, be swift to my aid.

CALL: Glory be to the Father, and to the Son, and to the Holy Spirit.

RESPONSE: As it was in the beginning, is now and ever shall be, world without end.

Amen.

Before the ending of the day,
Creator of the world, we pray
That with thy wonted favor thou
Wouldst be our guard and keeper now.

From all ill dreams defend our eyes,
From nightly fears and fantasies;
Tread underfoot our ghostly foe,
That no pollution we may know.

O Father, that we ask be done,
Through Jesus Christ, thine only Son;
Who, with the Holy Ghost and thee,
Doth live and reign eternally. Amen.

ANTIPHON: Into your hands, O Lord, I commend
my spirit.

Out of the depths I have cried to you, O Lord:
Lord, hear my voice!
Let your ears be attentive to the voice of my
supplication.

If you, O Lord, will mark iniquities,
Lord, who could stand it?
But with you is merciful forgiveness,
that we should revere you.

I have relied upon you, O Lord;
my soul has relied on his word.
My soul has hoped in the Lord,
more than watchman for the dawn.

More than watchman for the dawn
let Israel hope in the Lord
Because with the Lord there is mercy
and with him plentiful redemption.
And he shall redeem Israel
from all its iniquities.

PSALM 130

Eternal rest grant unto them, O Lord,
and let perpetual light shine on them.

ANTIPHON: Into your hands, O Lord, I commend
my spirit.

SHORT READING

They shall see God's face, and his name shall be on their foreheads. And night shall be no more; they shall not need the light of the lamp nor the light of the sun, because the Lord God shall enlighten them, and they shall reign forever and ever.

REVELATION 22:4–5

THE NUNC DIMITTIS

ANTIPHON: Save us, O Lord, while we wake, and watch over us as we sleep, that we may pass the night with Christ and rest in peace.

Lord, ✠ now let your servant depart in peace,
    according to your promise;
for my eyes have seen your salvation,
    which you have prepared in the presence of
        all peoples,
a light for revelation to the Gentiles,
    and for glory to your people Israel.

LUKE 2:29–32

Eternal rest grant unto them, O Lord,
    and let perpetual light shine on them.

ANTIPHON: Save us, O Lord, while we wake, and watch over us as we sleep, that we may pass the night with Christ and rest in peace.

Let us pray.

Visit this house, O Lord, we pray, and drive far from it the deadly power of the enemy. May your holy angels dwell here instead, that we may be preserved in peace with your blessing on us always. Through Christ our Lord. Amen.

Say the antiphon in honor of our Lady (see p.577–82), or use the following:

We fly to thy patronage, holy mother of God.
Despise not our petitions in our necessities
But deliver us from every evil,
O glorious and blessed Virgin!

OFFICE OF SAINTS

VIGILS
The night office

CALL: O Lord, ✠ open my lips.

RESPONSE: And my mouth shall declare
your praise.

ANTIPHON: Blessed is the one whose will is the
law of the Lord.

Blessed is the man who does not abide
    in the council of the ungodly,
nor stand in the way of sinners,
    nor sit in the company of scoffers,
but whose will is in the law of the Lord
    and on his law meditates day and night.

And he shall be like a tree
    that is planted near running waters,

which shall bring forth its fruit in due season,
and whose leaves shall not fall.
Whatsoever he shall do shall prosper.

Not so the wicked, not so,
but they shall be like the dust
that the wind drives from the face of the earth.
Therefore the wicked shall not rise again in judgment,
nor sinners in the council of the just.

For the Lord knows the way of the just,
and the way of the wicked shall perish.

PSALM 1

Glory be . . .

ANTIPHON: Blessed is the one whose will is the law of the Lord.

CALL: The Lord shall lead them in a straight way,

RESPONSE: And show them the kingdom of God.

FIRST READING
Read one chapter from the Scriptures.

RESPONSE TO THE READING

CALL: Whoever is baptized in Christ has put on Christ;

RESPONSE: You are all one in Christ Jesus.

CALL: Neither Jew nor Greek, neither male nor female;

RESPONSE: You are all one in Christ Jesus.

SECOND READING
Choose a spiritual reading.

RESPONSE TO THE READING

> CALL: You are light in the Lord: walk as children of the light.
>
> **RESPONSE:** And the fruit of the light is goodness, justice, and truth.
>
> CALL: You are the light of the world: let your light shine!
>
> **RESPONSE:** And the fruit of the light is goodness, justice, and truth.

Let us pray.

O God, who alone is holy, and without whom nothing is good, by the intercession of Saint [N.] grant that we may, by imitating his/her virtues, become like him/her, whose feast we celebrate with joy. Through Christ our Lord. Amen.

> CALL: Let us bless the Lord.
>
> **RESPONSE:** Thanks be to God.

LAUDS
Morning prayer

CALL: O God, ✠ come to my assistance.

RESPONSE: O Lord, be swift to my aid.

CALL: Glory be to the Father, and to the Son, and to the Holy Spirit.

RESPONSE: As it was in the beginning, is now and ever shall be, world without end. Amen.

For all the Saints, who from their labors rest,
Who thee by faith before the world confessed
Thy name, O Jesus, be forever blest.
Alleluia!

O may thy soldiers, faithful, true and bold,
Fight as the Saints who nobly fought of old,
And win, with them, the victor's crown of gold.
Alleluia!

O blest communion! fellowship divine!
We feebly struggle, they in glory shine;
Yet all are one in thee, for all are thine.
  Alleluia!

But lo! there breaks a yet more glorious day;
The Saints triumphant rise in bright array:
The King of Glory passes on his way.
  Alleluia!

From earth's wide bounds, from ocean's farthest coast,
Through gates of pearl streams in the countless host,
Singing to Father, Son and Holy Ghost.
  Alleluia!

W. W. HOW

ANTIPHON: The saints shall rejoice in glory.

Sing to the Lord a new song,
    let his praise be sung in the assembly of the saints!

Let Israel rejoice in him that made her,
    and let the children of Zion be joyful in their king.
Let them praise his name in choir,
    and sing to him with timbrel and psaltery.

For the Lord is well pleased with his people:
    he will exalt the meek with salvation.
The saints shall rejoice in their glory,
    they shall be joyful in their beds.

The high praises of God shall be in their mouth:
    and two-edged swords in their hands,
To execute judgment upon the nations,
    chastisements among the people!

To bind their kings with fetters,
    and their nobles with manacles of iron.

To bring upon them the judgment that is written:
  this glory is for all his saints.

PSALM 149

Glory be . . .

ANTIPHON: The saints shall rejoice in glory.

SHORT READING
I beseech you therefore, brethren, by the mercy of God,
that you present your bodies as a living sacrifice, holy and
pleasing to God, your reasonable service. Do not be conformed to this world but be reformed by newness of
mind, that you may prove what is the good and acceptable
and perfect will of God.

ROMANS 12:1–2

THE BENEDICTUS
Blessed ✛ be the Lord, the God of Israel,
  who has visited and redeemed his people,
and has lifted up a horn of salvation for us
  in the family of his servant David.
For this he swore through the mouths of holy men,
  those who were prophets, from the beginning:
There would be salvation from our foes,
  and from the hand of all those who hate us;
to comfort our fathers,
  and to honor his holy covenant,
which oath once he swore to Abraham, our father,
  that he would grant us,
that freed from the hand of our enemies,
  and without fear, we may serve him,
    in holiness and justice in his very presence
    all our days.

And you, my son, will be named Prophet of the
  Most High;
      for you will go before the presence of the Lord
      to prepare his way,
to teach knowledge of salvation to his people
      that their sins may be forgiven,
      through the merciful heart of our God,
when the Daystar shall visit us from on high
      to enlighten those who sit in darkness
      and in the shadow of death,
      and guide our feet to the way of peace.

LUKE 1:68–79

Glory be . . .

INTERCESSIONS

Offer these intercessions, or pray for other needs.

CALL:	Grant that we may come to share in the glory of your saints. *(Pause for prayer.)*
RESPONSE:	Lord, may your saints intercede for us.
CALL:	Grant that we be heroic in our faith, hope, and love. *(Pause.)*
RESPONSE:	Lord, may your saints intercede for us.
CALL:	May we faithfully meditate on your word, as your saints did. *(Pause.)*
RESPONSE:	Lord, may your saints intercede for us.
CALL:	Grant that those who invoke the protection of Saint [N.] may experience his/her help. *(Pause.)*
RESPONSE:	Lord, may your saints intercede for us.

Lord, have mercy.
Christ, have mercy.
Lord, have mercy.

Our Father . . .

Let us pray.

O God, who alone is holy, and without whom nothing is good, by the intercession of Saint [N.] grant that we may, by imitating his/her virtues, become like him/her, whose feast we celebrate with joy. Through Christ our Lord. Amen.

CALL: Let us bless the Lord.
RESPONSE: Thanks be to God.

TERCE
Midmorning prayer

CALL: O God, ✛ come to my assistance.
RESPONSE: O Lord, be swift to my aid.
CALL: Glory be to the Father, and to the Son,
and to the Holy Spirit.
RESPONSE: As it was in the beginning, is now and
ever shall be, world without end.
Amen.

Come, Holy Ghost, with God the Son
And God the Father, ever one;
Shed forth thy grace within our breast
And dwell with us a ready guest.

By every power, by heart and tongue,
By act and deed, thy praise be sung;
Inflame with perfect love each sense
That others' souls may kindle thence.

O Father, that we ask be done,
Through Jesus Christ, thine only Son;
Who, with the Holy Ghost and thee,
Doth live and reign eternally. Amen.

ANTIPHON: Blessed is the man who fears the Lord.

Blessed is the man who fears the Lord;
    he will delight greatly in his commandments.
His posterity shall be mighty upon earth;
    the generation of the righteous shall be blessed.
Glory and wealth shall be in his house;
    and his justice remains forever and ever.
For the righteous he is like a lamp risen up in darkness;
    he is merciful, compassionate, and just.
Happy is the man who shows pity and lends,
    who orders his affairs with care;
    he shall stand firm forever.
The just one shall be in everlasting remembrance;
    No evil tidings shall he fear.
His heart is ever ready to hope in the Lord;
    His heart is strong: he shall not be moved
    until he sees the destruction of his enemies.
He has given, given freely to the poor:
    his justice remains forever and ever:
    his horn shall be raised in glory.
The wicked shall see and be angry,
    he shall gnash his teeth and pine away:
    the desire of the wicked shall perish.

PSALM 112

Glory be . . .

ANTIPHON: Blessed is the man who fears the Lord.

SHORT READING

And the Lord said to Samuel, "Do not look on his face nor on the height of his stature, . . . for the Lord does not see as man sees; man looks on the appearance, but the Lord beholds the heart."

1 SAMUEL 16:7

Let us pray.

O God, who alone is holy, and without whom nothing is good, by the intercession of Saint [N.] grant that we may, by imitating his/her virtues, become like him/her, whose feast we celebrate with joy. Through Christ our Lord. Amen.

> *CALL:* Let us bless the Lord.
> **RESPONSE:** Thanks be to God.

SEXT
Midday prayer

CALL: O God, ✛ come to my assistance.
RESPONSE: O Lord, be swift to my aid.
CALL: Glory be to the Father, and to the Son,
            and to the Holy Spirit.
RESPONSE: As it was in the beginning, is now and
            ever shall be, world without end. Amen.

O God of truth, O Lord of might,
Who orderest time and change aright,
And send'st the early morning ray,
And light'st the glow of perfect day:

Extinguish thou each sinful fire,
And banish every ill desire;
And while thou keep'st the body whole,
Shed forth thy peace upon the soul.

O Father, that we ask be done,
Through Jesus Christ, thine only Son;
Who, with the Holy Ghost and thee,
Doth live and reign eternally. Amen.

> **ANTIPHON:** The Lord has given food to those who
> fear him.

I will praise you, Lord, with my whole heart
    in the council of the just, and in the congregation.
Great are the works of the Lord:
    to be studied by all who love them.
His work is praise and magnificence:
    his justice continues forever and ever.
He has remembered his wonderful works,
    being a merciful and gracious Lord:
    he has given food to those who fear him.
He will always be mindful of his covenant,
    he will show to his people the power of his works,
    that he may give them the inheritance of the
        nations.
The works of his hands are truth and justice,
    All his commands are faithful, firm forevermore,
    made in truth and equity.
He has sent redemption to his people:
    he has commanded his covenant forever.
Holy and terrible is his name:
    the fear of the Lord is the beginning of wisdom,
Well understood by all who observe it:
    his praise endures forever and ever.

PSALM 111

Glory be . . .

> **ANTIPHON:** The Lord has given food to those who
> fear him.

SHORT READING

Thus says the Lord: "Heaven is my throne and the earth is my footstool; what is the house that you will build for me, and what is this place of my rest? My hand has made all these things, and so all these things are mine," says the Lord. "But whom will I respect? The one that is poor and little, contrite in spirit, and who trembles at my word."

ISAIAH 66:1–2

Let us pray.

O God, who alone is holy, and without whom nothing is good, by the intercession of Saint [N.] grant that we may, by imitating his/her virtues, become like him/her, whose feast we celebrate with joy. Through Christ our Lord. Amen.

CALL: Let us bless the Lord.
RESPONSE: Thanks be to God.

NONE
Midafternoon prayer

CALL:	O God, ✝ come to my assistance.
RESPONSE:	O Lord, be swift to my aid.
CALL:	Glory be to the Father, and to the Son, and to the Holy Spirit.
RESPONSE:	As it was in the beginning, is now and ever shall be, world without end. Amen.

O God, Creation's secret force,
Thyself unmoved, all motion's source,
Who from the morn till evening ray
Through all its changes guid'st the day:

Grant us, when this short life is past,
The glorious evening that shall last;
That, by a holy death attained,
Eternal glory may be gained.

O Father, that we ask be done,
Through Jesus Christ, thine only Son;
Who, with the Holy Ghost and thee,
Doth live and reign eternally. Amen.

> **ANTIPHON:** The just shall dwell in the tent of the Lord.

Lord, who shall dwell in your tent?
> Or who shall rest on your holy hill?
He that walks without blemish,
> He whose works are just.
He that speaks truth in his heart,
> and has not used deceit with his tongue,
nor has done evil to his neighbor,
> nor taken up a quarrel with his friend.
In his sight, malignancy is brought to nothing,
> but he glorifies those who fear the Lord.
He keeps his oaths to his neighbors, though it hurt him,
> he does not put his money to usury
> nor take bribes against the innocent.
Whoever does these things shall stand firm forevermore.

PSALM 15

Glory be . . .

> **ANTIPHON:** The just shall dwell in the tent of the Lord.

SHORT READING

For the rest, brethren, whatever is true, whatever modest, whatever just, whatever holy, whatever lovely, whatever of good repute, if there is any virtue, if there is anything worthy of praise, think on these things. The things that you have learned and received and heard and seen in me, do; and the God of peace shall be with you.

PHILIPPIANS 4:8–9

Let us pray.

O God, who alone is holy, and without whom nothing is good, by the intercession of Saint [N.] grant that we may, by imitating his/her virtues, become like him/her, whose feast we celebrate with joy. Through Christ our Lord. Amen.

CALL: Let us bless the Lord.
RESPONSE: Thanks be to God.

VESPERS
Evening prayer

CALL:	O God, ✝ come to my assistance.
RESPONSE:	O Lord, be swift to my aid.
CALL:	Glory be to the Father, and to the Son, and to the Holy Spirit.
RESPONSE:	As it was in the beginning, is now and ever shall be, world without end. Amen.

Give me the wings of faith to rise
    Within the veil, and see
The saints above, how great their joys,
    How bright their glories be.

Once they were mourning here below,
    And wet their couch with tears;
They wrestled hard, as we do now,
    With sins, and doubts, and fears.

I ask them whence their victory came;
　　They, with united breath,
Ascribe their conquest to the Lamb,
　　Their triumph to his death.

Our glorious Leader claims our praise
　　For his own pattern given;
While the long cloud of witnesses
　　Show the same path to Heaven.

ISAAC WATTS

ANTIPHON:　Let every spirit praise the Lord.

Praise the Lord in his holy place:
　　praise him in the firmament of his power.
Praise him for his mighty acts,
　　praise him according to the excellence of his
　　　greatness.

Praise him with the sound of trumpet,
　　praise him with psaltery and harp.
Praise him with timbrel and choir,
　　praise him with strings and organs.
Praise him on well-sounding cymbals,
　　praise him on cymbals of joy.

Let everything that breathes praise the Lord!

PSALM 150

Glory be . . .

ANTIPHON:　Let every spirit praise the Lord.

SHORT READING
We know that to those who love God, all things work
together for good, to such as, according to his purpose,
are called to be saints. For those whom he foreknew
he also predestined to be conformed to the image of his

Son, in order that he might be the firstborn among many brethren. And those whom he predestined he also called; and those whom he called he also justified; and those whom he justified he also glorified.

ROMANS 8:28–30

THE MAGNIFICAT

My ✠ soul magnifies the Lord,
 my spirit rejoices in God who is my Savior,
 who has looked upon the humility of his
  handmaiden.
Behold, all generations from now
 will acknowledge me blessed,
For the mighty one has done great things for me:
 Holy is his name!
His mercy is from one generation to the next on those
 who fear him.
 Mighty is his arm!
He has scattered the proud in the imagination of
 their hearts,
 and has put down the powerful from their thrones,
 exalting those of humble degree.
The hungry he has filled with good things,
 but the rich he has dismissed with nothing.
Remembering his mercy, he has helped his servant Israel,
 as he promised to our fathers,
 to Abraham and to his posterity forevermore.

LUKE 1:46–55

Glory be . . .

INTERCESSIONS
Offer these intercessions, or pray for other needs.

  CALL: Grant us strength to pursue holiness of
      life. *(Pause for prayer.)*

RESPONSE: Lord, make us holy as you are holy.
CALL: Make us more effective witnesses to your kingdom. *(Pause.)*
RESPONSE: Lord, make us holy as you are holy.
CALL: Send us more saints, Lord, to tell us of your kingdom. *(Pause.)*
RESPONSE: Lord, make us holy as you are holy.
CALL: Admit to the company of your saints those we love who have died. *(Pause.)*
RESPONSE: Lord, make us holy as you are holy.

Lord, have mercy.
Christ, have mercy.
Lord, have mercy.

Our Father . . .

Let us pray.

O God, who alone is holy, and without whom nothing is good, by the intercession of Saint [N.] grant that we may, by imitating his/her virtues, become like him/her, whose feast we celebrate with joy. Through Christ our Lord. Amen.

CALL: Let us bless the Lord.
RESPONSE: Thanks be to God.

COMPLINE
Night prayer

CALL: O God, ✠ come to my assistance.
RESPONSE: O Lord, be swift to my aid.
CALL: Glory be to the Father, and to the Son,
            and to the Holy Spirit.
RESPONSE: As it was in the beginning, is now and
            ever shall be, world without end. Amen.

Make an examination of conscience, and perform an act of penance.

Before the ending of the day,
Creator of the world, we pray
That with thy wonted favor thou
Wouldst be our guard and keeper now.

From all ill dreams defend our eyes,
From nightly fears and fantasies;
Tread underfoot our ghostly foe,

That no pollution we may know.

O Father, that we ask be done,
Through Jesus Christ, thine only Son;
Who, with the Holy Ghost and thee,
Doth live and reign eternally. Amen.

ANTIPHON: Bless the Lord throughout the night.

Behold, bless the Lord,
     all you servants of the Lord,
who stand in the house of the Lord,
     in the courts of the house of our God by night.

Lift up your hands to the holy places,
     and bless the Lord.

May the Lord bless you out of Zion,
     he that made both heaven and earth.

PSALM 134

Glory be . . .

ANTIPHON: Bless the Lord throughout the night.

SHORT READING
They shall see God's face, and his name shall be on their
foreheads. And night shall be no more; they shall not need
the light of the lamp nor the light of the sun, because the
Lord God shall enlighten them, and they shall reign forever and ever.

REVELATION 22:4–5

THE NUNC DIMITTIS
ANTIPHON: Save us, O Lord, while we wake, and
watch over us as we sleep, that we
may pass the night with Christ and
rest in peace.

Lord, ✠ now let your servant depart in peace,
    according to your promise;
for my eyes have seen your salvation,
    which you have prepared in the presence of
    all peoples,
a light for revelation to the Gentiles,
    and for glory to your people Israel.

LUKE 2:29–32

Glory be . . .

ANTIPHON: Save us, O Lord, while we wake, and watch over us as we sleep, that we may pass the night with Christ and rest in peace.

Let us pray.

Visit this house, O Lord, we pray, and drive far from it the deadly power of the enemy. May your holy angels dwell here instead, that we may be preserved in peace with your blessing on us always. Through Christ our Lord. Amen.

Say the antiphon in honor of our Lady (see pp. 577–82), or use the following:

We fly to thy patronage, holy mother of God.
Despise not our petitions in our necessities
But deliver us from every evil,
O glorious and blessed Virgin!

PART TWO

PRAYERS FOR ALL OCCASIONS

PRAYERS OF BLESSING AND PRAISE

PRAYERS OF BLESSING AND PRAISE

CONTENTS

IN PRAISE OF GOD'S CREATION

Canticle of the Sun

Most High!
Most Mighty!
Most Just Lord!
To you be all praise, glory, worship, and blessing.
Yours they are, and unworthy is our praise.

Be praised, my Lord, in all that you have made!

Be praised for Brother Sun who lights our day.
His beauty, his radiance, his splendor
Surely are but reflections of yours.

Be praised, my Lord, for Sister Moon
and for the stars which shine clearly
decking the heavens with loveliness.

Be praised, my Lord for our Sister, Water
who humbly serves our many needs
yet is so precious and so pure.

Be praised, my Lord, for our Brother, Fire
who lightens our darkness, who brightens and cheers,
who is strength and power.

Be praised, my Lord, for our Mother the Earth
who feeds and tends us,
who sends forth fruit, many-hued flowers, and grasses.

Be praised, my Lord, in those who forgive for your sake,
and in those who bear troubles and sickness.

255

O blessed are those who peacefully persevere
To gain a crown from you, Most High Lord.

Be praised, my Lord, for our Sister Death,
Death of the body that none may escape.
Pity those that die in sin.
Blessed are those found walking in virtue.

Praise the Lord! Bless the Lord! Give thanks to the Lord!
Serve him with great humility!

ST. FRANCIS OF ASSISI

There is an Irish tradition that each Easter Sunday morning the sun dances as it rises, in joy at the Lord's resurrection. The compiler knows people who claim to have seen this. This is one account, from *The Sun Dances*.

The glorious gold-bright sun was after rising on the crests of the great hills, and it was changing color—green, purple, red, blood-red, white, intense-white, and gold-white, like the glory of the God of the elements to the children of men. It was dancing up and down in exultation at the joyous resurrection of the beloved Savior of victory.

To be thus privileged, a person must ascend to the top of the highest hill before sunrise, and believe that the God who makes the small blade of grass to grow is the same God who makes the large, massive sun to move.

BARBARA MACPHIE

Hildegard of Bingen

A ray of shining light,
    Of pure creative energy
Poured through the open window

    Of God's grace,
Stirring the spirit of Hildegard

And filling her mind with warmth,
    Insight and fullness

Her spirit awoke,
Her mind expanded,
Her heart refreshed with the dew
    Of her baptism
Rejoiced in the beauty of creation,
Her soul experienced the wonder
    Of Christ's risen life.

She found freedom in faith,
Freedom like the freedom of a feather
    Blown about by the breath of God,
While the soft springs of the Spirit
Moistened her wilting heart.
Germinating the divine seed within her,
    Making what had withered green.

A mirror of dazzling light,
A "symphonia" of divine harmony,
    A spring of living water,
A source of joy and healing
A living symbol of a loving heart,
    A green branch for all time—
Became this "Sybil of the Rhine."

T. J. RHIDIAN JONES

OFFERING ONESELF

God's will would I do,
My own will bridle;

God's due would I give,
My own due yield;

God's path would I ponder,
My own death remember;

Christ's agony would I meditate,
My love to God make warmer;

Christ's cross would I carry,
My own cross forget;

Repentance of sin would I make,
Early repentance choose;

A bridle to my tongue would I put,
A bridle on my thoughts I would keep;

God's judgment would I judge,
My own judgment guard;

Christ's redemption would I seize,
My own ransom work;

The love of Christ would I feel,
My own love know.

CELTIC PRAYER

Two prayers of St. Ignatius of Loyola

Teach us, good Lord, to serve you as you deserve; to give and not to count the cost, to fight and not to heed the wounds, to toil and not to seek for rest, to labor and not ask for any reward, save that of knowing that we do your will.

Receive, O Lord, my memory, my will, my understanding, and entire liberty. You have given me all I have, and I surrender all to your divine will, that you may dispose of me as it shall please you. Give me only your love and your grace, and I shall be happy, and shall have no more to ask.

———— • ————

The Universal Prayer

Lord, I believe, but I would believe more firmly;
I hope, but I would hope more surely;
I love, but I would love more ardently;
I repent, but I would repent more passionately.

I adore you as my first beginning;
I long for you as my final end;
I honor you as my constant benefactor;
I call on you as my prompt defender.

Direct me according to your wisdom,
Correct me according to your justice,
Comfort me according to your mercy,
Protect me according to your power.

I offer you my thinking, Lord, that it be fixed on you.
I offer you my speaking, Lord, that it have you for
  its theme;
I offer you my actions, Lord, that they may be
  yours alone;

I offer you my crosses, Lord, that I may bear them for
  your sake.

I desire to do whatever you ask of me,
Simply because you ask it,
In the way you ask it to be done,
And for as long as you wish it.

I pray you, Lord, to enlighten my understanding,
to impassion my will,
to purify my heart,
and sanctify my soul.

May I repent the evil that is past,
and shun temptations to come;
correct my evil tendencies
and grow in all virtues.

Grant me, gracious Lord, to love what is yours,
and detach myself from what is mine,
Give me zeal toward my neighbor,
and contempt for worldliness.

Grant me obedience to those over me,
and graciousness to those under me.
Make me true to my friends,
and merciful to my enemies.

May I conquer self-indulgence with self-control,
Selfishness with generosity,
Anger with gentleness,
and coldness with warmth.

Make me prudent in advice,
Constant in dangers,
Patient in adversity
and unassuming in prosperity.

Make me attentive when I pray,
Moderate when celebrating
Generous in giving,
and true to my commitments.

May I keep my innocence within,
and my modesty without;
May my conversation be pure
and my life well-ordered.

May I keep my appetites in check,
Let me treasure your grace,
Let me keep your law,
that I may come to your salvation.

Teach me how fleeting is this world,
how wonderful the next;
how insignificant are the things of time,
how lasting those of eternity.

Grant me to well prepare for death
with a proper fear of judgment
that I may fly from the fires of hell
and come to the joys of paradise.

Through Christ our Lord. Amen.

ATTRIBUTED TO POPE CLEMENT XI

TO GOD THE FATHER

The Our Father

And it came to pass that as Jesus was in a certain place praying, when he ceased, one of his disciples said to him, "Lord, teach us to pray, as John taught his disciples." And he said to them, "When you pray, say: 'Father, hallowed be thy name. Thy kingdom come. Give us this day our daily bread; and forgive us our sins, for we also forgive every one that is indebted to us; and lead us not into temptation.'"

LUKE 11:1–4

The more familiar version from St. Matthew's Gospel

Jesus said, "Thus shall you pray: 'Our Father who art in heaven, hallowed be thy name. Thy kingdom come. Thy will be done on earth as it is in heaven. Give us this day our daily bread. And forgive us our debts, as we also forgive our debtors. And lead us not into temptation, but deliver us from evil.'"

MATTHEW 6:9–13

Pater noster,
Qui es in caelis.
Sanctificetur nomen tuum.
Adveniat regnum tuum.
Fiat voluntas tua sicut in caelo et in terra.
Panem nostrum quotidianum da nobis hodie
Et dimitte nobis debita nostra
Sicut et nos dimittimus debitoribus nostris,

Et ne nos inducas in tentationem
Sed libera nos a malo.
Amen.

—— • ——

Which is the best of all prayers?
The best of all prayers is the "Our Father" or the
Lord's Prayer.
Who made the Lord's Prayer?
Jesus Christ himself made the Lord's Prayer.
In the Lord's Prayer who is called "our Father"?
In the Lord's Prayer God is called "our Father."
Why is God called "our Father"?
God is called "our Father" because he is the Father of all
Christians, whom he has made his children
by Holy Baptism.
Is God also the Father of all mankind?
God is also the Father of all mankind because he made
them all, and loves and preserves them all.
**Why do we say "our" Father, and not "my"
Father?**
We say "our" Father, and not "my" Father because, being
all brethren, we are to pray not for ourselves only, but
also for all others.
**When we say "hallowed be thy name," what do
we pray for?**
When we say "hallowed be thy name," we pray that God
may be known, loved, and served by all his creatures.
**When we say "thy kingdom come," what do we
pray for?**
When we say "thy kingdom come," we pray that God
may come and reign in the hearts of all by his grace in
this world, and bring us all hereafter to his
heavenly kingdom.

When we say "thy will be done on earth as it is in heaven," what do we pray for?
When we say "thy will be done on earth as it is in heaven," we pray that God may enable us by his grace to do his will in all things, as the blessed do in heaven.
When we say "give us this day our daily bread," what do we pray for?
When we say "give us this day our daily bread," we pray that God may give us daily all that is necessary for soul and body.
When we say "forgive us our trespasses, as we forgive those who trespass against us," what do we pray for?
When we say "forgive us our trespasses, as we forgive those who trespass against us," we pray that God may forgive us our sins, as we forgive others the injuries they do to us.
When we say "lead us not into temptation," what do we pray for?
When we say "lead us not into temptation," we pray that God may give us grace not to yield to temptation.
When we say "deliver us from evil," what do we pray for?
When we say "deliver us from evil," we pray that God may free us from all evil, both of soul and body.

A CATECHISM OF CHRISTIAN DOCTRINE

—•—

I knew a nun who could only make vocal prayer, yet, while keeping to this, she enjoyed all the rest as well. Unless she used oral prayer, her thoughts wandered to an unbearable extent—yet I wish we all made such mental prayer as she did! She spent two or three hours in reciting certain Pater Nosters and a few other prayers in honor of our Lord's blood-sheddings. One day she came to me in great distress because she did not know how to make mental prayer nor could she contemplate, but was only able to pray orally. I questioned her and found that she enjoyed pure contemplation while saying the Pater Noster, and that occasionally God raised her to perfect union with himself. This was evidenced by her conduct, for she lived so holy a life that I thank God for it, and I even envied her such vocal prayer. If this was the fact (as I assure you it was), let not any of you who are the foes of contemplatives feel sure that you run no risk being raised to contemplation yourselves if you say your vocal prayers as well as you ought and keep a good conscience.

ST. TERESA OF AVILA

Our Father, which in heaven art,
Lord, Hallowed be thy Name.
Thy kingdom come, thy will be done
In earth, even as the same
In heaven is. Give us, O Lord,
Our daily bread this day.
As we forgive our debtors,
So forgive our debts, we pray.
Into temptation lead us not,
From evil keep us free:
For kingdom, power and glory is
Thine to eternity.

STERNHOLD AND HOPKINS,
METRICAL PSALMS, 1767

TO OUR LORD JESUS CHRIST

Be thou a light unto my eyes, music to mine ears, sweetness to my taste, and full contentment to my heart. Be thou my sunshine in the day, my food at table, my repose in the night, my clothing in nakedness, and my succor in all necessities. Lord Jesus, I give thee my body, my soul, my substance, my fame, my friends, my liberty, and my life. Dispose of me and all that is mine as it may seem best to thee and to the glory of thy blessed name.

JOHN COSIN

To Christ the King

O Christ Jesus, I acknowledge you to be the King of the universe; all that has been made is created for your rule. Exercise over me all your sovereign rights. I hereby renew the promises of my baptism, renouncing Satan and all his works and empty promises, and I engage myself to lead from now on a truly Christian life. And especially I undertake to bring about the triumph of the Kingdom of God and serve your Church to that end, so far as in me lies. Divine Heart of Jesus, I offer you my poor actions that all may acknowledge your sacred kingly power. In such a way may the kingdom of your peace be firmly established throughout all the earth. Amen.

O my sweet Savior Christ, which in thine undeserved love toward mankind, so kindly wouldst suffer the painful death of the cross, suffer not me to be cold nor lukewarm in love again toward thee.

ST. THOMAS MORE

Lord Jesus, let me know myself and know thee,
And desire nothing save only thee.
Let me hate myself and love thee.
Let me do everything for the sake of thee.
Let me humble myself and exalt thee.
Let me think nothing except thee.
Let me die to myself and live in thee.
Let me accept whatever happens as from thee.
Let me banish self and follow thee,
And ever desire to follow thee.
Let me fly from myself and take refuge in thee,
That I may deserve to be defended by thee.
Let me fear for myself, let me fear thee,
And let me be among those who are chosen by thee.
Let me distrust myself and put my trust in thee.
Let me be willing to obey for the sake of thee.
Let me cling to nothing save only to thee,
And let me be poor because of thee.

Look upon me, that I may love thee.
Call me that I may see thee,
And forever enjoy thee. Amen.

ST. AUGUSTINE

—— • ——

Most sweet Jesus, pierce the interior of my soul with the sweet wound of your love, that my soul may ever languish, and be dissolved with your love, and with the desire of possessing you, and long to quit this life that it may come to be perfectly united with you in a blessed eternity. Grant that my heart may be ever fixed on you, my only hope, my riches, my peace, my refuge, my confidence, my treasure, and my inheritance. Amen.

ST. BONAVENTURE

—— • ——

O my Lord and Savior, in thy arms I am safe; keep me and I have nothing to fear; give me up and I have nothing to hope for. I know not what will come upon me before I die. I know nothing about the future, but I rely upon thee. I pray thee to give me what is good for me; I pray thee to take from me whatever may imperil my salvation; I pray thee not to make me rich, I pray thee not to make me very poor; but I leave it all to thee, because thou knowest and I do not. If thou bringest pain or sorrow on me, give me grace to bear it well—keep me from fretfulness, and self-ishness. If thou givest me health and strength and success in this world, keep me ever on my guard lest these great gifts carry me away from thee.

O thou who didst die on the cross for me, even for me, sinner as I am, give me to know thee, to believe in thee, to love thee, to serve thee; ever to aim at setting forth thy glory; to live for thee; to set a good example to all around me, give me to die just at that time and in that way which is most for thy glory, and best for my salvation.

J. H. NEWMAN

I believe, O my Savior, that thou knowest just what is best for me. I believe that thou lovest me better than I do myself, that thou art all-wise in thy providence, and powerful in thy protection. I am as ignorant as Peter as to what is to happen to me in time to come; but I resign myself entirely to my ignorance, and thank thee with all my heart that thou hast taken me out of my own keeping, and, instead of putting such a serious charge upon me, hast bidden me put myself into thy hands. I can ask nothing better than this, to be thy care, not my own.

J. H. NEWMAN

O Jesus! You are my true friend, my only friend. You take part in all my misfortunes; you take them on yourself, you know how to change them into blessings. You listen to me with the greatest kindness when I relate my troubles to you, and you have always balm to pour on my wounds. I find you at all times; I find you everywhere. You never go away; if I have to change my dwelling, I find you there wherever I go. You are never weary of listening to me; you are never tired of doing me good. I am certain of being loved by you, if I love you; my goods are nothing to you, and by bestowing yours on me, you never grow poor. However miserable I may be, no one more noble or clever or even holier can come between you and me, and deprive me of your friendship; and death, which tears us away from all other friends, will unite me forever to you. All the humiliations attached to old age or to the loss of honor will never detach you from me; on the contrary, I shall then enjoy You more fully, and you will never be closer to me than when everything seems to conspire against me, to overwhelm me, and to cast me down. You bear with all my faults with extreme patience, and even my want of fidelity and my ingratitude do not wound you to such a degree as to make you unwilling to receive me back when I return to you. O Jesus, grant that I may die praising you, that I may die loving you, that I may die for the love of you. Amen.

ST. CLAUDE DE LA COLOMBIÈRE

A prayer on the most sweet name of Jesus

O most sweet and most loving Jesus. Jesus is a good name, a precious name, a name which none may utter except in the Holy Spirit, O most sweet and most soothing Jesus. O lovable and admirable, O great and healthful name of Jesus. Jesus is a holy name, a name full of delight, a name of good hope, a name that gives strength to the sinner. What else is the name of Jesus but Savior? Therefore, Jesus, for thine own sake be to me Jesus. Good Jesus, sweet Jesus, kindly Jesus; for the sake of this thy name, do to me according to thy name. Thou who didst form me, lest I perish, be to me Jesus. Good Jesus, best Jesus, Jesus have mercy on me while yet there is time for mercy: do not condemn me at the day of judgment. Open the eyes of my mind, that I may learn to despise with a pure heart everything that is merely of earth, whether pleasing or displeasing, and may think only of the things that are of heaven and eternal; and may my soul attain the strength to be forever intent upon the contemplation of eternal blessings. Faithful Jesus, kindly Jesus,

Jesus full of mercy, admit me into the number of thy elect; that with them I may deserve to serve and praise and glorify thee now and forever. Amen.

FIFTEENTH-CENTURY PRAYER

O Deus Ego Amo Te

O God, I love thee mightily,
Not only for thy saving me,
Nor yet because who love not thee
Must burn throughout eternity.
Thou, thou, my Jesu, once didst me
Embrace upon the bitter tree.
For me the nails, the soldier's spear
With injury and insult, bear—
In pain all pain exceeding,
In sweating and in bleeding,
Yea, very death, and that for me
    A sinner all unheeding!
O Jesu, should I not love thee
Who thus hast dealt so lovingly—
Not hoping some reward to see,
Nor lest I my damnation be;
But, as thyself hast loved me
So love I now and always thee,
Because my King alone thou art
Because, O God, mine own thou art!

R. H. BENSON

Thanks be to thee, my Lord Jesus Christ,
For all the benefits
which thou hast given me;
For all the pains and insults

which thou hast borne for me;
O most merciful Redeemer,
Friend and Brother,
May I know thee more clearly,
Love thee more dearly,
And follow thee more nearly. Amen.

ST. RICHARD OF CHICHESTER

TO THE HOLY SPIRIT

Veni, Sancte Spiritus, reple tuorum corda fidelium, et tui amoris in eis ignem accende.

CALL: Emitte spiritum tuum, et creabuntur.
RESPONSE: Et renovabis faciem terrae.

Oremus.

Deus, qui corda fidelium Sancti Spiritus illustratione docuisti, da nobis in eodem Spiritu recta sapere, et de eius semper

Come, Holy Spirit, fill the hearts of thy faithful, and kindle in them the fire of thy love.

CALL: Send forth thy Spirit and they shall be created.
RESPONSE: And thou shalt renew the face of the earth.

Let us pray.

O God, who hast taught the hearts of the faithful by the light of the Holy Spirit, grant that by the gift of the same Spirit we may be always truly wise and ever

consolatione gaudere.   rejoice in his consolation.
Per Christum Dominum   Through Christ our Lord.
nostrum. Amen.   Amen.

*An ancient translation of the same prayer from
an English primer of about 1400*

Come, Holy Ghost, fulfill the hearts of thy true servants,
and lighten the fire of thy love in them

> CALL: Send out thy ghost and they shall
>   be made.
> **RESPONSE:** And thou shalt make new the
>   face of the earth.

Pray we.

God that taughtest the hearts of thy true servants by the
lightening of the Holy Ghost: grant us to savor rightfulness
in the same Ghost, and to be joyful evermore of his holy
comfort. By Christ our Lord. Amen.

In the hour of my distress,
When temptations me oppress,
And when I my sins confess,
Sweet Spirit comfort me!

When I lie within my bed,
Sick in heart and sick in head,
And with doubts discomforted,
Sweet Spirit comfort me!

When the house doth sigh and weep,
And the world is drowned in sleep,
Yet mine eyes the watch do keep,
Sweet Spirit comfort me!

When the artless Doctor sees
No one hope but of his fees,
And his skill runs on the lees,
Sweet Spirit comfort me!

When his potion and his pill,
Has, or none, or little skill,
Meet for nothing but to kill,
Sweet Spirit comfort me!

When the passing-bell doth toll,
And the Furies in a shoal,
Come to fright a parting soul,
Sweet Spirit comfort me!

When the tapers now burn blue,
And the comforters are few,
And that number more than true,
Sweet Spirit comfort me!

When the priest his last hath prayed,
And I nod to what is said,
'Cause my speech is now decayed,
Sweet Spirit comfort me!

When (God knows) I'm tossed about,
Either with despair or doubt,
Yet before the glass be out,
Sweet Spirit comfort me!

When the Tempter me pursu'th
With the sins of all my youth,
And half damns me with untruth,
Sweet Spirit comfort me!

When the flames and hellish cries
Fright mine ears and fright mine eyes,

And all terrors me surprise,
Sweet Spirit comfort me!

When the judgment is revealed,
And that opened which was sealed,
When to thee I have appealed,
Sweet Spirit comfort me!

ROBERT HERRICK

— • —

My God, I adore thee, as the third person of the ever-blessed Trinity. Thou art that living love, wherewith the Father and the Son love each other. And thou art the author of supernatural love in our hearts. Increase in me this grace of love, in spite of all my unworthiness. It is more precious than anything else in the world. I accept it in place of all the world can give me. It is my life.

J. H. NEWMAN

— • —

Come, Holy Spirit, fill my heart with your holy gifts. Let my weakness be penetrated with your strength this very day, that I may fulfill all the duties of my state conscientiously, that I may do what is right and just.

Let my charity be such as to offend no one, and hurt no one's feelings; so generous as to pardon sincerely any wrong done to me. Assist me, O Holy Spirit, in all my trials of life, enlighten me in my ignorance, advise me in my doubts, strengthen me in my weakness, help me in all my needs, protect me in temptations and console me in afflictions. Graciously hear me, O Holy Spirit, and pour your light into my heart, my soul and my mind.

Assist me to live a holy life and to grow in goodness and grace. Amen.

— • —

Veni Creator
  Spiritus
Mentes tuorum
  visita
Imple superna
  gratia
Quae tu creasti,
  pectora.
Qui diceris
  Paraclitus
Altissimi donum
  Dei,
Fons vivus, ignis,
  caritas
et spiritalis unctio.

Tu septiformis
  munere,
Digitus Paternae dexterae.
Tu rite promissum
  Patris,
Sermone ditans guttura.

Accende lumen
  sensibus,
Infunde amorem
  cordibus.
Infirma nostri
  corporis
Virtute fifirmans perpeti.

Hostem repellas
  longius,
Pacemque dones protinus,

Come Holy Ghost, creator,
  come
From thy bright heavenly
  throne.
Come take possession of
  our souls
And make them all thine
  own.
Thou who art called the
  Paraclete
Best gift of God above,
The living spring, the living
  fire,
Sweet unction, and true
  love.

Thou who art sevenfold in
  thy grace,
Finger of God's right hand,
His promise, teaching little
  ones
To speak and understand.

O guide our minds with
  thy blest light,
With love our hearts
  inflame,
And with they strength
  which ne'er decays
Confirm our mortal frame.

Far from us drive our
  deadly foe,
True peace unto us bring,

Ductore sic te praevio Vitemus omne noxium.	And through all perils lead us safe Beneath thy sacred wing.
Per te sciamus da Patrem, Noscamus atque Filium, Teque utriusque spiritum Credamus omni tempore.	Through thee may we the Father know, Through thee the eternal Son. And thee, the Spirit of them both Thrice-blessed, three in one.
Deo Patris sit gloria, Et Filio qui a mortuis Surrexit, ac Paraclito In saeculorum saecula. Amen.	All glory to the Father be, With his co-equal Son: The same to thee, great Paraclete, While endless ages run.

ATTRIBUTED TO RABANUS MAURUS, 776–856
(TRANSLATOR UNKNOWN)

— • —

Come, Holy Spirit, and make your home within my heart. Cast out all that is unworthy of your presence, and make it a fit temple for your holy habitation.

— • —

Creator Spirit, by whose aid
The world's foundations first were laid,
Come visit every pious mind;
Come pour thy joys on humankind;
From sin and sorrow set us free,
And make thy temples worthy thee. . . .

Plenteous of grace, descend from high,
Rich in thy sevenfold energy,

Thou strength of his almighty hand,
Whose power does heaven and earth command!
Proceeding Spirit, our defense,
Who dost the gift of tongues dispense,
And crown'st thy gift with eloquence!

Refine and purge our earthy parts;
But, O, inflame and fire our hearts!
Our frailties help, our vice control,
Submit the senses to the soul;
And when rebellious they are grown,
Then lay thy hand and hold them down.

Chase from our minds the infernal foe,
And peace, the fruit of love, bestow;
And lest our feet should step astray,
Protect and guide us in the way.

Make us eternal truths receive,
And practice all that we believe:
Give us thyself that we may see
The Father and the Son, by thee.

Immortal honor, endless fame,
Attend the Almighty Father's Name:
The Savior Son be glorified,
Who for lost man's redemption died;
And equal adoration be,
Eternal Paraclete, to thee.

JOHN DRYDEN, 1631–1700
(BASED ON THE VENI CREATOR SPIRITUS)

For the seven gifts of the Holy Spirit

O Lord Jesus Christ, who, before ascending into heaven did promise to send the Holy Spirit to finish your work in the souls of your apostles and disciples, deign to grant the same Holy Spirit to me, to perfect in my soul the work of your grace and your love.

Grant me the Spirit of *Wisdom*—that I may not be attached to the perishable things of this world, but aspire only after the things that are eternal.

The Spirit of *Understanding*—to enlighten my mind with the light of your divine truth.

The Spirit of *Counsel*—that I may ever choose the surest way of pleasing God and gaining heaven.

The Spirit of *Fortitude*—that I may bear my cross with you, and that I may overcome with courage all the obstacles that oppose my salvation.

The Spirit of *Knowledge*—that I may know God, and know myself, and grow perfect in the science of the Saints.

The Spirit of *Piety*—that I may find the service of God sweet and amiable.

The Spirit of *Fear*—that I may be filled with a loving reverence toward God, and may avoid anything that may displease him.

Mark me, dear Lord, with the sign of your true disciples, and animate me in all things with your Spirit. Amen.

—•—

O my God, I give myself to thee, with all my liberty, all my intellect and heart and will. O Holy Spirit of God, take me as thy disciple, guide me, illuminate me, sanctify me. Bind my hands that I may not do evil, cover my eyes that I may see it with pleasure no more, sanctify my heart that evil may not rest within me. Be thou my God and my Guide. Wheresoever thou leadest me I will go, whatsoever thou forbiddest I will renounce, and whatsoever thou commandest in thy strength I will do. Amen.

— • —

Descend, O Holy Spirit, and create a new Pentecost among us. Help us to be witnesses to Christ, O heavenly comforter, that his kingdom may stretch to the ends of the earth, and last forever. Through the same Christ our Lord.

— • —

Veni Sancte Spiritus

Come, Holy Ghost, send down those beams
Which sweetly flow in silent streams
    From thy bright throne above;
O come, thou Father of the poor,
O come, thou source of all our store;
    Come, fill our hearts with love.

O thou, of comforters the best,
O thou, the soul's delightful guest,
    The pilgrim's sweet relief;
Thou art our rest in toil and sweat,
Refreshment in excessive heat,
    And solace in our grief.

O Sacred Light! shoot home thy darts,
O pierce the center of these hearts
    Whose faith aspires to thee.
Without thy Godhead, nothing can
Have any price or worth in man,
    Nothing can harmless be.

Lord wash our sinful stains away,
Water from Heaven our barren clay,

Our wounds, our bruises, heal;
To thy sweet yoke, our stiff necks bow
Warm with thy fire our hearts of snow
Our wandering feet repeal.

O grant thy faithful, dearest Lord,
Whose only hope is thy sure word,
The seven gifts of thy Spirit;
Grant us in life, to obey thy grace,
Grant us in death, to see thy Face
And endless joys inherit. Amen.

To the Holy and Undivided Trinity

The Trisagion

Holy God!
Holy mighty one!
Holy, immortal one,
have mercy on us!

— • —

Glory be to the Father, and to the Son and to the Holy Spirit, as it was in the beginning, is now and ever shall be, world without end. Amen.

— • —

Most holy Trinity, Godhead indivisible, Father, Son and Holy Spirit, our first beginning and our last end, you have made us in accord with your own image and likeness. Grant that all the thoughts of our minds, all the words of our tongues, all the affections of our hearts and all the actions of our being may always be conformed to your holy will. Thus, after we have seen you here below in creation, and in a dark manner by means of faith, we may come at last to contemplate you face-to-face forever in heaven.

— • —

St. Patrick's Breastplate

I bind unto myself today
the strong name of the Trinity
by invocation of the same
the Three in One and One in Three.
of whom all nature hath creation,
eternal Father, Spirit, Word.
Praise to the Lord of my salvation:
Salvation is of Christ the Lord. Amen.

ST. PATRICK, C. 373–463
(TRANSLATED BY CECIL FRANCIS ALEXANDER)

It is right and proper that we worship the Father, and the Son, and the Holy Spirit, one in essence and undivided Trinity. It is right and proper to sing to you, to bless you, to honor you, to thank you and worship you in every place of your rule; for you are God who is mysterious, incomprehensible, invisible, limitless, together with your only-begotten Son, and the Holy Spirit. You brought us out of nothing into being, and again raised up the fallen, overlooking nothing until you brought us to heaven, and granted us the coming kingdom. For all this we give you thanks, with your only-begotten Son, and your Holy Spirit, for all the gifts, seen and unseen, which have been granted us, those which we know of and those of which we do not. We thank you also for this worship, which you condescend to accept from our poor hands, even though thousands of Archangels stand before you, and hundreds of thousands of Angels, Cherubim and Seraphim, with six wings and countless eyes, who soar aloft, singing the triumphant song, calling aloud, lifting their voices and saying: Holy, Holy, Holy is the Lord of Hosts; heaven and earth are full of his glory. Hosanna in the highest. Blessed is he who comes in the name of the Lord. Hosanna in the highest.

LITURGY OF ST. JOHN CHRYSOSTOM

I praise you, Father all-powerful!
I praise you, Divine Son, our Lord and Savior!
I praise you, Spirit of love!

O God, three persons, be near me in the temple of my soul, you reveal yourself in the depths of my being, draw me to share in your life and your love. Your power is beyond all words to describe, your glory is measureless, your mercy is without limits, your love for mankind is beyond all telling. Look down upon me and in your kindness grant to me the riches of your compassion and mercy, a share in your divine life. May I come to live more fully the life I profess and come to the glory of your kingdom.

ACTS OF FAITH, HOPE, AND CHARITY

O almighty and eternal God, grant to us the increase of faith, hope, and charity; and that we may deserve to obtain what you promise, make us love whatever you command, through Christ our Lord. Amen.

— • —

O my God, I firmly believe that you are one God in three divine Persons, Father, Son, and Holy Spirit; I believe that your divine Son became man and died for our sins, and that he will come to judge the living and the dead. I believe these and all the truths which the holy Catholic Church teaches, because you revealed them, who can neither deceive nor be deceived. Amen.

— • —

I firmly believe there is one God; and that in this one God there are three persons, the Father, the Son, and the Holy Spirit; that the Son took to himself the nature of man from the womb of the Virgin Mary, by the operation of the power of the Holy Spirit, and that in this our human nature he was crucified and died for us, that afterward he rose again and ascended into heaven, from whence he shall come to repay the just with everlasting glory and the wicked with everlasting punishment. Moreover, I believe whatsoever the Catholic Church proposes to be believed, and this because God, who is the sovereign truth that can never deceive or be deceived, has revealed all these things to this his Church.

—— • ——

O my God I believe in you and in all that your Church teaches, because you have said it, and your word is true.

—— • ——

O my God, relying on your infinite goodness and promises, I hope to obtain pardon of my sins, the help of your grace, and life everlasting, through the merits of Jesus Christ, my Lord and Redeemer. Amen.

—— • ——

O my God, relying on your almighty power and your infinite mercy and goodness, and because you are faithful to your promises, I trust in you that you will grant me the forgiveness of my sins through the merits of Jesus Christ your Son; and that you will give me the assistance of your grace, with which I will labor to continue to the end in the diligent exercise of all good works, and may deserve to obtain in heaven the glory which you have promised.

—— • ——

O my God, I hope in you, for grace and for glory, because of your promises, your mercy and your power.

—— • ——

O my God, I love you above all things, with my whole heart and soul, because you are all good and worthy of all my love. I love my neighbor as myself for the love of you. I forgive all who have injured me and I ask pardon of all whom I have injured. Amen.

—— • ——

O Lord my God, I love you with my whole heart, and above all things, because you, O God, are the Sovereign good and for your own infinite perfections are most worthy of all love. For your sake, I also love my neighbor as myself.

AT THE BEGINNING OF THE DAY

In the name of the Father, the Son, ✠ and the Holy Spirit. Amen.

—•—

Lord, teach us to pray.   LUKE 11:1

—•—

If, when we wish to make any request to men in power, we presume not to do except with humility and reverence; how much more ought we with all lowliness and purity of devotion to offer our supplications to the Lord God of all things? And let us remember that not for our much speaking, but for our purity of heart and tears of compunction shall we be heard. Our prayer, therefore, ought to be short and pure, except it be perchance prolonged by the inspiration of Divine Grace.

RULE OF ST. BENEDICT

—•—

My Lord and my God, I firmly believe that you are here, that you see me, that you hear me. I adore you with profound reverence; I beg your pardon for my sins and the grace to spend this time of prayer fruitfully. My immaculate Mother, St. Joseph my father and lord, my guardian angel, intercede for me.

—•—

Actiones nostras

Direct, O Lord, our actions by your holy inspirations, and carry them on by your gracious assistance that every prayer and work of ours may begin always with you, and through you be happily ended. Amen.

ROMAN RITUAL

—— • ——

O my God, I offer to you all the duties that I am about to perform, that they may be to your greater glory, and to the honor of your blessed Mother. Amen.

—— • ——

My God, I firmly believe that you are here and perfectly see me, and that you observe all my actions, all my thoughts, and the most secret motions of my heart. Though I am a sinner who has often offended you, do not, I pray, turn me away, out of that very goodness and generosity which at this time has called me to you. Give me grace, then, to pray as I ought.

—— • ——

Take my life, and let it be
Consecrated, Lord, to thee.
Take my hands, and let them move
At the impulse of thy love.
Take my feet and let them be
"Swift and beautiful" for thee.
Take my voice and let it sing
Always, only for my King.
Take my lips and let them be
Filled with messages from thee.
Take my moments and my days,
Let them flow in ceaseless praise.

Take my intellect, and use
Every power as thou shalt choose.
Take my will, and make it thine,
It shall be no longer mine.
Take my heart—it is thine own,
Let it be thy royal throne.
Take my love—O Lord, O pour
At thy feet its treasure store.
Take myself, and I will be
Ever, only—all for thee.

FRANCES R. HAVERGAL

———•———

Pray as you can, and not as you can't!

DOM JOHN CHAPMAN

———•———

Teach me, dearest Lord, to seek for you, and then show yourself when I search. For I cannot seek unless you show me how, nor find you but when you reveal yourself. Let me long for you with all my heart, and yearn for you as I seek: O fill me utterly with love when I find you!

ST. AMBROSE

———•———

THROUGH THE DAY

MORNING

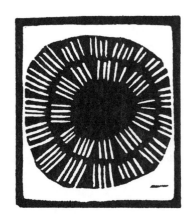

A short road to perfection

It is the saying of holy men that, if we wish to be perfect, we have nothing more to do than to perform the ordinary duties of the day well. A short road to perfection—short, not because easy, but because pertinent and intelligible. There are no short ways to perfection, but there are sure ones.

I think this is an instruction which may be of great practical use to persons like ourselves. It is easy to have vague ideas what perfection is, which serve well enough to talk about, when we do not intend to aim at it; but as soon as a person really desires and sets about seeking it himself, he is dissatisfied with anything but what is tangible and clear, and constitutes some sort of direction toward the practice of it.

We must bear in mind what is meant by perfection. It does not mean any extraordinary service, anything out

292

of the way, or especially heroic—not all have the opportunity of heroic acts, of sufferings—but it means what the word perfection ordinarily means. By perfect we mean that which has no flaw in it, that which is complete, that which is consistent, that which is sound—we mean the opposite to imperfect. As we know well what *im*perfection in religious service means, we know by the contrast what is meant by perfection.

He, then, is perfect who does the work of the day perfectly, and we need not go beyond this to seek for perfection. You need not go out of the *round* of the day.

I insist on this because I think it will simplify our views and fix our exertions on a definite aim. If you ask me what you are to do in order to be perfect, I say, first—Do not lie in bed beyond the due time of rising; give your first thoughts to God; make a good visit to the Blessed Sacrament; say the Angelus devoutly; eat and drink to God's glory; say the Rosary well; be recollected; put out bad thoughts; make your evening meditation well; examine yourself daily; go to bed in good time, and you are already perfect.

J. H. NEWMAN

—•—

These things I will think over in my heart, and therefore I will hope: the mercies of the Lord never come to an end, his compassions never fail; they are new every morning; great is your faithfulness. "The Lord is my portion," said my soul, "therefore I will wait for him."

LAMENTATIONS 3:21–24

—•—

O my God, through the most pure heart of Mary, I offer thee all the prayers, works and sufferings of this day for the intentions of thy divine heart in the holy Mass.

TRADITIONAL PRAYER

Most holy and adorable Trinity, one God in three persons, I praise you and give you thanks for all the favors you have bestowed on me. Your goodness has preserved me until now. I offer you my whole being, and in particular all my thoughts, words, and deeds, together with all the trials I may undergo this day. Give them your blessing. May your divine love animate them and may they serve your greater glory.

I make this morning offering in union with the divine intentions of Jesus Christ who offers himself daily in the holy sacrifice of the Mass, and in union with Mary, his virgin Mother and our Mother, who was always the faithful handmaid of the Lord. Amen.

Morning offering of St. Leonard of Port Maurice

O my eternal God, behold me prostrate before your immense majesty in humblest adoration. I offer you all my thoughts, words and actions of this day; and I intend to do all for your love, for your glory, to fulfill your divine will, to serve you, to praise you and to bless you; to be enlightened in the mysteries of the holy faith, to secure my salvation, and to hope in your mercy; to satisfy your divine justice for my sins, so many and so grievous; to give help to the holy souls in Purgatory, and to obtain the grace of a true conversion for all sinners: in short, I intend to do this day every thing in union with those most pure intentions which Jesus and Mary had in life, and all the saints who are in heaven, and all the just who are upon earth; and I should wish to be able to subscribe with my own blood this my intention, and to repeat it as many times every moment as there will be moments in eternity. Accept, O my beloved God, this my good desire; give me your holy blessing, with powerful grace not to commit mortal sin throughout the whole course of my life, but particularly on this day, on which I desire, and intend to gain all the indulgences which I can, and to assist spiritally at all the Masses which shall be celebrated today throughout the whole world, applying them all as help to the holy souls in Purgatory that they may be freed from those pains. Amen.

—— • ——

I offer to thee, O my God, the life and death of thine only Son, and with them these, mine affections and resolutions, my thoughts, words, deeds, and sufferings of this day and of all my life, in honor of thine adorable majesty, in thanksgiving for all thy benefits, in satisfaction for my sins, and to obtain the assistance of thy grace; that, persevering to the end in doing thy holy will, I may love and enjoy thee forever in thy glory.

—— • ——

O my God, I offer you my thoughts, words, actions, and sufferings; and I beseech you to give me your grace that I may not offend you this day, but may faithfully serve you and do your holy will in all things. Amen.

—— • ——

Grant, O Lord, that none may love you less this day because of me; that never word or act of mine may turn one soul from thee; and, ever daring, yet one more grace would I implore that many souls this day, because of me, may love thee more. Amen.

—•—

Father, unless you help me I shall do no good today whatever, but great evil.

ST. PHILIP NERI

—•—

Give us, Lord, a humble, quiet, peaceable, patient, tender and charitable mind, and in all our thoughts, words and deeds a taste of the Holy Spirit. Give us, Lord, a lively faith, a firm hope, a fervent charity, a love of you. Take from us all lukewarmness in meditation, dullness in prayer. Give us fervor and delight in thinking of you and your grace, your tender compassion toward us. The things that we pray for, good Lord, give us grace to labor for. Through Jesus Christ our Lord.

ST. THOMAS MORE

—•—

God be in my head,
    And in my understanding;
God be in mine eyes,
    And in my looking;
God be in my mouth
    And in my speaking;
God be in my heart,
    And in my thinking;
God be at my end and at my departing.

SARUM PRIMER

—•—

God, our Father, we are very feeble and not inclined to any virtuous or gallant undertaking. Fortify our weakness, we beg, that we may be valiant in this spiritual war; help us against our own neglect and timorousness, and protect us from the treachery of our unfaithful hearts, for the love of Jesus Christ our Lord. Amen.

THOMAS À KEMPIS

Actiones nostras

Direct, we beseech you, Lord, our actions by your holy inspiration and further them with your gracious assistance, that our every word and work may always begin with you, and through you be happily ended. Amen.

ROMAN BREVIARY

Lord, I give you my feet to go your way,
my body to do whatever you want me to do,
my tongue to say whatever you want me to say.
Now take away from me whatever I do not need.

Lord, God Almighty, since you have brought us safely to the beginning of this day, defend us as this day proceeds by your mighty power, so that we do not fall into any sin, but that all our words, our thoughts and actions may be so governed, as to be ever righteous in your sight. Through Christ our Lord. Amen.

ROMAN BREVIARY

Angel of God, my guardian dear
To whom God's love commits me here,
Ever this day be at my side
To light and guard, to rule and guide.
Amen.

Use me, my Savior, for whatever purpose and in whatever way thou mayest require. Here is my poor heart, an empty vessel; fill it with thy grace. Here is my sinful, troubled soul; quicken it and refresh it with thy love. Take my heart for thine abode; my mouth to spread abroad the glory of thy name; my love and all my powers for the advancement of thy believing people and never suffer the steadfastness and confidence of my faith to abate.

DWIGHT MOODY

THE ANGELUS

This devotion in honor of the Incarnation is traditionally said in the morning, at noon, and in the evening.

OTHER THAN DURING EASTERTIDE

CALL: The angel of the Lord declared unto Mary,

RESPONSE: And she conceived of the Holy Spirit.

Hail Mary . . .

CALL: Behold the handmaid of the Lord,

RESPONSE: Be it done unto me according to your word.

Hail Mary . . .

CALL: And the Word was made flesh,

RESPONSE: And dwelt among us.

Hail Mary . . .

CALL: Pray for us, O holy mother of God,

RESPONSE: That we may be made worthy of the promises of Christ.

Let us pray.

Pour forth, we beg you, O Lord, your grace into our hearts: that we, to whom the incarnation of Christ your Son was made known by the message of an angel, may by his passion and cross be brought to the glory of his resurrection. Through the same Christ our Lord. Amen.

DURING THE EASTER SEASON: *REGINA CAELI*

Queen of Heaven, rejoice, alleluia:
For he whom you merited to bear, alleluia,
Has risen, as he said, alleluia.
Pray for us to God, alleluia.

> *CALL:* Rejoice and be glad, O Virgin Mary, alleluia.
>
> **RESPONSE:** Because the Lord is truly risen, alleluia.

Let us pray.

O God, who by the resurrection of your Son, our Lord Jesus Christ, granted joy to the whole world: grant, we beg you, that through the intercession of the Virgin Mary, his mother, we may lay hold of the joys of eternal life. Through the same Christ our Lord. Amen.

BEFORE WORK

Lord, thou knowest how busy I must be this day. If I forget thee, do not thou forget me.

JACOB ASTLEY AT THE BATTLE OF EDGEHILL, 1642

Almighty God, the giver of all good things, without whose help all labor is ineffectual, and without whose grace all wisdom folly, grant, we beseech thee, that in all our undertakings, thy Holy Spirit may not be withheld from us: but that we may promote thy glory, and the salvation both of ourselves and others. Grant this, O Lord, for the sake of Jesus Christ our Lord.

SAMUEL JOHNSON

I know not, O my God, what may befall me today, but I am well convinced that nothing will happen which thou hast not foreseen and ordained from eternity. I adore thy eternal and impenetrable designs, I submit to them for thy love, I sacrifice myself in union with the sacrifice of Jesus Christ my divine Savior. I ask in his holy name for patience and resignation in my sufferings, and perfect conformity of my will to thine in all things, past, present and to come.

My God, I have nothing worthy of thy acceptance to offer thee, I know nothing, I can do nothing. I have but my heart to give thee; I may be deprived of health, reputation and even life, but my heart is my own. I consecrate it to thee, hoping never to resume it and desiring not to live if not for thee. Amen.

ELIZABETH OF FRANCE, SISTER TO LOUIS XVI

A prayer of St. Thomas Aquinas before work

O Thou Creator, of whom my tongue is powerless to tell, thou who from the infinite depths of thy wisdom hast fashioned the choirs of angels, and arranged them marvelously above the highest heavens, each in its proper rank; thou who hast set all things most perfectly and beautifully in place; thou, I pray, who art acclaimed as the true fount of light and wisdom, from whom all things take their origin, pour out thy clear radiance upon the obscurity of my mind. Take away the double darkness in which I was born, of sin, that is, and of ignorance. Thou, who makest the lips of babes to utter praise, give eloquence to my lips and pour out the grace of thy blessing upon my speech. Grant me intelligence to learn, memory to retain, method and ease to understand, facility to explain, and abundant fluency to speak. Give me knowledge as I begin, guide me in the progress of my work, and bring me out with my task well done, O thou who art true God and true man. Amen.

TRANSLATED BY JEROME BERTRAM

— • —

A prayer of St. Thomas Aquinas before beginning study

O incomprehensible Creator, the true fountain of light and only author of all knowledge, enlighten, we pray, our understanding, and remove from us all darkness of ignorance. Give us a diligent and obedient spirit, quickness to grasp subtleties, capacity to remember and the powerful assistance of thy holy grace, that what we learn we may apply to the honor of our own souls, through Jesus Christ our Lord. Amen.

— • —

O my God, I offer to thee the duties I am going to perform, to thy greater honor and glory. I desire to praise and glorify thy holy name and that of thy holy Mother now and forever. Amen.

— • —

A prayer before reading the Scriptures

Lord, may your sacred Scriptures be my delight; turn to me, my God. You are fullness of day to those that can see; you are light to the blind; you are power to the strong, strength to the weak: turn to me. Listen to my cry from the depths. There are so many mysteries in the Scriptures, and yet it was not without purpose that you wished them to be written. Let me praise you for all the truths I discover in these sacred books. Help me to listen to the voice of prayer; refresh me as I meditate on the wonders of your law; from the beginning of time when you created the heavens and the earth to the moment when I shall reign with you in your holy city forever.

ST. AUGUSTINE

— • —

Enkindle in our hearts, Master and lover of mankind, the pure light of thy divine knowledge, and open the eyes of our understanding, that we may comprehend the teachings of thy gospel: instill in us a fear of thy blessed commandments that, trampling all desires of the flesh, we might live a spiritual life, thinking and doing all those things which are pleasing to thy holy will. For thou art the light of our souls and of our bodies, O Christ our God, and to thee do we offer glory, together with thy eternal Father, and to thy most holy, good and life-giving Spirit, now, and always, and forever and ever. Amen.

LITURGY OF ST. JOHN CHRYSOSTOM

— • —

GRACE BEFORE AND AFTER MEALS

FORMAL GRACE BEFORE MEALS

CALL: Bless the Lord!
RESPONSE: Bless the Lord!

BEFORE THE MIDDAY MEAL

CALL: The eyes of all look to you, O Lord,
RESPONSE: And you grant them food when it is needed. You open wide your hand and fill all your creatures with blessings.

Lord, have mercy.
Christ, have mercy.
Lord, have mercy.

Our Father . . .

Let us pray.

BEFORE THE EVENING MEAL

CALL: The poor shall eat and have their fill,
RESPONSE: And shall praise the Lord who has blessed them, for they shall live forever and ever.

Bless us, O Lord, ✠ and these thy gifts which we are about to receive from thy bounty. Through Christ our Lord. Amen.

The cook or another person says the following:

Lord, give us your blessing!

Whoever presides replies:

May the king of eternal glory make us partakers one day of his heavenly banquet.

RESPONSE: Amen.

May the king of eternal glory draw us to share in the banquet of everlasting life.

RESPONSE: Amen.

FORMAL GRACE AFTER MEALS

AFTER THE MIDDAY MEAL

CALL: All your works, Lord, proclaim your goodness.
RESPONSE: And all your holy people rejoice in you.

AFTER THE EVENING MEAL

CALL: The good and merciful Lord has caused us to remember his goodness:
RESPONSE: He has given food to those who love him.

We give you thanks, O Lord, for all your benefits, who lives and reigns forever and ever. Amen.

Praise the Lord, all you nations,
Praise him, all you peoples.
For his mercy has been shown forth toward us,
And the Lord keeps his word forever.

PSALM 117

Glory be . . .

Lord, have mercy.
Christ, have mercy.
Lord, have mercy.

Our Father . . .

CALL: The Lord gives freely to the poor.
RESPONSE: And his justice shall last forever.
CALL: I will bless the Lord at all times.
RESPONSE: His praise shall be always on my lips.
CALL: My soul will ever praise the Lord.
RESPONSE: The redeemed shall hear it and be glad.
CALL: Bless the Lord with me.
RESPONSE: Let us praise his name together.
CALL: May the name of the Lord be blessed.
RESPONSE: Now and forevermore.

Reward, O Lord, with eternal life all those who have been good to us, for the sake of your holy name. Amen.

CALL: Let us bless the Lord.
RESPONSE: Thanks be to God.
CALL: May the souls of the faithful departed, through the mercy of God, rest in peace.
RESPONSE: Amen.

SIMPLE GRACE BEFORE MEALS

Bless us, O Lord, ✠ and these thy gifts which we are about to receive from thy bounty. Through Christ our Lord. Amen.

Bless us, gracious Lord,
Bless this food, set before us,
Bless those who have prepared it
And give bread to those who have none.

To God who gives our daily bread
A thankful song we raise,
And pray that he who sends us food
May fill our hearts with praise.

THOMAS TALLIS

———•———

SIMPLE GRACE AFTER MEALS

We give thee thanks, almighty God, for these and all thy benefits, who livest and reignest world without end. Amen. May the souls of the faithful departed, through the mercy of God rest in peace. Amen.

———•———

We give you thanks, generous Lord,
for the food which we have shared.
Make us openhanded to those in need,
and ever grateful for the good things you give us.
Through Christ our Lord. Amen.

———•———

A Celtic grace

Be with me, O God at breaking of bread,
Be with me, O God at close of our meal,
Let no whit adown my body
That may hurt my sorrowing soul.

———•———

BRIEF PRAYERS

These short prayers expressing love and praise of God are also called aspirations since they can be said in a single breath. They may also be offered mentally. They help us "pray constantly," keeping the presence of God before us at all times.

We adore you, O Christ, and we bless you; because by your holy Cross you have redeemed the world.

ROMAN BREVIARY

——•——

May the Holy Trinity be blessed.

ROMAN MISSAL

——•——

Christ conquers! Christ reigns! Christ commands!

——•——

O Heart of Jesus, burning with love for us, inflame our hearts with love for you.

——•——

O Heart of Jesus, I place my trust in you.

——•——

O Heart of Jesus, all for you.

——•——

Most Sacred Heart of Jesus, have mercy on us.

——•——

My God and my all.

——•——

O God, have mercy on me, a sinner.

LUKE 18:13

——•——

Grant that I may praise you, O sacred Virgin; give me strength against your enemies.

ROMAN BREVIARY

———•———

Teach me to do your will, because you are my God.

PSALM 143:10

———•———

O Lord, increase our faith.

LUKE 17:5

———•———

O Lord, may we be of one mind in truth and of one heart in charity.

———•———

O Lord, save us, lest we perish.

MATTHEW 8:25

———•———

My Lord and my God.

JOHN 20:28

———•———

Sweet Heart of Jesus, be my salvation.

———•———

Glory be to the Father, and to the Son, and to the Holy Spirit.

———•———

Jesus, Mary, Joseph, I give you my heart and my soul.
Jesus, Mary, Joseph, assist me in my last agony.
Jesus, Mary, Joseph, may I breathe forth my soul in peace with you.

ROMAN RITUAL

———•———

Jesus, meek and humble of heart, make my heart like your heart.

ROMAN RITUAL

———•———

May the Most Blessed Sacrament be praised and adored forever.

———•———

Stay with us, O Lord.

LUKE 24:29

———•———

Mother of Sorrows, pray for us.

———•———

My Mother, my Hope.

———•———

Send, O Lord, laborers into your harvest.

SEE MATTHEW 9:38

———•———

May the Virgin Mary together with her loving Child bless us.

ROMAN BREVIARY

———•———

Hail, O Cross, our only hope!

ROMAN BREVIARY

———•———

Pray for us, O Holy Mother of God, that we may be made worthy of the promises of Christ.

ROMAN RITUAL

———•———

Father, into your hands I commend my spirit.

LUKE 23:46; SEE PSALM 31:5

Merciful Lord Jesus, grant them everlasting rest.

ROMAN MISSAL

Queen conceived without original sin, pray for us.

ROMAN RITUAL

Holy Mother of God, Mary ever Virgin, intercede for us.

ROMAN BREVIARY

Holy Mary, pray for us.

ROMAN RITUAL

You are the Christ, the Son of the living God.

MATTHEW 16:16

The Golden Arrow

Use this prayer when you hear a blasphemy.

May the most holy, most sacred, most adorable, most mysterious and unutterable name of God be praised, blessed, loved, adored, glorified in heaven, on earth and in hell, by all God's creatures, and by the Sacred Heart of our Lord and Savior Jesus Christ in the most holy sacrament of the altar. Amen.

EVENING

If you are really fighting, you need to make an examination of conscience. Take care of the daily examination: find out if you feel the sorrow of love, for not getting to know our Lord as you should.

BLESSED JOSÉ MARIA DE BALAGUER

Blessed Jesus, still my soul in you. Reign in me, O mighty Calm. Rule in me, O gentle King, O peaceful King. Give me self-control, strong self-control over what I say, what I think, what I do. Deliver me, beloved Lord, from fractiousness, irritability, lack of gentleness and by your own profound patience, give the same to me, with a soul that loves to be still in you. Make me again in your likeness, in this as in everything. Amen. O rest in the Lord forever, my soul, for he is the eternal repose of the saints.

ST. JOHN OF THE CROSS

Blessed Jesus, make me love you entirely. Let me deeply consider the greatness of your love toward me. Sweet Jesus, possess my heart, hold and keep it only to you. O Blessed Lord, you have overcome me; you have utterly bound me by your grace and manifold benefits to be your servant. From now on, I will never leave you. Amen.

ST. JOHN FISHER

Thou being of marvels,
Shield me with might,
Thou being of statutes
And of stars.

Compass me this night,
Both soul and body,
Compass me this night
And on every night.

Compass me aright
Between earth and sky,
Between the mystery of thy laws
And mine eye of blindness;

Both that which mine eye sees
And that which it reads not;
Both that which is clear
And is not clear to my devotion.

CELTIC PRAYER

The Pillar of the Cloud

Lead, Kindly Light, amid the encircling gloom
    Lead thou me on!
The night is dark, and I am far from home—
    Lead thou me on!
Keep thou my feet; I do not ask to see
The distant scene—one step enough for me.

I was not ever thus, nor pray'd that thou
    Shouldst lead me on.
I loved to choose and see my path, but now
    Lead thou me on!
I loved the garish day, and, spite of fears,
Pride ruled my will: remember not past years.

So long thy power hath blest me, sure it still
    Will lead me on,
O'er moor and fen, o'er crag and torrent, till
    The night is gone;

And with the morn those angel faces smile
Which I have loved long since, and lost awhile.

J. H. NEWMAN

THROUGH THE YEAR

ADVENT

During the four-week Advent season, we prepare for Christ's two comings: his second coming at the end of time and his first coming, the Incarnation, at Christmas. Advent begins on the Sunday that falls on or closest to November 30 and ends with the first evening prayer of Christmas. The first two weeks of Advent, when the prayers below are typically said, are associated with Christ's second coming.

Stir up your power, we beseech you, O Lord, and come, that we may be protected from the dangers to which our sins expose us, and thus we may be saved.

———•———

Grant the will, we beseech you, almighty God, to your faithful people, that, running to meet the coming of your Anointed with the gift of good works, we may be found worthy to be gathered at his right hand and thus possess the heavenly kingdom.

———•———

Almighty God, give us grace that we may cast away the works of darkness, and put upon us the armor of light, now

315

in the time of this mortal life, in which thy Son Jesus Christ came to visit us in great humility; that in the last day, when he shall come again in his glorious majesty to judge both the quick and the dead, we may rise to life immortal.

———•———

Lo! He comes with clouds descending,
    Once for favored sinners slain;
thousand thousand Saints attending
    Swell the triumph of his train:
        Alleluia!
God appears, on earth to reign.

Every eye shall now behold him
    Robed in dreadful majesty;
Those who set at nought and sold him
    Pierced and nailed him to the tree;
        Deeply wailing
Shall the true Messiah see.

Those dear tokens of his passion
    Still his dazzling body bears,
Cause of endless exultation
    To his ransomed worshippers:
        With what rapture
Gaze we on those glorious scars!

Yea, amen! let all adore thee,
    High on thine eternal throne;
Savior, take the power and glory:
    Claim the kingdom for thine own
        O come quickly!
Alleluia! Come, Lord, come!

C. WESLEY AND J. CENNICK

———•———

Lord Jesus Christ, the world's true sun, always rising, never setting, whose life-giving warmth engenders, preserves, nourishes and gladdens all things in heaven and on earth, shine into my soul, I pray: scatter the night of sin and the clouds of error; blaze within me, so that I may go on my way without stumbling, taking no part in shameful deeds done in the dark, but ever walking as one born to the light. Amen.

ERASMUS

The second phase of Advent changes to the preparation for the coming of Christ at Christmas. The best-known devotions for this period are the O Antiphons, a mosaic of biblical verses from the prophetic and wisdom books, each beginning with the invocative O. These seven antiphons are prayed daily between December 17 and 23 and are sung before and after the Magnificat at vespers. They are ancient prayers dating from the eighth century.

December 17

O Sapientia, quae ex ore Altissimi prodisti, attingens a fine usque ad finem, fortiter suaviter disponensque omnia: veni ad docendum nos viam prudentiae.

Wisdom, who came forth from the mouth of the Most High, and reaching from beginning to end, strongly and sweetly orders all things: come and teach us the way of prudence.

December 18

O Adonai, et Dux domus Israel, qui Moysi in igne flammae rubi apparuisti, et ei in Sina legem dedisti: veni ad redimendum nos in brachio extento.

O Lord, and leader of the house of Israel, who appeared to Moses in the burning bush, and gave him the law on Mount Sinai, come and save us with outstretched arm.

December 19

O radix Iesse, qui stas
in signum populorum,
quem continebunt reges
os suum, quem gentes
deprecabuntur: veni ad
liberandum nos, iam
noli tardare.

O root of Jesse, raised
as a supersign to the
people, to put kings to
silence and to whom all
nations shall have recourse:
come without delay and
save us.

December 20

O clavis David, et
sceptrum domus Israel:
qui aperis et nemo
claudit, claudis et nemo
aperit, et educ vinctum
de domo carceris,
sedentem in tenebris et
umbra mortis.

O key of David, and scepter
of the house of Israel, who
opens that none may close,
closes that none may
open: come and lead the
captive from prison, who
sits in darkness and the
shadow of death.

December 21

O Oriens, splendor lucis
aeternae, et sol iustitiae:
veni et illumina
sedentes in tenebris
et umbra mortis.

O Daystar, radiance of the
eternal light, and sun of
justice, come and shine on
those who sit in darkness
and the shadow of death.

December 22

O Rex gentium, et
desideratus earum,
lapisque angularis, qui
facis utraque unum:

O King of the people, and
their desire, O cornerstone
binding each together,
come and save mankind

veni et salva hominem, quem de limo formasti.	whom you formed from the dust.

— • —

December 23

O Emmanuel, Rex et legifer noster, exspectatio gentium, et Salvator earum: veni ad salvandum nos Domine Deus noster.	O God-with-us, our king and lawgiver, the expected of nations and their Savior: come and save us, O Lord our God.

— • —

Rorate caeli desuper, et nubes pluant justum.	Drop down dew, you heavens: clouds, rain the just one.
CALL: Ne irascaris Domine, ne ultra memineris iniquitatis: ecce civitas Sancti facta est deserta: Sion deserta facta est: Jerusalem desolata est: domus sanctificationis tuae et gloriae tuae, ubi laudaverunt te patres nostri.	*CALL:* Be not angry, O Lord, remember our sin no more: behold your holy city is abandoned: Zion is deserted: Jerusalem stands lonely, that house of your holiness and of your glory where our forefathers praised you.
CALL: Peccavimus, et facti sumus tamquam immundus nos, et cecidimus quasi folium universi: et iniquitates nostrae quasi ventus abstulerunt nos:	*CALL:* We have sinned, and as bad as those who afflicted us; so we have fallen like the leaves of any tree, blown away because of our sins: you have hidden your

abscondisti faciem tuam a nobis, et allisisti nos in manu iniquitatis nostrae.

CALL: Vide Domine affictionem populi tui, et mitte quem missurus es: emitte Agnum dominatorem terrae, de petra deserti ad montem filiae Sion: ut auferat ipse iugum captivitatis nostrae.

CALL: Consolamini, consolamini, popule meus: cito veniet salus tua: quare moerore consumeris, quia innovavit te dolor? Salvabo te, noli timere, ego enim sum Dominus Deus tuus, Sanctus Israel, redemptor tuus.

face from us, and made us bear the consequence of our sins.

CALL: See the sadness of your people, O Lord, and send us the one promised: send us a Lamb to rule the earth, from the rocky desert to the mount of the daughter of Zion, that he may remove the yoke of our captivity.

CALL: Comfort ye; be comforted my people: your salvation quickly comes: Why are you eaten up with weeping: why renew your sorrow? I will save you, do not be afraid, for I am the Lord your God, the Holy One of Israel, your redeemer.

CHRISTMAS

Before the crib

Devoutly we approach your cradle, Lord, to find the one of whom the prophets spoke, and here behold the mighty God of thunders lying helpless on the straw. O grant us some of this humility that we may conquer mightily the reign of sin within us. And grant us, too, the protection of your gentle mother, whose tender eye and loving heart attend your every wish.

———•———

Hail and blessed be the hour and moment in which the Son of God was born of the most pure Virgin Mary at midnight in Bethlehem, in piercing cold. In that hour vouchsafe, O my God, to hear my prayer and grant my desires, through the merits of our Savior, Jesus Christ and of his blessed mother.

———•———

The Nativity of Christ

Behold the father is his daughter's son,
　　The bird that built the nest is hatch'd therein,
The old of years an hour hath not outrun,
　　Eternal life to live doth now begin,
The word is dumb, the mirth of heaven doth weep,
Might feeble is, and force doth faintly creep.

O dying souls! behold your living spring!
　　O dazzled eyes! behold your son of grace!
Dull ears attend what word this word doth bring!
　　Up, heavy hearts, with joy your joy embrace!
From death, from dark, from deafness, from despairs,
This life, this light, this word, this joy repairs.

Gift better than himself God doth not know,
    Gift better that his God no man can see;
This gift doth here the giver given bestow,
    Gift to this gift let each receiver be:
God is my gift, himself he freely gave me,
God's gift am I, and none but God shall have me.

Man alter'd was by sin from man to beast;
    Beast's food is hay, hay is all mortal flesh;
Now God is flesh, and lives in manger press'd,
    As hay the brutest sinner to refresh:
Oh happy field wherein this fodder grew,
Whose taste doth us from beasts to men renew!

ST. ROBERT SOUTHWELL

O glorious Mother of God and Queen of Heaven, my especial patroness, I greet you through the most tender and affectionate heart of your beloved Son Jesus, and I commend myself this day to your maternal love. In every danger and difficulty, in every trial and temptation, help me, O merciful, O loving, O gentle Virgin Mary. Through your sacred virginity and Immaculate Conception obtain for us purity both of soul and body.

Holy the womb that bare him,
Holy the breasts that fed,
But holier still the royal heart
That in his passion bled.

J. H. NEWMAN

HOLY FAMILY
First Sunday after Christmas

Jesus, Mary, and Joseph, guide our families here on earth. Jesus, Mary, and Joseph, make our lives and our homes like yours. Jesus, Mary, and Joseph, make our home life a foretaste of heaven here on earth.

—— • ——

Almighty God, whose only-begotten Son was born of a virgin and submitted himself to the authority and vocation of a carpenter, grant us a share in his humility so that we may be raised to share the joyful company of that same Virgin and Carpenter in your heavenly kingdom. Through the same Christ our Lord. Amen.

—— • ——

EPIPHANY
January 6

All-powerful God, who manifested your only-begotten Son to the gentiles by the light of a star, grant in your mercy that we who know you now only by faith may when we die see your glorious Godhead in its fullness. Through the same Christ our Lord. Amen.

ROMAN LITURGY

Your birth, O Christ our God, arose upon the world as the light of knowledge, for those that worshiped the stars, learned from a star to adore you, the Sun of righteousness, and to recognize in you the Daystar from on high. Glory to you O Lord.

The Virgin today gives birth to the one who is above nature, and earth offers a lowly home to the transcendent. The angels and the shepherds sing glory, and the Magi follow the star: for to us is born a Son, God himself who is before all time.

BYZANTINE MENAION

PURIFICATION
February 2

Now, dismiss your servant O Lord,
  according to your word, in peace:
because my eyes have seen your salvation
  which you have prepared before the face of
    all peoples,
a light for the revelation to the Gentiles
  and the glory of your people Israel.

LUKE 2:29–32

The Angel-lights of Christmas morn
Which shot across the sky,
Away they pass at Candlemas,
They sparkle and they die.

Comfort of earth is brief at best,
Although it be divine;
Like funeral lights for Christmas gone
Old Simeon's tapers shine.

And then for eight long weeks and more
We wait in twilight grey,
Till the high candle sheds a beam
On Holy Saturday.

We wait along the penance-tide
Of solemn fast and prayer;
While song is hush'd and lights grow dim
In the sin-laden air.

And while the sword in Mary's soul
Is driven home, we hide

In our own hearts, and count the wounds
Of passion and of pride.

And still, though Candlemas be spent
And Alleluias o'er,
Mary is music in our need,
And Jesus light in store.

J. H. NEWMAN

LENT

Before beginning Lent with a good confession
Heavenly Father; sackcloth and ashes are a little old-fashioned these days: help me to tear my sins instead of my clothes, and put on good works of prayer, fasting, and almsgiving instead of ashes. From this moment I intend to be all yours, living like Jesus and never sinning again.

———— • ————

Attende Domine et miserere, quia peccavimus tibi.

Pay heed, O Lord, and have mercy, for we have sinned against you.

CALL: Ad te Rex summe, omnium Redemptor, oculos nostros sublevamus flentes: exaudi, Christe, supplicantum preces.

CALL: To you, O highest King, redeemer of all, we lift our weeping eyes: hear, O Christ, the pleading of your people.

CALL: Dextera Patris, lapis angularis, via salutis, ianua caelestis, ablue nostri maculas delicti.

CALL: O right hand of the Father, O cornerstone, O way of salvation, O gate of heaven, wash away the stain of our sin.

CALL: Rogamus, Deus, tuam maiestatem: auribus sacris gemitus exaudi: crimina nostra placidus indulge.

CALL: We pray your majesty, O God, to hear our weeping cries: for our sins, be gracious and forgiving.

CALL: Tibi fatemur crimina admissa: contrito

CALL: To you we acknowledge our sins,

corde pandimus occulta:
tua Redemptor, pietas
ignoscat.

CALL: Innocens captus,
nec repugnans ductus,
testibus falsis pro impiis
damnatus: quos
redemisti, tu conserva
Christe.

with contrite hearts we
open our hearts: be gentle,
O our Redeemer!

CALL: O innocent captive,
not refusing to be taken,
and condemned for the
guilty by false witnesses,
preserve, O Christ, those
whom you have redeemed.

EASTER

Seeing that Christ has risen, let us worship the holy Lord Jesus, the sinless one. We adore your cross, O Christ, and we praise and glorify your holy resurrection. For you are our God, and we know no other but you, we call upon your name. Come, all faithful people, and let us worship Christ's holy resurrection; for through the cross joy has come into the world. Always blessing the Lord, let us praise his rising; for having undergone crucifixion for us, through death itself he destroyed death.

Although you descended into the tomb, Immortal One, yet you have destroyed the power of hell; and you have risen as a conqueror, Christ our God, proclaiming to the women who went to anoint your body: rejoice! and leaving peace on your Apostles: you who bring the dead to life.

BYZANTINE PENTECOSTAL

RESPONSE: Alleluia! Alleluia! Alleluia!

O filii et filiae
   Rex caelestis,
    Rex
    gloriae
Morte surrexit
  hodie.
    Alleluia!
	O sons and daughters of
	  the king,
	Whom heav'nly hosts
	  in glory sing,
	Today the grave hath lost
	  its sting.
	    Alleluia.

Et mane prima
  sabbati,
Ad ostium
  monumenti
	On that first morning
	  of the week,
	Before the day began
	  to break,

Accesserunt
  discipuli.
    Alleluia!
	Disciples went their
	  Lord to seek.
	    Alleluia.

Et Maria
  Magdalene,
Et Jacobi, et Salome
Venerunt corpus ungere.
    Alleluia!
	There Mary went, called
	  Magdalene
	Mary of James, and Salome
	For to anoint him and array.
	    Alleluia.

In albis sedens
  Angelus
Praedixit
  mulieribus:
In Galilaea est
  Dominus.
    Alleluia!
	An angel white bade
	  sorrow flee,
	For thus he spake unto
	  the three:
	"Your Lord is gone to
	  Galilee."
	    Alleluia.

Et Joannes
  Apostolus
Cucurrit Petro citius
Monumento
  venit prius.
    Alleluia!
	So John th'Apostle
	  fleeting fled
	And slower Peter thither led
	He reached the tomb
	  a while ahead.
	    Alleluia.

Discipulis
  adstantibus,
In medio stetit
  Christus
Dicens: Pax vobis
  omnibus.
    Alleluia!
	That night th'Apostles
	  met in fear,
	Amidst them came the
	  Lord so dear
	And said: "Peace be unto
	  you here."
	    Alleluia.

Ut intellexit
  Didymus
	When Thomas afterwards
	  had heard

Quia surrexerat
  Jesus,
Remansit fere
  dubius.
    Alleluia!

Vide, Thoma, vide
  latus,
Vide pedes, vide
  manus,
Noli esse
  incredulus.
    Alleluia!

Quando Thomas
  Christi latus,
Pedes vidit atque
  manus,
Dixit: Tu es
  Deus meus.
    Alleluia!

Beati qui non
  viderunt
Et firmiter
  crediderunt
Vitam aeternam
  habebunt.
    Alleluia!

In hoc festo
  sanctissimo
Sit laus et
  jubilatio,
Benedicamus
  Domino.

That Jesus had fulfilled
  his word,
He doubted if it were
  the Lord.
    Alleluia.

"Thomas, behold my side,"
  said he,
"My hands, my feet, my
  body see,
"And doubt not, but believe
  in me."
    Alleluia.

No longer Thomas then
  denied.
He saw the feet, the hands,
  the side;
"Thou art my Lord and
  God," he cried.
    Alleluia.

Blessed are they that have
  not seen
And yet whose faith has
  constant been,
In life eternal they shall
  reign.
    Alleluia.

On this most holy day
  of days,
To God your heart and
  voices raise
In laud and jubilee and
  praise.

Alleluia!	Alleluia.
Ex quibus nos humillimas	And we with holy Church unite
Devotas atque debitas	As evermore is just and right
Deo dicamus gratias.	In glory to the King of Light.
Alleluia!	Alleluia.

TRANSLATED BY J. M. NEALE

—— • ——

A collect for Easter Sunday

O God, who this day through the victory of your only-begotten Son over death opened a passage for us to eternity, grant that our prayers, inspired by your protecting grace, may by your grace become effective. Through Christ our Lord. Amen.

—— • ——

Almighty God, who, in the death and glorious resurrection of Christ your Son has opened for us the way to salvation, grant that we may also die to our sins and so rise with him to everlasting life. Through the same Christ our Lord.

—— • ——

For altar servers on Easter Sunday

Exhausted, Lord, on your sanctuary, we offer our tired-out liturgical efforts to your greater glory, and while the dried candle wax gets well trodden into the carpet, and the vestments lie in untidy piles at the bottom of cupboards, we beg you to accept what we have done in your honor. Overlook our tantrums, our skimping this or overdoing that, and raise up our humble fumblings in your sight as being, perhaps, a faint shadow of the worship of heaven, for thus it was intended. On this your rising day, O Lord, accept our praise. Amen. Alleluia!

PENTECOST

Whitsuntide

Holy Spirit from above
Sweet Comforter most dear
Inspire us with your love;
To restless souls draw near

Holy Spirit from above
Your sevenfold gifts impart
Inspire us with your love
Seek out the pure in heart

Holy Spirit from above
Tongue of eternal fire
Inspire us with your love
Become our souls' desire

Holy Spirit from above
Grant us to know your peace
Life-giving Holy Dove
Bid all our striving cease

T. J. RHIDIAN JONES

See also prayers to the Holy Spirit (pp. 273–82).

PRAYERS FOR PARTICULAR NEEDS

PRAYERS FOR PARTICULAR NEEDS

CONTENTS

FOR PARENTS, CHILDREN, AND FAMILIES

Parents' prayer to the Holy Family

Jesus, Son of the Eternal Father, we most fervently implore you to take our children under your special care and enclose them in the love of your sacred Heart. Rule and guide them that they may live according to our holy faith, that they may not waver in their confidence in you and may ever remain faithful in your love.

O Mary, blessed Mother of Jesus, grant to our children a place in your pure maternal heart. Spread over them your protecting mantle when danger threatens their innocence; keep them firm when they are tempted to stray from the path of virtue; and should they have the misfortune to fall, raise them up again and reconcile them with your divine Son.

Holy foster father, St. Joseph, watch over our children. Protect them from the assaults of the wicked enemy, and deliver them from all dangers of soul and body.

Mary and Joseph, dear parents of the holy Child Jesus, intercede for us that we may be a good example and bring up our children in the love and fear of God, and one day attain with them the beatific vision in Heaven. Amen.

—— • ——

Father, we bless you for this our family. Keep us strong and united in your love. May all our quarrels be little ones, and our forgiveness great. Unite us one day with the Holy Family in your kingdom forever. Amen.

—— • ——

A prayer of engaged couples

Father, in my heart, love has come alive for a person you made, and whom you too know and love. It was you who brought me to meet her/him and come to know her/him as once, in Paradise, you brought Eve and Adam together so that man should not remain alone. I want to thank you for this gift. It fills me with profound joy. It makes me like you who are love itself, and brings me to understand the value of life you have given me. Help me not to squander the riches you have stored in my heart. Teach me that love is a gift that must not be suffocated by selfishness; that love is pure and strong and must not be soiled or corrupted; that love is fruitful and should, beginning even now, open up a new life for myself and for the person who has chosen me. Loving Father, I pray for the person who is thinking of me and waiting for me, and who has placed in me complete trust for the future. I pray for this person who will walk along the path of life with me; help us to be worthy of one another and to be an encouragement and example to one another. Help us to prepare for marriage, for its grandeur and for its responsibilities, so that the love which fills us body and spirit may rule our lives forevermore.

— • —

For parents, at the birth of a child

Blessed be God the Father of our Lord Jesus Christ! Almighty God we praise and thank you for once more repeating your miracle of creation. May this beloved child grow strong and healthy, wise and happy, and above all, holy. Mother Mary, watch over this child. And we greet our child's Guardian Angel: welcome to our family! We place our child in your care, to keep him/her from sin all his/her life. And we pray for ourselves: may our joy in our child never grow less: may we be good parents: friends as well as adults. May we never fail to set good example, so that we all, parents and child may come to your heavenly kingdom.

— • —

A child's prayer

This prayer has been taught to children in the compiler's family for many generations.

Little Jesus, meek and mild,
Look on me, a little child.
Pity mine, and pity me,
Suffer me to come to thee.
Heart of Jesus, I adore thee;
Heart of Mary, I implore thee;
Heart of Joseph, pure and just:
In these three hearts I put my trust.

— • —

A prayer to St. Monica for our lapsed children
St. Monica's wayward son became one of the Church's greatest theologians.

Blessed Monica, mother of St. Augustine, we give thanks to our Father in heaven who looked with mercy upon your tears over your wayward son. His conversion and heroic sanctification were the fruit of your prayers. Dear St. Monica we now ask you to pray with us for all those sons and daughters that have wandered away from God and to add your prayers to those of all mothers who are worried over their children. Pray also for us that, following your example, we may, in the company of our children, one day enjoy the eternal vision of our Father in heaven. Amen.

TERENCE CARDINAL COOKE

In Times of Trouble

May the most just, most high, and most amiable will of God be done, praised, and eternally exalted in all things. Amen.

— • —

An act of self-abandonment

O my God, I believe in your infinite goodness; not only that goodness which embraces the world, but also in that particular and personal goodness which extends to me, poor creature that I am, and which disposes everything for my greatest good. For this reason, Lord, even when I cannot see, perceive or understand, I believe that what and where I am and everything that happens to me is the work of your love. With all my will, I prefer this to all other situations which would be more pleasant for me, but which do not come from you. I commend myself into your hands: do with me what you please, leaving me no other consolation than that of obeying you. Amen.

— • —

On a disastrous event

O Jesus, I am come to seek consolation from you, my most tender and most faithful friend. You can see how dejected I am, from what has happened. Grant me strength, I beseech you, that I may be able to bear my affliction with fortitude, and receive it in your spirit. I adore your divine justice, which has overtaken me; I receive with respect and submission all its chastisements; I return thanks for them as

341

I would for so many signs and testimonies of the love of God. I accept them in the spirit of homage, and with the view of honoring your own labors and sufferings. I offer them through your hand, and in union with your sufferings to my heavenly Father as a penance for my sins, sincerely acknowledging that I have deserved much worse. I praise his goodness for having treated me with so much gentleness, and readily submit to whatever else he may please to inflict on me in the future. I only beg of him strength to bear them in the manner I ought, and the undeserved favor of not being punished during eternity. Amen.

— • —

For those who do us harm

Lord God, it is your will that we should love even those who speak or act against us. Help us to observe the commandments of the new law, returning good for evil and learning to forgive as your Son forgave those who persecuted him. Through the same Christ our Lord. Amen.

— • —

Almighty God, hear your people who cry to you in their affliction, but for the glory of your name turn again to us, and help us in our tribulation through Christ our Lord. Amen.

— • —

My most loving God, I offer you this trial and commend it to you with that same intention with which you brought it down to me from the Heart of Jesus, beseeching you to record it for me on high, together with my deepest thankfulness. Amen.

ST. MECHTILDE

— • —

Almighty God, have mercy on all that bear me evil will, and would me harm, and their faults and mine together by such easy, tender, merciful means, as thine infinite wisdom best can devise, vouchsafe to amend and redress and make us saved souls in heaven together, where we may ever live and love together with thee and thy blessed saints, O glorious Trinity, for the bitter passion of our sweet Savior Christ. Lord, give me patience in tribulation and grace in everything to conform my will to thine, that I may truly say, "Thy will be done on earth as it is in heaven." The things, good Lord, that I pray for, give me grace to labor for. Amen.

ST. THOMAS MORE

On distractions and coldness in prayer

Do not be troubled or uneasy in consequence of your coldness and tepidity; all these trials which you feel in prayer, when accepted with patience, glorify God. Remember the beautiful psalm in which the prophet calls on the ice, snow and tempests to praise the Lord! Our Lord is so tender and loving; he knows so well what we are made of, and he thinks of such little things.

OLIVAINT

This prayer of St. Thomas More was written in the margin of his book of hours after his troubles had begun and he had resigned his offices at court.

Give me thy grace, Good God, to set the world at nought, to set my mind fast upon thee and not to hang upon the words of men's mouths, to be content to be solitary, not to long for worldly company, little by little utterly to cast off the world, and rid my mind of all besides thee, not to long to hear any worldly things, but that the hearing of worldly fantasies may be to me displeasing, gladly to be thinking of God, piteously to call for his help, to lean unto the comfort of God, busily to labor to love him, to know my own vileness and wretchedness, to humble and abase myself under the mighty hand of God, to bewail my past sins, for the purging of them patiently to suffer adversity, gladly to bear my purgatory here, to be joyful in tribulations, to walk the narrow way that leadeth to life, to bear the cross with Christ, to have the last things in remembrance, to have ever before mine eye my death that is ever at hand, to make death no stranger to me, to foresee and consider the everlasting fire of hell, to pray for pardon before the Judge do come, to have continually in mind the passion Christ suffered for me, for his benefits incessantly to give him thanks, to buy the time again that I have lost, to abstain from vain conversations, to eschew light foolish mirth and gladness, recreations not necessary to cut off, to set the loss of worldly substance, friends, liberty, life and all at right nought for the winning of Christ, to think my worst enemies my best friends, for the brethren of Joseph could never have done him so much good with their love and favor as they did him with their malice and hatred.

These wishes are more to be desired by every man than all the treasure of all the princes and kings, Christian and heathen, were it gathered and laid together all upon one heap.

ST. THOMAS MORE

Lord, make me an instrument of your peace: where there is hatred, let me sow love; where there is injury, let me sow pardon; where there is doubt, let me sow faith; where there is despair, let me give hope; where there is darkness, let me give light; where there is sadness, let me give joy.

O Divine Master, grant that I may try not to be comforted, but to comfort; not to be understood, but to understand; not to be loved, but to love. Because it is in giving that we receive, it is in forgiving that we are forgiven, and it is in dying that we are born to eternal life.

ATTRIBUTED TO ST. FRANCIS OF ASSISI

—•—

O blessed Jesus, make me understand and remember that whatsoever we gain, if we lose you, all is lost, and whatsoever we lose, if we gain you, all is gained.

ST. THOMAS COTTAM

—•—

Lord, give me patience in tribulation.
Let the memory of your Passion,
and of those bitter pains you suffered for me,
strengthen my patience
and support me
in this tribulation and adversity.

ST. JOHN FORREST

—•—

A black sonnet

No worst, there is none. Pitched past pitch of grief,
More pangs will, schooled at forepangs, wilder wring.
Comforter, where, where is your comforting?
Mary, mother of us, where is your relief?
My cries heave, herds-long; huddle in a main, a chief
Woe, world-sorrow; on an age-old anvil wince and sing—
Then lull, then leave off. Fury had shrieked "No ling-
Ering! Let me be fell: force I must be brief."

O the mind, mind has mountains; cliffs of fall
Frightful, sheer, no–man-fathomed. Hold them cheap
May who ne'er hung there. Nor does long our small
Durance deal with that steep or deep. Here! creep,
Wretch, under a comfort serves in a whirlwind: all
Life death does end and each day dies with sleep.

GERARD MANLEY HOPKINS, S.J.

—•—

In all things may the most holy, the most just, and the most lovable will of God be done, praised, and exalted above all forever. Thy will be done, O Lord, thy will be done. The Lord has given, the Lord has taken away: blessed be the name of the Lord.

—•—

IN SICKNESS

O Lord Jesus Christ, I receive this sickness which you are pleased to grant me, as coming from your fatherly hand. It is your will, and therefore I submit—"not my will, but yours be done." May it be to the honor of your holy name, and for the good of my soul. I here offer myself with an entire submission to all that you will; to suffer whatever you please, as long as you please, and in what manner you please; for I am your child, O Lord, who has often and most ungratefully offended you, and whom you might justly have visited with your severest punishments. Oh, let your justice be tempered with mercy and let your heavenly grace come to my assistance to support me under this affliction! Fortify my soul with strength from above, that I may bear with true Christian patience all the uneasiness, pains, nuisances, and troubles which I endure; preserve me from all temptations and murmuring thoughts, that in this time of affliction I may in no way offend you, and grant that this and all other earthly trials may be the means of preparing my soul for its passage into eternity, that being purified from all my sins, I may believe in you, hope in you, love you above all things, and finally, through your infinite merits, be admitted into the company of the blessed in heaven, there to praise you forever and ever. Amen.

Lord God, I do not know why you have given me this sickness: I just ask your grace to bear it with fortitude, and to give as little trouble as possible to those who care for me. I offer to you such pains as I may suffer today together with the pains that Jesus offered on the cross for the salvation of the world. May my pain be, as it were, an ease and a comfort to him.

——— • ———

Heavenly Father, accept my pains this day as a prayer for this intention of mine *(name the intention close to your heart)*. Accept it, dearest Lord, and grant my prayer for the merits of our beloved Savior Jesus Christ, who willingly offered his pains for my salvation. Amen.

——— • ———

Lord, thy will be done, I take this for my sins. I offer up to thee my sufferings, together with all that my Savior has suffered for me; and I beg of thee, through his sufferings, to have mercy on me. Free me from this illness and pain if thou wilt, and if it be for my good. Thou lovest me too much to let me suffer unless it be for my good. Therefore, O Lord, I trust myself to thee; do with me as thou pleasest. In sickness, and in health, I wish to love thee always.

——— • ———

Footprints

One night, a man had a dream. He dreamed that he was walking along the beach with the Lord. Across the sky flashed scenes from his life. For each scene he noticed two sets of footprints in the sand. He noticed that many times along the path of his life there was only one set of footprints. He also noticed that this happened at the very lowest and saddest times in his life. This really bothered him, and he questioned the Lord about it: "Lord, you said that once I'd decided to follow you, you'd walk with me all the way. But I have noticed that during the most troublesome times of my life there is only one set of footprints. I don't understand why when I needed you most you would leave me." The Lord replied, "My son, my precious child; I love you and I would never leave you. During your times of trial and suffering, when you see only one set of footprints, it was then that I carried you."

— • —

Look down O Lord on me, poor man.
In thee I live and move and am.
O clear my soul and conscience,
That I in thee my peace may find.
Rest to my heart, joy to my mind,
Freed from my sins and mine offense!

WILLIAM BYRD

— • —

FOR THE DYING AND THE DEAD

FOR A HAPPY DEATH

My Lord God, resignedly and willingly, I accept at thy hand with all its anxieties, pains, and sufferings, whatever kind of death it shall please thee to be mine. Amen.

———•———

Jesus, Mary, and Joseph, I give you my heart
   and my soul.
Jesus, Mary, and Joseph, assist me in my last agony.
Jesus, Mary, and Joseph, may I breathe forth my soul in peace with you. Amen.

———•———

O my Lord and Savior, support me in that hour in the strong arms of thy sacraments, and by the fresh fragrance of thy consolations. Let the absolving words be said over me, and the holy oil sign and seal me, and thy own body be my food, and thy blood my sprinkling; and let my sweet Mother, Mary, breathe on me, and my Angel whisper peace to me, and my glorious saints . . . smile upon me; that in them all, and through I them all, I may receive the gift of perseverance, and die, as I desire to live, in thy faith, in thy Church, in thy service, and in thy love. Amen.

J. H. NEWMAN

———•———

Good Lord, give me the grace so to spend my life, that when the day of my death shall come, though I feel pain in my body, I may feel comfort in soul; and with faithful hope of thy mercy, with due love toward thee, and charity toward the world, I may, through thy grace, depart into thy glory.

ST. THOMAS MORE

Hymn to God My God, in My Sickness

Since I am coming to that holy room,
    Where, with thy quire of saints forevermore,
I shall be made thy music; as I come
    I tune the instrument here at the door,
    And what I must do then, think here before.

Whilst my physicians by their love are grown
    Cosmographers, and I their map, who lie
Flat on this bed, that by them may be shown
    That this is my South-west discovery
    Per fretum febris, by these straits to die,

I joy, that in these straits, I see my West;
    For, though their currents yield return to none,
What shall my West hurt me? As West and East
    In all flat maps (and I am one) are one,
    So death doth touch the resurrection.

Is the Pacific Sea my home? Or are
    The Eastern riches? Is Jerusalem?
Anyan, and Magellan, and Gibraltar,
    All straits, and none but straits, are ways to them,
    Whether where Japhet dwelt, or Cham, or Sem.

We think that Paradise and Calvary,
    Christ's cross and Adam's tree, stood in one place;

Look, Lord, and find both Adams met in me;
  As the first Adam's sweat surrounds my face,
  May the last Adam's blood my soul embrace.

So, in his purple wrapp'd receive me, Lord,
  By these his thorns give me his other crown
And as to other's soul I preach'd thy word.
  Be this my text, my sermon to mine own,
  Therefore that he may raise the Lord throws down.

JOHN DONNE

A Litany for the Dying

Kyrie eleison, Christe eleison, Kyrie eleison.
Holy Mary, pray for him.
All holy Angels, pray for him.
Holy Abraham, pray for him.
St. John Baptist, St. Joseph, pray for him.
St. Peter, St. Paul, St. Andrew, St. John,
All Apostles, all Evangelists, pray for him.
All holy Disciples of the Lord, pray for him.
All holy Innocents, pray for him.
All holy Martyrs, all holy Confessors,
All holy Hermits, all holy Virgins,
All ye saints of God, pray for him.
Be merciful, be gracious; spare him, Lord.
Be merciful, be gracious; Lord, deliver him
From the sins that are past;
From thy frown and thine ire;
From the perils of dying;
From any complying
With sin, or denying
His God, or relying
On self, at the last;

From the nethermost fire;
From all that is evil;
From power of the devil;
Thy servant deliver,
For once and forever.
By thy birth, and by thy Cross,
Rescue him from endless loss;
By thy death and burial,
Save him from a final fall;
By thy rising from the tomb,
By thy mounting up above,
By the Spirit's gracious love,
Save him in the day of doom.

Rescue him, O Lord, in this his evil hour,
As of old so many by thy gracious power:—Amen.
Enoch and Elias from the common doom; Amen.
Noe from the waters in a saving home; Amen.
Abraham from th'abounding guilt of Heathenesse; Amen.
Job from all his multiform and fell distress; Amen.
Isaac, when his father's knife was raised to slay; Amen.
Lot from burning Sodom on its judgment-day; Amen.
Moses from the land of bondage and despair; Amen.
Daniel from the hungry lions in their lair; Amen.
And the children Three amid the furnace-flame; Amen.
Chaste Susanna from the slander and the shame; Amen.
David from Golia and the wrath of Saul; Amen.
And the two Apostles from their prison-thrall; Amen.
Thecla from her torments; Amen.
—so, to show thy power,
Rescue this thy servant in his evil hour.

ROMAN RITUAL (TRANSLATED BY J. H. NEWMAN IN
THE DREAM OF GERONTIUS)

All-powerful and merciful Father, in the death of Christ you have opened a gateway to eternal life. Look kindly upon our brother/sister who is suffering his/her last agony. United to the passion and death of your Son, and saved by the blood he shed, may he/she come before you with confidence. Through the same Christ our Lord. Amen.

FOR THE DEAD

Profisciscere, anima Christiana, de hoc mundo
Go forth upon thy journey, Christian soul!
Go from this world! Go, in the name of God
The omnipotent Father, who created thee!
Go, in the name of Jesus Christ, our Lord,
Son of the living God, who bled for thee!
Go, in the name of the Holy Spirit, who
Hath been poured out on thee! Go, in the name
Of Angels and Archangels; in the name
Of Thrones and Dominations; in the name
Of Princedoms and of Powers; and in the name
Of Cherubim and Seraphim, go forth!
Go, in the name of Patriarchs and Prophets;
And of Apostles and Evangelists,
Of Martyrs and Confessors; in the name
Of holy Monks and Hermits; in the name
Of holy Virgins; and all Saints of God,
Both men and women, go! Go on thy course;
And may thy place to-day be found in peace,
And may thy dwelling be the Holy Mount
Of Zion—through the Same, through Christ, our Lord.
ROMAN RITUAL (TRANSLATED BY J. H. NEWMAN IN
THE DREAM OF GERONTIUS)

God of all spirits and of all flesh, who trampled upon
death, and overthrew the devil, giving life to the world: O
Lord, grant rest to the soul of your departed servant [N.],
in a place of light, in a place of pasture, in a place of rest,
from whence pain, sadness and tears have all fled; and forgive him/her all sins, whether committed in thought, word

or deed, O good God that loves humanity: for there is no one living who is sinless: you alone are without sin; your justice is eternal justice, and your word is truth. For you yourself are the resurrection, and the life, and the rest of your departed servant [N.], O Christ our God, and to you we offer glory, together with your eternal Father, and your most holy, good, and life-giving Spirit, now, and always, and for ages unending. Amen.

BYZANTINE PRAYER

O divine Lord, whose adorable heart ardently sighs for the happiness of your children, we humbly pray that you remember the souls of your servants for whom we pray; command that your holy angels receive them and convey them to a place of rest and peace. Amen.

May the bright company of angels bear your soul
   to paradise.
May the glorious band of apostles greet you at the gates.
May the white-robed army of martyrs welcome you
   as you come.
May the cheerful throngs of saints lighten your
   heart forever.
May those you have loved and lost be glad of
   your coming.
May Mary enfold you in her tender arms, and lead you
   to Jesus your love forever, and for whom you have
   longed all this while.
May your home be in the heavenly Jerusalem this day
   and forever.
Rest in peace, [N.] God keep you in his care. Amen.

May the souls of the faithful departed, through the mercy of God, rest in peace. Amen.

— • —

De Profundis

Out of the depths I have cried unto thee O Lord:
 Lord, hear my voice.
Let thine ears be attentive:
 to the voice of my supplication.
If thou, O Lord, shalt observe iniquities
 Lord, who shall endure it?
For with thee there is merciful forgiveness:
 and by reason of thy law I have waited for thee,
 O Lord.
My soul hath waited on his word:
 my soul hath hoped in the Lord.
From the morning watch even unto night
 let Israel hope in the Lord.
For with the Lord there is mercy:
 and with him is plentiful redemption.
And he shall redeem Israel:
 from all his iniquities.

CALL: Eternal rest grant unto them, O Lord,
RESPONSE: And let perpetual light shine on them.
CALL: May they rest in peace.
RESPONSE: Amen.
CALL: O Lord, hear my prayer.
RESPONSE: And let my cry come unto thee.

Let us pray.

O God, the Creator and Redeemer of all the faithful; grant to the souls of thy servants departed the remission of all their sins, that through pious supplications they may obtain the pardon that they have always desired. Who livest and reignest, world without end. Amen.

— • —

On the day of a person's death or burial

O God, whose nature is always to have mercy and to spare, we humbly pray to you for the soul of your servant [N.] whom you have this day called out of the world, that you would not deliver him/her up into the hands of the enemy, nor forget him/her eternally, but command him/her to be received by your holy angels, and to be carried to Paradise, his/her true country; that as in you [N.] had faith and hope he/she may not suffer the pains of loss, but may take possession of everlasting joys. Through Christ our Lord. Amen.

— • —

On the anniversary of a death

O Lord, the God of mercy and pardon, grant to the soul of your servant the happiness of rest and the brightness of light. Through Christ our Lord. Amen.

— • —

For one recently deceased

Grant your forgiveness, Lord, to the soul of your servant [N.] that, being dead to this world, he/she may live now to you alone, and whatever sins he/she committed through human frailty, do you, in your mercy, absolve. Through Christ our Lord. Amen.

— • —

For a bishop or a priest

O God, who amongst your apostolic priests raised up your servant [N.] to the dignity of a bishop, [or a priest,] grant, we pray, that he may also be admitted in heaven to their everlasting fellowship. Through Christ our Lord. Amen.

———•———

For a father and mother

O God, who commanded us to honor our father and mother, have mercy on the souls of my father and mother; and grant that I may see them in the glory of eternity. Through Christ our Lord. Amen.

———•———

For friends, relations, and benefactors

O God, the giver of pardon and lover of the salvation of mankind, we ask your clemency on behalf of our friends, relations, and benefactors who have departed this life; that the Blessed Virgin Mary and all the saints interceding for them, they may come to the fellowship of eternal happiness. Through Christ our Lord. Amen.

———•———

IN SORROW AND REPENTANCE

ACTS OF CONTRITION

O my God, because you are so good, I am very sorry that I have sinned against you, and with the help of your grace I will not sin again.

TRADITIONAL PRAYER

O my God, I am sorry and beg pardon for all my sins, and detest them above all things, because they deserve your dreadful punishments, because they have crucified my loving Savior Jesus Christ, and, most of all, because they offend your infinite goodness: and I firmly resolve, by the help of your grace, never to offend you again and carefully to avoid the occasions of sin. Amen.

O my God, who is infinitely good and always hates sin, I beg pardon from my heart for all my offenses against you. I detest them all and am heartily sorry for them because they offend your infinite goodness: and I firmly resolve, by the help of your grace, never more to offend you and carefully to avoid the occasions of sin. Amen.

—— • ——

O my God, I love you with my whole heart and above all things. I am heartily sorry that I have offended you. May I never offend you more. O may I love you without ceasing, and make it my delight to do in all things your most holy will. Amen.

TRADITIONAL PRAYER

—— • ——

My God, I am sorry for my sins with all my heart. In choosing to do wrong and failing to do good, I have sinned against you whom I should love above all things. I firmly intend, with your help, to do penance, to sin no more, and to avoid whatever leads me to sin. Our Savior Jesus Christ suffered and died for us. In his name, my God, have mercy. Amen.

—— • ——

Jesus, you knew all my miseries before your eyes were fixed on me and yet you did not turn away from my wretchedness; rather, because of it, you loved me with a love more sweet and tender. Jesus, I beg pardon for having corresponded so little to your love; Jesus, I beg of you to forgive and to purify my actions in your divine blood; Jesus, I am deeply grieved at having offended you because you are infinitely holy; Jesus, I repent with heartfelt sorrow, and I promise to do all in my power to avoid these faults in the future.

REVEALED TO JOSEPHA MENENDEZ AND
ADAPTED BY REX BAKER

O how late have I loved you, O love forever ancient and forever new, how late have I loved you!

ST. AUGUSTINE

Before Confession

Lord, be merciful to me a sinner! All I have comes from you: my home, my family, my food, my clothing, even my life, and I have repaid your goodness with my sins. Deeply I regret my ingratitude, and I beg grace to make some amends, beginning with this sacrament of penance. Help me to unburden myself of anything that stands between us and to be truly sorry. My Jesus, mercy! Mary, help!

———•———

Heavenly and forgiving Father: see here before you your prodigal child! I have squandered your wonderful gifts of grace, and can expect nothing more from your already overflowing goodness. But here I am, begging once more for your forgiveness. Treat me as one of your hired servants. I deserve nothing more.

———•———

Batter my heart, three-person'd God; for you
As yet but knock, breathe, shine, and seek to mend;
That I may rise, and stand, o'erthrow me, and bend
Your force, to break, blow, burn and make me new.
I, like an usurped town, to another due,
Labor to admit you, but O, to no end,
Reason, your viceroy in me, me should defend,
But is captiv'd, and proves weak or untrue.
Yet dearly I love you, and would be loved fain,
But am betroth'd unto your enemy:
Divorce me, untie, or break that knot again,
Take me to you, imprison me, for I
Except you enthrall me, never shall be free,
Nor ever chaste, except you ravish me.

John Donne

———•———

Lord Jesus Christ, whose arms were extended on the cross out of love for me, here I am, acknowledging that it was I who drove those nails into your hands and feet by my sins. Help me truly to cleanse my soul in this sacrament of Confession, hiding nothing from you who were hung naked on the cross for me, and with true sorrow together with a resolute determination never to repeat my faults.

—•—

Come, Holy Spirit, and reveal me truly to myself. Show me the truth: let me see myself as you see me. Show me my soul in all its disfigurement that I may take it to be healed and made beautiful again as once you made it in baptism.

—•—

O God, who opened the eyes of the blind, open the eyes of my heart, so as to drive from me all the darkness of wickedness and vice, the very appearance of defilement, that I may raise up my eyes on high toward the beauty of your holy glory.

COPTIC LITURGY OF ST. MARK

—•—

Quaerens me sedisti lassus,	You sought me to exhaustion,
Redimisti crucem passus;	And redeemed me with your cross;
Tantus labor non sit cassus.	Let not such a labor be in vain!

FROM THE DIES IRAE

—•—

AFTER CONFESSION

Bless the Lord, O my soul, and all that is within me,
  bless his holy name!
Bless the Lord, O my soul, and never forget
  all his goodness!
For the Lord is kindly, long-suffering and of great mercy.
Bless the Lord, O my soul, and all that is within me,
  bless his holy name!
    Blessed are you, O Lord!
                    LITURGY OF ST. JOHN CHRYSOSTOM

The Magnificat

My ✠ soul magnifies the Lord,
    my spirit rejoices in God who is my Savior,
    who has looked upon the humility of his
      handmaiden.
Behold, all generations from now
    will acknowledge me blessed,
For the mighty one has done great things for me:
    Holy is his name!
His mercy is from one generation to the next on those
  who fear him.
    Mighty is his arm!
He has scattered the proud in the imagination of
  their hearts,
    and has put down the powerful from their thrones,
    exalting those of humble degree.
The hungry he has filled with good things,
    but the rich he has dismissed with nothing.

Remembering his mercy, he has helped his servant
  Israel,
    as he promised to our fathers,
    to Abraham and to his posterity forevermore.

LUKE 1:46–55

Glory be . . .

—·—

A prayer to the Holy Spirit, the life of the soul

My God, I adore you, Eternal Paraclete, the light and the
life of my soul. You might have been content with merely giving me good suggestions, inspiring grace and help-
ing from without. But in your infinite compassion you
have from the first entered into my soul, and taken possession of it. You will go from me, if I sin, and I shall be left
to my own miserable self. God forbid, I will use what you
have given me; I will call on you when tried and tempted. Through you I will never forsake you.

J. H. NEWMAN

—·—

THE SEVEN PENITENTIAL PSALMS

For centuries, Christians have used these seven psalms to express repentance and sorrow for sin. They are known by Latin titles taken from the first few words of the Latin texts. These psalms can be prayed whenever repentance seems appropriate, particularly during Lent and before or after the sacrament of reconciliation. They are given here in the traditional Douai-Challoner version.

ANTIPHON: Remember not, O Lord, our offenses, nor those of our parents, and take not revenge of our sins.

Domine, ne in furore

O Lord, rebuke me not in thine indignation,
    nor chastise me in thy wrath.
Have mercy on me, O Lord, for I am weak;
    heal me, O Lord, for my bones are troubled.
And my soul is troubled exceedingly;
    but thou, O Lord, how long?
Turn to me, O Lord, and deliver my soul:
    oh, save me for thy mercy's sake.
For there is no one in death that is mindful of thee;
    and who shall acknowledge thee in hell?
I have labored in my groanings;
    every night I will wash my bed,
    I will water my couch with my tears.
Mine eyes are troubled through indignation;
    I have grown old amongst all mine enemies.
Depart from me, all ye workers of iniquity;
    for the Lord hath heard the voice of my weeping.
The Lord hath heard my supplication;
    the Lord hath received my prayer.
Let all mine enemies be ashamed,
    and be very much troubled;

let them be turned back
and be ashamed very speedily.

Psalm 6

Glory be . . .

———— • ————

Beati quorum

Blessed are they whose iniquities are forgiven,
    and whose sins are covered.
Blessed is the man to whom the Lord hath not
  imputed sin,
    and in whose spirit there is no guile.
Because I was silent, my bones grew old;
    whilst I cried out all the day long.
For day and night thy hand was heavy upon me;
    I am turned in mine anguish, whilst the thorn
      is fastened.
I have acknowledged my sin to thee;
    and mine injustice I have not concealed.
I said, I will confess against myself mine injustice
  to the Lord;
    and thou hast forgiven the wickedness of my sin.
For this shall every one that is holy pray to thee:
    in a seasonable time.
And yet in a flood of many waters,
    they shall not come nigh unto him.
Thou art my refuge from the trouble which hath
  encompassed me;
    my joy, deliver me from them that surround me.
I will give thee understanding,
    and I will instruct thee in this way in which thou
      shalt go:
    I will fix mine eyes upon thee.

Do not become like the horse and the mule,
    which have no understanding.
With bit and bridle bind fast their jaws,
    who come not near unto thee.
Many are the scourges of the sinner;
      but mercy shall encompass him that hopeth
     in the Lord.
Be glad in the Lord, and rejoice, ye just;
    and glory, all ye right of heart.

PSALM 32

Glory be . . .

— • —

Domine, ne in furore

Rebuke me not, O Lord, in thine indignation;
    nor chastise me in thy wrath.
For thine arrows are fastened in me,
    and thy hand hath been strong upon me.
There is no health in my flesh, because of thy wrath;
    there is no peace for my bones, because of my sins.
For mine iniquities are gone over my head;
    and as a heavy burden, are become heavy upon me.
My sores are putrefied and corrupted,
    because of my foolishness.
I am become miserable, and am bowed down even
 to the end:
    I walked sorrowful all the day long.
For my loins are filled with illusions;
    and there is no health in my flesh.
I am afflicted and humbled exceedingly;
    I roared with the groaning of my heart.
Lord, all my desire is before thee;
    and my groaning is not hidden from thee.

My heart is troubled, my strength hath left me;
>and the light of mine eyes itself is not with me.
My friends and my neighbors have drawn near,
>and have stood against me.
And they that were near me stood afar off;
>and they that sought my soul used violence.
And they that sought evils to me spoke vain things;
>and studied deceits all the day long.
But I, as a deaf man, heard not;
>and was as a dumb man, not opening his mouth.
And I became as a man that heareth not;
>and that hath no reproofs in his mouth.
For in thee, O Lord, have I hoped:
>thou wilt hear me, O Lord my God.
For I said, lest at any time mine enemies rejoice over me;
>and whilst my feet are moved,
>they speak great things against me.
For I am ready for scourges;
>and my sorrow is continually before me.
For I will declare mine iniquity;
>and I will think for my sin.
But mine enemies live, and are stronger than I;
>and they that hate me wrongfully are multiplied.
They that render evil for good have detracted me,
>because I followed goodness.
Forsake me not, O Lord my God:
>do not thou depart from me.
Attend unto my help,
>O Lord, the God of my salvation.

PSALM 38

Glory be . . .

Miserere

Have mercy on me, O God, according to thy
  great mercy;
        and according to the multitude of thy tender
          mercies
        blot out mine iniquity.
Wash me yet more from mine iniquity,
        and cleanse me from my sin.
For I know mine iniquity,
        and my sin is always before me.
To thee only have I sinned,
        and have done evil before thee;
that thou mayest be justified in thy words,
        and mayest overcome when thou art judged.
For behold I was conceived in iniquities;
        and in sins did my mother conceive me.
For behold, thou hast loved truth;
        the uncertain and hidden things of thy wisdom
        thou hast made manifest to me.
Thou shalt sprinkle me with hyssop, and I shall
  be cleansed;
        thou shalt wash me, and I shall be made whiter
          than snow.
To my hearing thou shalt give joy and gladness;
        and the bones that have been humbled shall rejoice.
Turn away thy face from my sins,
        and blot out all mine iniquities.
Create a clean heart in me, O God,
        and renew a right spirit within me.
Cast me not away from thy face,
        and take not thy Holy Spirit from me.
Restore unto me the joy of thy saving mercy,
        and strengthen me with a perfect spirit.

I will teach the unjust thy ways;
 and the wicked shall be converted to thee.
Deliver me from the guilt of blood,
 O God, thou God of my salvation;
 and my tongue shall extol thy justice.
O Lord, thou wilt open my lips;
 and my mouth shall declare thy praise.
For if thou hadst desired sacrifice,
 I would indeed have given it;
 with burnt-offerings thou wilt not be delighted.
A sacrifice to God is an afflicted spirit:
 a contrite and humble heart, O God, thou wilt
  not despise.
Deal favorably, O Lord, in thy good will with Zion,
 that the walls of Jerusalem may be built up.
Then shalt thou accept the sacrifice of justice,
 oblations, and whole burnt-offerings;
 then shall they lay calves upon thine altar.

PSALM 51

Glory be . . .

— • —

Domine, exaudi

Hear, O Lord, my prayer,
 and let my cry come unto thee.
Turn not away thy face from me;
 in the day when I am in trouble,
 incline thine ear to me.
In whatever day I shall call upon thee,
 hear me speedily.
For my days are vanished like smoke;
 and my bones are grown dry like fuel for the fire.
I am smitten as grass, and my heart is withered,

because I forgot to eat my bread.
Through the voice of my groaning,
 my bone hath cleaved to my flesh.
I am become like a pelican of the wilderness;
 I am like a night raven in the house.
I have watched and am become as a sparrow,
 all alone on the house top.
All the day long mine enemies reproached me,
 and they that praised me did swear against me.
For I did eat ashes like bread,
 and mingled my drink with weeping.
Because of thine anger and indignation;
 for having lifted me up thou hast thrown me down.
My days have declined like a shadow,
 and I am withered like grass.
But thou, O Lord, endurest forever;
 and thy remembrance to all generations.
Thou shalt arise and have mercy on Zion;
 for it is time to have mercy on it, yes, the
  time is come.
For the stones thereof have pleased thy servants,
 and they shall have pity on the earth thereof.
And the Gentiles shall fear thy name, Lord,
 and all the kings of the earth thy glory.
For the Lord hath built up Zion;
 and he shall be seen in his glory.
He hath had regard to the prayer of the humble;
 and he hath not despised their petition.
Let these things be written unto another generation;
 and the people that shall be created shall praise
  the Lord.
Because he hath looked forth from his high sanctuary;
 from heaven the Lord hath looked upon the earth.

That he might hear the groans of them that are
  in fetters;
      that he might release the children of the slain.
That they may declare the Name of the Lord in Zion,
      and his praise in Jerusalem.
When the people assemble together,
      and kings, to serve the Lord,
      he answered them in the way of his strength.
Declare unto me
      the fewness of my days.
Call me not away in the midst of my days;
      thy years are unto generation and generation.
In the beginning, O Lord, thou foundedst the earth;
      and the heavens are the works of thy hands.
They shall perish, but thou remainest;
      and all of them shall grow old like a garment.
And as a vesture thou shalt change them,
      and they shall be changed;
but thou art always the self-same,
      and thy years shall not fail.
The children of thy servants shall continue,
      and their seed shall be directed forever.

PSALM 102

Glory be . . .

— • —

De profundis

Out of the depths I have cried to thee, O Lord:
      Lord, hear my voice.
Let thine ears be attentive
      to the voice of my supplication.
If thou, O Lord, shalt observe iniquities:
      Lord, who shall endure it?

For with thee there is merciful forgiveness:
>   and by reason of thy law
>   I have waited for thee, O Lord.
My soul hath relied on his word:
>   my soul hath hoped in the Lord.
From the morning watch even until night,
>   let Israel hope in the Lord.
Because with the Lord there is mercy,
>   and with him plentiful redemption.
And he shall redeem Israel
>   from all his iniquities.

PSALM 130

Glory be . . .

—•—

Domine, exaudi

Hear, O Lord, my prayer;
>   give ear to my supplication in thy truth;
>   hear me in thy justice.
And enter not into judgment with thy servant:
>   for in thy sight no man living shall be justified.
For the enemy hath persecuted my soul;
>   he hath brought down my life to the earth.
He hath made me to dwell in darkness,
>   as those that have been dead of old.
And my spirit is in anguish within me,
>   my heart within me is troubled.
I remembered the days of old,
>   I meditated on all thy works;
>   I mused upon the works of thy hands.
I stretched forth my hands to thee;
>   my soul is as earth without water unto thee.

Hear me speedily, O Lord;
> my spirit hath fainted away.

Turn not away thy face from me,
> lest I be like unto them that go down into the pit.

Cause me to hear thy mercy in the morning,
> for in thee have I hoped.

Make the way known to me wherein I should walk;
> for I have lifted up my soul to thee.

Deliver me from mine enemies, O Lord;
> to thee have I fled:
> teach me to do thy will, for thou art my God.

Thy good spirit shall lead me into the right land;
> for thy Name's sake, O Lord,
> Thou wilt quicken me in thy justice.

Thou wilt bring my soul out of trouble;
> and in thy mercy thou wilt destroy mine enemies.

And thou wilt cut off all them that afflict my soul;
> for I am thy servant.

PSALM 143

Glory be . . .

———•———

ANTIPHON: Remember not, O Lord, our offenses,
nor those of our parents, and take not
revenge of our sins.

———•———

FOR THE CHURCH

O God, our refuge and strength, look down on thy people who cry to thee, and by the intercession of the glorious and blessed ever-virgin Mary, of St. Joseph her spouse, of thy holy apostles Peter and Paul and of all the saints, in mercy and goodness hear our prayers for the conversion of sinners and for the liberty and exaltation of our holy mother the Church. Amen.

——•——

For the pope

O God, the pastor and governor of all the faithful, mercifully look down upon your servant John Paul, whom you have been pleased to confirm as the chief pastor of your flock on earth, grant we pray, that both by word and example he may edify those over whom he is set, and together with the flock committed to his care, may attain everlasting life, through Christ our Lord. Amen.

——•——

For the bishop

Almighty and everlasting God, who alone works great marvels, send down upon your servants the Bishops of your Church, and especially upon [N.] the Bishop of this diocese the spirit of your sanctifying grace, and so that they may truly please you, pour on them the refreshing dew of your blessing, through Christ our Lord. Amen.

———•———

Dearest Lord, we thank you for the prayer and ministry of our Bishop [N.] Be a tower of strength to him, that he may be the same to us. Make him a fearless defender of the faith committed to his charge, and a holy and humble father in God to us his spiritual children. Make him a worthy successor of the apostles, to the end of his own salvation and ours.

———•———

For priests

O Jesus, great King, good shepherd, eternal priest, living bread, my wisdom, my hope, my reward; with Mary my Mother I adore your wounded heart, I thank you for your seven holy sacraments, and I pray for all priests who minister them. In charity remember those whose charity has aided me: some have guided, warned, instructed, absolved me, some have remembered me in their supplications, tears, and sacrifices; some have commended their life, their agony, their judgment, their purgatory to my prayers. Preserve them for the glory of your name for they have proclaimed your praise. Look upon them with mercy, for they have shown mercy; gladden them in their troubles, for they have brought joy to the sorrowful; keep unstained their anointed hands, for they have blessed; keep unearthly their hearts sealed with the sublime marks of your priesthood. Bless their labors, the souls they love, the souls they seek, the souls they pray for. May those to whom they have ministered be here their joy and consolation, and in heaven their beautiful crown. Amen.

For religious sisters

Our Father, we offer this prayer in thanksgiving for Sisters, whose unique role of consecrated dedication to the Church is so in keeping with their fulfillment as christian witnesses and christian women. We rejoice in their courage and vision, manifested by their efforts to express religious community as an answer to the special needs of your Church today. We pray that they will have the clarity of vision and the courage of conviction to be open to the working of the Holy Spirit, so that their lives will express a spirit of living prayer and the power of true christian witness. We ask that by their leadership they will be looked on as symbols of hope in a world which is uncertain and troubled. Finally, we pray that they will be heartened by the living presence of Christ, in whom "we live and move and have our being," so that their lives will be a unique testimony to the value of religious community in the pilgrim Church. Amen.

TERENCE CARDINAL COOKE

Lord Jesus Christ, Savior of the world! We humbly beg you to manifest in your Church the Spirit whom you so abundantly bestowed upon your apostles. Call, we pray you, very many to your priesthood and to the religious life. And may zeal for your glory and the salvation of souls inflame these whom you have chosen. By your Spirit strengthen them, that they may be saints in your likeness. Amen.

Stir up in your Church, O Lord, the devotion and fortitude needed to make worthy ministers for your altar and powerful preachers of your word. In your kindness be attentive to our prayers and offerings that the stewards of your mysteries may increase in number and persevere to the end in loving you. Grant that those whom you have chosen as ministers of the redemption may, with pure minds, be worthy servants of your boundless love. Amen.

TERENCE CARDINAL COOKE

———•———

Jesus, High Priest and Redeemer forever, we beg you to call young men and women to your service as priests and religious. May they be inspired by the lives of dedicated priests, brothers, and sisters. Give to parents the grace of generosity and trust toward you and their children so that their sons and daughters may be helped to choose their vocations in life with wisdom and freedom.

Lord, you told us that "the harvest indeed is great but the laborers are few. Pray, therefore, the Lord of the harvest, to send laborers into his harvest." We ask that we may know and follow the vocation to which you have called us. We pray particularly for those called to serve as priests, brothers, and sisters; those whom you have called, those you are calling now, and those you will call in the future. May they be open and responsive to the call of serving your people. We ask this through Christ, our Lord. Amen.

———•———

Lord Jesus Christ, Savior of the world, through thy gentle heart we humbly beseech thee, the Eternal Shepherd, not to desert thy flock in its afflictions, but to enliven it with that spirit which thou didst pour out in such abundance on thine apostles. Call, we pray thee, more and more souls to enter the priestly and religious orders, and may those whom thou callest be fired with zeal for the salvation of souls, by virtue be sanctified, and by thy spirit be strengthened against every obstacle.

For Christian unity

O God, the Father of our Savior, Jesus Christ, give us the grace seriously to take to heart the great dangers we are in by our unhappy divisions. Remove from us all hatred and prejudice and whatever else may keep us from union and concord. As there is but one Body and one Spirit, one hope of our calling, one Lord, one faith, one baptism, one God and Father of us all, so may we all be of one heart and of one soul, united in one holy bond of truth and peace, of faith and charity. May we together glorify you through Christ our Lord. Amen.

TERENCE CARDINAL COOKE

For catechumens

O Lord our God, who dwells on high and yet looks down on the lowly, who sent salvation to the human race in the person of your only-begotten Son, our Lord and our God, Jesus Christ: look upon your servants, the catechumens, who bow their heads before you; make them worthy, in due time, of the washing of baptismal regeneration, of forgiveness of sins, and of the white garment of innocence; unite them with your Holy, Catholic and Apostolic Church and number them with your chosen flock, that they, too, together with us, may glorify your most honorable and majestic name, Father, Son, and Holy Spirit, now, and always, and for ages unending. Amen.

LITURGY OF ST. JOHN CHRYSOSTOM

FOR JUSTICE AND PEACE

The Beatitudes

Seeing the multitude, Jesus went up onto a mountain,
and when he sat down, his disciples came to him. And
  opening his mouth he taught them, saying:
Blessed are the poor in spirit, for theirs is the kingdom
  of heaven.
Blessed are the meek, for they shall possess the land.
Blessed are those who mourn, for they shall
  be comforted.
Blessed are those who hunger and thirst for justice, for
  they shall have their fill.
Blessed are the merciful, for they shall obtain mercy.
Blessed are the clean of heart, for they shall see God.
Blessed are the peacemakers, for they shall be called the
  children of God.
Blessed are those who suffer persecution for justice' sake,
  for theirs is the kingdom of heaven.
Blessed are you when men shall revile you and persecute
  you, and speak all that is evil against you falsely
  for my sake.
Be glad and rejoice, for your reward is very great in
  heaven, for so men persecuted the prophets who were
  before you.

MATTHEW 5:1–12

Prayer for Peace

Lord, make me an instrument of your peace! Where there is hatred, let me sow love; where there is injury, let me sow pardon; where there is doubt, faith; where there is despair, hope; where there is darkness, light; where there is sadness, joy. Amen.

ATTRIBUTED TO ST. FRANCIS OF ASSISI

Father, those who work for peace are called your sons. May we never tire in working for that justice which alone guarantees true and lasting peace. Through Christ our Lord. Amen.

Father, you have called men and women through their daily work, to share in your work of creation. May we recognize every person as our brother or sister, and, by the power of your Spirit, strive with them for a more just world where men and women will find work in accordance with the dignity of their vocation, and will contribute to the progress of all humanity. Through Christ our Lord. Amen.

Almighty and eternal God, may your grace enkindle in everyone a love for the many unfortunate people whom poverty and misery reduce to a condition of life unworthy of human beings. Arouse in the hearts of those who call you Father a hunger and thirst for social justice, and for fraternal love in deed and in truth. Grant, O Lord, peace in our days, peace to souls, peace to families, peace to our country, and peace among nations. Amen.

POPE PIUS XII

O God, our Father, you have set us over all the works of your hands. You have shared with us your creative power to build a world of peace and justice—a world in which everyone can live as brothers and sisters endowed with human dignity as members of your human family.

O God, our Father, bestow on us who live in this age of space a share in your vision. Grant that we, who have seen battlefields where we have sought to destroy one another and ghettos where many of us live without dignity or hope, may now look to the stars and see our world, as the astronauts did, as "small and blue and beautiful in the eternal silence in which it floats." Grant that we, who witness millions of homeless, hungry children in a world of unparalleled scientific achievements, may enjoy the prophetic vision which sees all the members of your human family as "riders on the earth together," brothers and sisters on "that bright loveliness in the eternal cold."

O God, our Father, inspire us with faith to believe that this vision of our earth can be fulfilled. Grant us the grace to believe firmly that you have given us sufficient resources for this purpose. Show us how to use them generously to provide food, decent shelter, education, and meaningful employment for all in your family.

O God, our Father, strengthen us with humility and wisdom. Teach us to be thankful for the precious mystery of life that you have made ours. Bless our efforts to promote the total development of each and every human being that all might reach the fullness of their potential and dignity as your sons and daughters. Amen.

TERENCE CARDINAL COOKE

ON CERTAIN OCCASIONS

THE BLESSING OF A HOUSE

CALL: Peace be to this place.
RESPONSE: And to all who dwell here.

It is customary to sprinkle each room with holy water as it is visited.

In the entrance hall

Almighty God, our most welcome visitor, bless the portals of this home. May those who cross the threshold in peace find within a ready welcome and an open heart. May this door keep out all sin and evil, so that within there may be only goodness and truth, and the presence of your kingdom. Through Christ our Lord. Amen.

In the main room of the house

Lord Jesus Christ, who found a ready welcome in the home of Martha and Mary, grant that in this room may be much laughter and good nature. May dissension never gain a foothold here, but may joyful companionship become for everyone a foretaste of heaven, where all the elect will rejoice in the communion of saints, praising God forever and ever. Amen.

— • —

In the kitchen

Teach us, good Lord, to grow in humility, and in the practical love of our fellow human beings. In this kitchen may we learn that it is truly more blessed to serve than to be served, and that fidelity and affection are most truly learned in the simplest ways. We ask this through Christ our Lord. Amen.

— • —

In the dining room

In this room, O Lord, give us a foretaste of your heavenly banquet, where none goes hungry, where none goes lonely, but all is satisfaction, communion, and joy. Grace this table with your blessing, Lord, and accept our thanks for what has been and will be received by those who sit here. We ask this through Christ our Lord. Amen.

— • —

On the stairs

O Lord, who never does allow the steps of the just to stumble, keep all who use these stairs safe. May they ascend also in the path of virtue, and thereby come eventually to heaven. We ask this through Christ our Lord. Amen.

— • —

In a bedroom

Guard our purity, O blessed Lord, and bless our sleep. Make us quick to keep your commandments, that when we finally fall asleep in death we may wake to eternal glory. Through Christ our Lord. Amen.

— • —

In a couple's bedroom

Bless this room, O Lord, where we remember the joy of the wedding day. Renew the grace of marriage, and move those who sleep here to the keeping of your commandments in the truest covenant of love. We ask this through Christ our Lord. Amen.

— • —

In the bathroom

Wash us, O Lord, and we will be truly clean. In this room, O Lord Jesus, may we remember the washing of baptism which brought us eternal life, and may we remember your words that inner cleanliness is more important than outer. Let us set aside vanity and self-centeredness, and make us fit citizens of your kingdom, where you live and reign forever and ever. Amen.

— • —

In the main room once more

Most blessed Trinity: we consecrate this home to your honor and glory. May it become for all who dwell here the place wherein they find the means of salvation. Mary, Mother of God, be a mother in this house; angels and saints, protect all who enter or dwell here with your powerful intercession.

— • —

An image of the Sacred Heart of Jesus may be placed and blessed at this point, with an act of consecration such as on page 575.

Our Father . . .

Hail Mary . . .

Let us pray.

Visit this house, O Lord, we pray, and drive far from it the deadly power of the enemy. May your holy angels dwell here instead, that we may be preserved in peace, with your blessing on us always. Through our Lord Jesus Christ your Son, who lives and reigns with you and the Holy Spirit, one God forever and ever. Amen.

A priest or deacon may add the following:

May almighty God bless this house and all who dwell here, the Father, the ✟ Son, and the Holy Spirit. Amen.

    CALL: Let us bless the Lord.
    RESPONSE: Thanks be to God.

MEETINGS

BEFORE A MEETING

Come, Holy Spirit, fill the hearts of your faithful, and kindle in them the fire of your love.

> CALL: Send forth your Spirit and they shall be created.
>
> RESPONSE: And you will renew the face of the earth.

Lord, have mercy.
Christ, have mercy.
Lord, have mercy.

Our Father . . .

> CALL: Remember your people, O Lord,
>
> RESPONSE: Who have been yours from of old.
>
> CALL: O Lord, hear my prayer,
>
> RESPONSE: And let my cry come to you.

Let us pray.

Illumine our minds, we beseech you, Lord, with the light of your glory, that we may be enabled to see what needs to be done, and be empowered to see it soon and fruitfully effected. Through Christ our Lord. Amen.

———•———

We have come, O Lord, Holy Spirit, we have come before you hampered indeed by our many and grievous sins, but for a special purpose gathered together in your name. Come to us and be with us and enter our hearts.

Teach us what we are to do and where we ought to tend; show us what we must accomplish, in order that, with your help, we may be able to please you in all things.

May you alone be the author and the finisher of our judgments, who alone with God the Father and his Son possess a glorious name.

Do not allow us to disturb the order of justice, you who love equity above all things. Let not ignorance draw us into devious paths. Let not partiality sway our minds or respect of riches or persons pervert our judgment.

But unite us to you effectually by the gift of your grace alone, that we may be one in you and never forsake the truth; inasmuch as we are gathered together in your name, so may we in all things hold fast to justice tempered by mercy, so that in this life our judgment may in no wise be at variance with you and in the life to come we may attain to everlasting rewards for deeds well done. Amen.

ROMAN PONTIFICAL

AFTER A MEETING

Lord, have mercy.
Christ, have mercy
Lord, have mercy.

Our Father . . .

CALL: Strengthen, O God what has been done among us,
RESPONSE: And give us help from your holy temple.
CALL: O Lord, hear my prayer,
RESPONSE: And let my cry come to you.

Let us pray.

Grant us, O Lord, the help of your grace, that since we have deliberated by the help of your inspiration, we may continue to acknowledge you, the author of all good, and thus see our good resolutions put into effect. Through Christ our Lord. Amen.

———•———

BEFORE PARISH MEETINGS

Heavenly Father, be present with us now. Let all our deliberations tend to your glory and the furtherance of the gospel. Let our discussions be charitable and our conclusions fruitful. May the breeze of your Holy Spirit breathe among us instead of long-windedness, let there be no fighting of corners or sacrificing long-term trust for short-term popularity. In short, dear Father, may this meeting end on time, with your kingdom furthered. Through the one who used few words but to great effect, Jesus Christ our Lord. Amen.

———•———

Before a Journey

Antiphon: In the way of peace and prosperity may the Lord, the almighty and merciful, direct our steps. And may the angel Raphael accompany us on our way, that we may return to our home in peace, safety, and joy.

The Benedictus

Blessed ✠ be the Lord, the God of Israel,
    who has visited and redeemed his people,
and has lifted up a horn of salvation for us
    in the family of his servant David.
For this he swore through the mouths of holy men,
    those who were prophets, from the beginning:
There would be salvation from our foes,
    and from the hand of all those who hate us;
to comfort our fathers,
    and to honor his holy covenant,
which oath once he swore to Abraham, our father,
    that he would grant us,
that freed from the hand of our enemies,
    and without fear, we may serve him,
    in holiness and justice in his very presence
      all our days.
And you, my son, will be named Prophet of the
  Most High;
    for you will go before the presence of the Lord
    to prepare his way,
to teach knowledge of salvation to his people
    that their sins may be forgiven,
    through the merciful heart of our God,

when the Daystar shall visit us from on high
to enlighten those who sit in darkness
and in the shadow of death,
and guide our feet to the way of peace.

LUKE 1:68–79

Glory be . . .

ANTIPHON: In the way of peace and prosperity may the Lord, the almighty and merciful, direct our steps. And may the angel Raphael accompany us on our way, that we may return to our home in peace, safety, and joy.

Lord, have mercy.
Christ, have mercy.
Lord, have mercy.

Our Father . . .

CALL: O Lord, save your servants,
RESPONSE: Who trust in you, O God.
CALL: Send us help, O Lord, from your holy place,
RESPONSE: And defend us out of Zion.
CALL: Be unto us, O Lord, a tower of strength,
RESPONSE: From the face of the enemy.
CALL: Do not let the enemy prevail against us.
RESPONSE: Nor let evildoers approach to hurt us.
CALL: Blessed be the Lord from day to day.
RESPONSE: God our salvation, make our way prosper before us.
CALL: Show us your ways, O Lord,

RESPONSE: And teach us your paths.

CALL: O, that our footsteps may be directed

RESPONSE: To keeping your righteous laws.

CALL: The crooked ways shall
be made straight,

RESPONSE: And the rough places smooth.

CALL: God has given his angels
charge over you,

RESPONSE: To keep you on your way.

CALL: O Lord, hear my prayer,

RESPONSE: And let my cry come to you.

Let us pray.

O God, who made the sons of Israel to walk with dry feet through the midst of the sea, and who opened to the three magi, by the guiding of a star, the way that led to your Son: grant to us, we beg, a prosperous journey and a time of tranquillity, that, attended by your holy angels, we may happily arrive at [N.] and finally at the haven of eternal salvation.

— • —

O God, who brought Abraham your son out of the land of the Chaldees, and preserved him unhurt through all his journeyings, we beseech you to keep us your servants safe; be to us our support in our setting out, our solace on the way, our shade in the heat, our shelter in the rain and cold, our transport in our weariness, our fortress in trouble, our staff on slippery paths, our harbor on stormy seas, that under your guidance we may safely reach our destination, and at length return home in safety.

— • —

Listen, O Lord, we beg, to our prayers, and arrange the way of your servants in the blessedness of your salvation, that amidst all the various changes of this our life and pilgrimage, we may ever be protected by your help.

———•———

Grant to your people, we beg you, almighty God, that they may walk onward in the way of salvation, and by following the exhortations of blessed John the Baptist, the forerunner, that they may come safely to the presence of the One of whom John spoke, Jesus Christ your Son, our Lord, who lives and reigns with you in the unity of the Holy Spirit, one God forever and ever. Amen.

> CALL: Let us proceed on our journey in peace.
> RESPONSE: In the name of the Lord. Amen

———•———

FOR CERTAIN INTENTIONS

When making an important decision

Lord Jesus Christ, open the eyes and ears of my heart, so that I may hear and understand your word and do your will, for in this world, Lord, I am a stranger and an exile. Hide not your commandments from me. Draw the veil from my eyes, and let me ponder the wonderful workings of your law. Make known to me the obscure and hidden ways of your wisdom and of my own heart. For in you, God, is my hope; enlighten my thoughts and my understanding. Amen.

— • —

Give me, O my Lord, that purity of conscience which alone can receive, which alone can improve thy inspirations. My ears are dull, so that I cannot hear thy voice. My eyes are dim, so that I cannot see thy tokens. Thou alone canst quicken my hearing, and purge my sight, and cleanse and renew my heart. Teach me, like Mary, to sit at thy feet, and to hear thy word. Give me that true wisdom which seeks thy will by prayer and meditation, by direct intercourse with thee, more than by reading and reasoning. Give me the discernment to know thy voice from the voice of strangers, and to rest upon it and to seek it in the first place as something external to myself; and answer me through my own mind, if I worship and rely on thee as above and beyond it.

J. H. NEWMAN

— • —

397

On choosing a state of life

O almighty God, whose wise and kind providence watches over every human event, be my light and my counsel in all my undertakings, particularly in the choice of a state of life. I know that on this important step my sanctification and salvation may in a great measure depend. I know that I am incapable of discerning what is truly best for me; and so I throw myself into your arms, beseeching you, my God, who sent me into this world only to love and serve you, to direct with your grace every moment and action of my life to the glorious purpose of my creation. I renounce most sincerely every other wish than to fulfill your will for my soul, whatever it may be; and I beseech you to give me the necessary grace, in the true spirit of a Christian, to qualify myself for any vocation your kindly providence may assign me. O my God, whenever it may become my duty to make a choice, be my light and my counsel, and mercifully *make the way known to me wherein I should walk, for I have lifted up my soul to you.* Preserve me from listening to the suggestions of my own self-love, or wordly prudence in preference to your holy and wiser inspirations. *Let your good Spirit lead me into the right way,* and your kind providence place me, not necessarily where I may be happiest according to the world, but in the state in which I shall love and serve you best, and meet with most abundant means for working out my salvation. This is all that I ask, and all that I desire; for what would it avail me to gain the whole world if, in the end, I were to lose my soul, and be so unfortunate as to prefer temporal advantages and worldly honors to the enjoyment of your divine presence in a happy eternity?

Most holy Virgin, take me under thy protection.
My Angel Guardian and Patron Saints pray for me.

My heavenly Father, I sincerely wish to dedicate my whole life to you, to please you in everything I do, and to guide my life by your will. I realize, Father, that you wish me to use the freedom you have given me. I am deeply concerned about my free choice of the state of life in which I can live most happily and serve you best. Guide me in my choice, O Lord, and help me to decide wisely. Give me also the strength to persevere in following my decision. I ask this grace through Jesus Christ your Son, who perfectly knew and fulfilled your will for him.

TERENCE CARDINAL COOKE

Before an important undertaking

O adorable Jesus, I come to thee before I commence this undertaking to implore thy Divine assistance, and to consecrate it, through thee, to the greater honor and glory of God: thou knowest that of myself I can do nothing, assist me therefore, I beseech thee, to accomplish the will of God—that divine will which was so dear to thee, as to be thy food whilst thou wert upon earth. Direct me particularly in the affair I am about to undertake, and teach me to act in a manner pleasing to thy divine Majesty—or rather, do thou thyself deign to act in and by me; govern me by thy wisdom; support me by thy power and by thy infinite goodness direct all my exertions on this and on every other occasion, to thy greater honor and glory, and my own eternal salvation. Amen.

When feeling tepid

Merciful God, almighty Father, so generous with your benefits to me, forgive the ingratitude with which I have repaid your goodness. Here I am before you with a dead, unfeeling heart, cold despite the warmth of your gentle and patient goodness. Turn again, merciful Father! Try once more! Make me hunger for you as the bread of life with all my longing. Make me desire to serve you only, make me long to do only what you desire me to do. Grant my prayer, beloved Lord, lest I die of this wretched chill.

ST. ANSELM

For rain in due season

Praise the Lord, for praising him is good;
     It is joyful and comely to sing his praise!

The Lord builds up Jerusalem,
     he will gather together the dispersal of Israel.
It is he who heals the brokenhearted,
     he binds up all their bruises.
He can tell the number of the stars,
     and calls each one by its name.

Great is our Lord, and great is his power;
     the acts of his wisdom are numberless.
The Lord lifts up the meek;
     and brings the wicked down to the dust.
Sing to the Lord with praise:
     sing to our God upon the harp.

It is he who covers the heavens with clouds;
     and prepares rain for the earth,
making grass to grow on the mountains
     and with herbs for the service of men.

He gives the beasts their food
     and feeds the young ravens that call upon him.
His delight is not in the power of the horse,
     nor his pleasure in the strength of a man's legs.

But the Lord takes pleasure in those who fear him,
    and in those who hope in his mercy.

PSALM 147:1–11

Glory be . . .

CALL: O Lord, cover the heavens with clouds,
RESPONSE: And prepare rain for the earth.
CALL: May it make grass to grow upon the
            mountains,
RESPONSE: And herbs for the service of men.
CALL: Water the hills from above,
RESPONSE: And the earth shall be filled with the
            fruit of your works.
CALL: O Lord, hear my prayer,
RESPONSE: And let my cry come to you.

Let us pray.

O God, in whom we live, move, and have our being, grant us seasonable rain, that when our temporal needs are sufficiently supplied, we may seek with more confidence after things eternal.

—•—

Grant us wholesome rain, O Lord, we beseech, and graciously pour forth showers from heaven on the parched face of the earth. Through our Lord Jesus Christ who lives and reigns with you in the unity of the Holy Spirit, one God, world without end. Amen.

—•—

For fine weather

God be merciful unto us, and bless us:
    may he cause the light of his countenance
    to shine upon us, and have mercy on us.

That we may know your way upon earth:
    your salvation in all the nations.

Let the people praise you, O God:
    let all the people praise you.

Let the nations be glad and rejoice:
    for you judge the people with justice,
    and govern the nations upon earth.

Let the people praise you, O God:
    let all the people praise you:
    the earth has yielded her fruit.

May God, our own God bless us, may God bless us:
    and may all the ends of the earth fear him.

PSALM 67

Glory be . . .

CALL: You brought, O Lord, your wind upon the earth,

RESPONSE: And the rain from heaven was restrained.

CALL: When I shall cover the sky with clouds,

RESPONSE: My rainbow shall appear and I will remember my covenant.

CALL: May your face shine upon your servants, O Lord,

RESPONSE: And bless those who hope in you.

CALL: O Lord, hear my prayer,

RESPONSE: And let my cry come to you.

Let us pray.

Graciously hear us, O Lord, who cry to you, and grant fair weather to your suppliants, that we who are justly afflicted for our sins may experience your mercy and clemency.

We beseech your clemency, almighty God, that you would restrain the inundation of waters and vouchsafe to show us the brightness of your countenance. Through our Lord Jesus Christ, who lives and reigns with you in the unity of the Holy Spirit, one God, world without end. Amen.

——— • ———

Almighty God, we beseech that we, who in our trouble put our trust in thy mercy, may be strengthened by your defense against all adversity.

——— • ———

For dear friends

Almighty God, who has poured the gift of love into the hearts of your faithful people, grant to [N.] [those] whom I love health of mind and body, that he/she [they] may come to love you with all [their] strength, and accomplish all that is pleasing to you. Through Christ our Lord. Amen.

——— • ———

To repel bitter thoughts

O God, almighty and yet most meek, hear my prayers and free my heart from bitter thoughts, and from all harmful wanderings of the imagination, that your Holy Spirit may find this his temple a more worthy home. Through Christ our Lord. Amen.

——— • ———

For the gift of charity

O God, who smooths the path for those that love you, grant to our hearts the gift of charity, that those things which have been undertaken through your inspiration may not be diverted through the interference of our selfishness. Through Christ our Lord. Amen.

——— • ———

For the gift of patience

O God, whose only-begotten Son conquered the pride of his enemies through his singular patience, grant, we beseech, that inspired by his example as we recall his sufferings, we may face our adversities with equanimity. Through the same Christ our Lord. Amen.

———— • ————

For continence

Purify our hearts and minds, O Lord, with the gift of your Holy Spirit, that we may serve you with a pure body and a clean soul. Through Christ our Lord. Amen.

———— • ————

In thanksgiving

O God, whose mercies are numberless and whose treasury of goodness is limitless, we give you grateful thanks for your countless blessings, and we pray that our wise use of your gifts may fit us for the joys of heaven. Through Christ our Lord. Amen.

———— • ————

For grace to do God's will

Grant me grace, O merciful God, to desire ardently all that is pleasing to you, to examine it prudently, to acknowledge it truthfully, and to accomplish it perfectly for the praise and glory of your name. Amen.

ST. THOMAS AQUINAS

———— • ————

DEVOTIONS

DEVOTIONS

CONTENTS

THE ROSARY

THE CLASSIC ROSARY

The rosary, the most common Catholic devotional prayer, consists of the recitation of fifteen decades of Hail Marys, each introduced by the Lord's Prayer and concluded with the doxology. Each decade is associated with a mystery, a meditation on some aspect of the life of Christ or Mary. These meditations are divided into three groups of five mysteries—the joyful, sorrowful, and glorious mysteries—commemorating Christ's incarnation, passion, and glorification. To assist memory, the prayers are usually counted on a string of beads.

The current form of the rosary dates from the sixteenth century, but its roots lie in older systems for counting prayers and guiding devotional meditation. The Dominican order especially promoted use of the rosary. The Feast of Our Lady of the Rosary is celebrated on October 7.

The rosary can be prayed both as a method of vocal prayer and as a guide to meditation. The prayers of the rosary, taken mostly from Scripture, praise Jesus and his mother. At the same time, the scenes from Jesus' life recalled in the mysteries are fruitful subjects for reflection and meditation.

—•—

THE PRAYERS OF THE ROSARY

The Apostles' Creed

I believe in God the Father Almighty, Creator of heaven and earth; and in Jesus Christ his only Son our Lord; who was conceived by the Holy Spirit, born of the Virgin Mary, suffered under Pontius Pilate, was crucified, dead, and buried; he descended into hell; the third day he rose again from the dead; he ascended into heaven, is seated at the right hand of God the Father Almighty; from thence he shall come to judge the living and the dead. I believe in the Holy Spirit; the holy Catholic Church; the communion of saints; the forgiveness of sins; the resurrection of the body; and life everlasting. Amen.

—•—

Our Father, who art in heaven. Hallowed be thy name; thy kingdom come; thy will be done on earth as it is in heaven; give us this day our daily bread; and forgive us our trespasses, as we forgive those who trespass against us; and lead us not into temptation, but deliver us from evil. Amen.

—•—

Hail Mary, full of grace, the Lord is with thee. Blessed art thou among women, and blessed is the fruit of thy womb, Jesus. Holy Mary, mother of God, pray for us sinners now and at the hour of our death. Amen.

—•—

Glory be to the Father, and to the Son, and to the Holy Spirit. As it was in the beginning, is now and ever shall be, world without end. Amen.

———•———

The Salve Regina

Hail, holy Queen, mother of mercy; hail, our life, our sweetness, and our hope! To thee do we cry, poor banished children of Eve, to thee do we send up our sighs, mourning and weeping in this vale of tears. Turn then, most gracious advocate, thine eyes of mercy toward us; and after this our exile, show unto us the blessed fruit of thy womb, Jesus. O clement, O loving, O sweet Virgin Mary.

———•———

THE USUAL METHOD OF RECITING THE ROSARY

Begin on the tail of the rosary beads.

Holding the crucifix: one Apostles' Creed
On the first bead: one Our Father
On the three grouped beads: one Hail Mary on
                                each bead
On the next single bead: one Glory Be

Many people ignore the tail and begin at this point.

The first mystery

On the same bead, begin
the first mystery with: one Our Father

Continue on to the loop of beads.

On the first set of ten beads: ten Hail Marys

Meditate on the first mystery.

On the single bead, finish
the mystery with: one Glory Be

The second to the fifth mysteries

On the same bead, begin
the second mystery with: one Our Father

Repeat the pattern of one Our Father, ten Hail Marys, and one Glory Be until you have completed the loop of beads and have meditated on five mysteries. Then conclude with the following prayers:

One Salve Regina (Hail, Holy Queen)

> *CALL:* Pray for us, holy mother of God,
>
> **RESPONSE:** That we may be made worthy of the promises of Christ.

Let us pray.

O God, whose only-begotten Son by his life, death, and resurrection has purchased for us the rewards of eternal life, grant, we beseech thee, that by meditating on the mysteries of the most holy rosary of the Blessed Virgin Mary we may both imitate what they contain and obtain what they promise, through the same Christ our Lord. Amen.

May the divine assistance remain always with us. Amen.

May the souls of the faithful departed, through the mercy of God, rest in peace. Amen.

THE FIFTEEN MYSTERIES OF THE HOLY ROSARY

THE FIVE JOYFUL MYSTERIES

The five joyful mysteries are customarily prayed on Mondays, Thursdays, and Sundays from the first Sunday of Advent to the Feast of the Presentation (February 2).

1. THE ANNUNCIATION

We recall how our blessed Lady learned from the angel Gabriel that she was to be the mother of Jesus, and how she willingly took on this difficult thing that God asked of her. We recall the conception of Jesus: the beginning of his earthly life.

2. THE VISITATION

We recall the visit that the expectant Mary paid to her cousin Elizabeth, who also was pregnant, bearing John the Baptist within her. As soon as Mary's greeting reached the ears of Elizabeth, we read, the child in Elizabeth's womb leaped for joy. Mary then gave great praise to God in the hymn known as the Magnificat.

—— • ——

3. THE NATIVITY

We recall the miserable and yet glorious birth of our Lord at Bethlehem in a stable, the song of the angels, the visits of the shepherds and the wise men from the East.

—— • ——

4. THE PRESENTATION

We recall how our Lord was presented in the temple as the law of Moses required, offering a young lamb or two turtledoves as a sacrifice to the Lord. We remember how Simeon and Anna recognized who Jesus was, and prophesied coming sorrow for our Lady.

—— • ——

5. THE FINDING OF THE CHILD JESUS IN THE TEMPLE

We recall how the child Jesus was lost in Jerusalem for three days and finally found by St. Joseph and our Lady in the temple, discussing with the doctors of the Law. We recall how Jesus gently rebuked his mother and foster father, saying that surely this was the place where he should be. We remember how Jesus went home with them and was subject to their authority. And we recall how Mary stored all these things in her heart.

—— • ——

THE FIVE SORROWFUL MYSTERIES

The five sorrowful mysteries are customarily prayed on Tuesdays, Fridays, and Sundays from the Feast of the Presentation (February 2) until Easter.

1. THE AGONY IN THE GARDEN

We recall that after the Last Supper, Jesus and his disciples went into the garden of Gethsemane, where Jesus prayed and his disciples slept. We recall how Jesus' distress was so great that he sweated blood, praying that the cup of suffering be taken away from him, but submitting to the will of God nonetheless.

——•——

2. THE SCOURGING AT THE PILLAR

We recall that, in hope that it might satisfy his persecutors, Pilate had Jesus brutally scourged. Truly each of our sins was another blow of the scourge.

——•——

3. THE CROWNING WITH THORNS

We recall that our Lord's eternal kingship was mocked by this parody of the coronation ceremony. We remember Jesus' saying, "My kingdom is not of this world."

—— • ——

4. THE CARRYING OF THE CROSS

We recall how the heavy cross was laid upon Jesus, who was already so weak that he could hardly stand. We remember that Simon of Cyrene helped him to bear it.

—— • ——

5. THE CRUCIFIXION AND DEATH OF OUR LORD

We recall Jesus' hours of agony on the cross, how he died, promising salvation to the penitent thief, how his side was pierced by a lance and his body taken down to be laid in the arms of his blessed mother.

—— • ——

THE FIVE GLORIOUS MYSTERIES

The glorious mysteries are customarily prayed on Wednesdays, Saturdays, and Sundays from Easter until Advent.

1. THE RESURRECTION

We recall that on the third day in the tomb, Jesus rose from the dead and appeared to Simon Peter, Mary Magdalene, and then many others.

———•———

2. THE ASCENSION

We recall that forty days after his resurrection, Jesus went body and soul to heaven, promising to send the Holy Spirit to his disciples.

———•———

3. THE COMING OF THE HOLY SPIRIT AT PENTECOST

We recall how the Holy Spirit descended in the form of

countless tongues of fire and inspired the disciples to set aside their fear and preach the gospel to all nations.

— • —

4. THE ASSUMPTION OF OUR BLESSED LADY INTO HEAVEN

We recall in this mystery how the mother of God was taken up to heaven body and soul when her earthly life was over: a forerunner of the resurrection of the body that awaits us all.

— • —

5. THE CORONATION OF OUR LADY AS QUEEN OF HEAVEN, AND THE GLORY OF THE SAINTS

We recall with gratitude the good things that God has promised for those who love him, the coming glory that awaits those who do his will in this life, and how it will last forever.

— • —

DEVOTIONS FOR THE MYSTERIES

The prayers and Scripture readings in the following section are offered as aids to meditation on the mysteries of the rosary. You are invited to choose the devotions that seem most suitable. The devotions include a Scripture passage related to the mystery that may be said along with the rosary prayer. Each passage is divided into ten smaller parts designated by a number (not corresponding to the number of the Scripture verse). You may pray a "Scripture rosary" by saying this small Scripture passage before each Hail Mary.

THE JOYFUL MYSTERIES

THE ANNUNCIATION

Let us contemplate in this mystery how the angel Gabriel saluted our Blessed Lady with the title Full of Grace, thus revealing Mary's Immaculate Conception, and how he declared to her the Incarnation of our Lord and Savior Jesus Christ, to which she willingly assented to be the means.

Suggestions for intercession: for an end to the evils of abortion, resignation to God's will in one's own life, humility, chastity.

— • —

O holy Mary, Queen of Virgins, through the most high mystery of the Incarnation of your beloved Son our Lord Jesus Christ, by which our salvation was so happily begun: obtain for us through your intercession, light to be aware of the greatness of the benefit which he has bestowed on us in making himself our Brother, and you, his own beloved Mother, our Mother also. Amen.

— • —

^{1} In the sixth month, the angel Gabriel was sent from God to a city of Galilee called Nazareth to a virgin espoused to a man whose name was Joseph of the house of David, and the virgin's name was Mary. ^{2} And the angel, entering, said to her: Hail, full of grace, the Lord is with you: Blessed are you among women. ^{3} She, having heard this, was troubled at his words, and considered in herself what manner of greeting this could be. ^{4} And the angel said to her: Fear not, Mary, for you have found grace with God. ^{5} Behold, you shall conceive in your womb and bring forth a son, and you shall call his name Jesus. ^{6} He shall be great, and shall be called the Son of the most High, and the Lord God shall give to him the throne of David his father, and he shall reign in the house of Jacob forever, and of his kingdom there shall be no end. ^{7} And Mary said to the angel: How shall this be done, because I am a virgin? ^{8} And the angel answered her: The Holy Spirit shall come upon you, and the power of the most High shall overshadow you. And therefore also the holy one who shall be born of you will be called the Son of God. ^{9} And behold, your cousin Elizabeth also has conceived a son in her old age, and this is the sixth month of pregnancy in her who was called barren. Nothing is impossible to God! ^{10} And Mary said: Behold the handmaid of the Lord: be it done to me according to your word. And the angel departed from her.

LUKE 1:26–38

O Lord, who when you came down to redeem our nature chose for yourself the most chaste womb of Mary to be the true tabernacle of God with men: grant, we beseech you, that by her holy intercession, our souls may be so filled with your grace, that we may be made temples of

God, who lives and reigns with you and the Holy Spirit, one God forever and ever. Amen.

———— • ————

THE VISITATION

Let us contemplate in this mystery how the Blessed Virgin Mary, understanding from the angel that her cousin Elizabeth had conceived, went with haste into the mountains of Judea to visit her and remained with her three months.

Suggestions for intercession: for those who visit people in need, the St. Vincent de Paul Society, stronger devotion to our Lady, gratitude to God, charity to our neighbor.

———— • ————

O holy Virgin, most spotless mirror of humility, by that great love which moved you to visit your holy cousin, St. Elizabeth: obtain for us, through your intercession, that our hearts being visited by your most holy Son, and freed from all sin, we may praise and give thanks forever. Amen.

———— • ————

[1] In those days, Mary rose up and went with haste into the hill country of Judea. [2] She entered into the house of Zechariah and greeted Elizabeth. [3] And it happened that when Elizabeth heard the salutation of Mary, the infant leaped in her womb. [4] Elizabeth was filled with the Holy Spirit and she cried out with a loud voice, [5] saying: Blessed are you among women, and blessed is the fruit of your womb! [6] And why should this be, that the mother of my Lord should come to me? [7] For behold, as soon as the voice of your greeting sounded in my ears, the infant in my womb leaped for joy. [8] And blessed are you who has believed that those things shall be accomplished that were

promised you by the Lord. ^{9} And Mary said: My soul magnifies the Lord, and my spirit has rejoiced in God my savior. ^{10} Mary stayed with her about three months, and then returned to her own house.

LUKE 1:39–47, 56

O Lord, who in the visitation of Mary poured forth your heavenly graces on the house of Zechariah and Elizabeth, sanctify us by your sacred and most loving presence, as you sanctified your holy servant John, and give us grace so to instruct others in righteousness, and to edify them by our holy life, as to escape from all danger of pride or vainglory, who live and reign forever and ever. Amen.

THE NATIVITY

Let us contemplate in this mystery how the Blessed Virgin Mary, when the time of her delivery was come, brought forth our Redeemer, Jesus Christ, and laid him in a manger, because there was no room for them in the inn at Bethlehem.

Suggestions for intercession: for the poor, the gift of wisdom, priests who bring our Lord into the world on the altars at Mass, humility.

O most pure Mother of God, through your virginal and most joyful delivery, whereby you gave to the world your only Son our Savior: we beseech, obtain for us, through your intercession, the grace to lead such pure and holy lives in this world, that we may become worthy to sing without ceasing, both day and night, the mercies of your Son, and his benefits to us through you. Amen.

^{1} Joseph went up from Galilee, from the city of Nazareth into Judea, to the city of David called Bethlehem, because he was of the house and family of David, to be enrolled with Mary his espoused wife, who was with child. ^{2} And it came to pass that when they were there, her time of expectancy ended, that her child could be delivered. ^{3} And she brought forth her firstborn son, and wrapped him up in swaddling clothes, and laid him in a manger because there was no room for them in the inn. ^{4} And there were in the same country shepherds watching and keeping vigil over their sheep. ^{5} And behold: an angel of the Lord stood by them, and the glory of the Lord shone round about them, and they feared with a great fear. ^{6} But the angel said to them: Do not fear, for behold, I bring you good tidings of great joy that shall be to all the people. ^{7} For this day is born to you a Savior who is Christ the Lord, in the city of David. ^{8} And this shall be a sign to you: you will find the infant wrapped in swaddling cloths and laid in a manger. ^{9} And suddenly there was with the angel a multitude of the heavenly army, praising God and saying: Glory to God in the highest, and on earth peace to men of goodwill. ^{10} And it came to pass that after the angels had gone back into heaven, the shepherds said to one another: Let us go over to Bethlehem, and see this thing that has come to pass, which the Lord has shown to us. And they went with haste, and they found Mary and Joseph, and the infant lying in the manger.

LUKE 2:4–16

We give you thanks, most loving Jesus, because for our sake you chose to be born in a poor stable and to be wrapped in swaddling cloths, laid in a manger, and fed at your

Mother's breasts. Grant, dearest Lord, that we may become like little children, humble and poor in spirit. Grant that we may, like the Magi from the East, seek after you with diligence, and find you in the cradle of our hearts, and there adore you, offering up the gold of charity, the incense of devotion, and the myrrh of penance. Amen.

— • —

THE PRESENTATION

Let us contemplate in this mystery how the Blessed Virgin Mary, on the day of her purification, presented the child Jesus in the temple, where holy Simeon, giving thanks to God with great devotion, received him into his arms.

Suggestions for intercession: for generosity, seeing the Lord even in the strangest situations, children in need, our own children, obedience to the commands of the Lord.

— • —

O holy Virgin, most admirable lady, and pattern of obedience, who presented in the temple the Lord of the temple, obtain for us from your beloved Son, that with holy Simeon and devout Anna, we may praise and glorify him forever.

— • —

1 And after eight days were passed, when the child was to be circumcised, they called his name Jesus, which he had been called by the angel before he was conceived in the womb. 2 And after the days of her purification were accomplished according to the law of Moses, they carried him to Jerusalem to present him to the Lord . . . 3 and to offer a sacrifice, as it is written in the law of the Lord, a pair of turtledoves or two young pigeons. 4 And behold, there was a man in Jerusalem named Simeon, and this man

was just and devout, waiting for the consolation of Israel, and the Holy Spirit was in him. 5 He had received an answer from the Holy Spirit, that he should not see death before he had seen the Anointed of the Lord. 6 And the Spirit inspired him to come into the temple. 7 When his parents brought in the child Jesus, to do for him according to the custom of the law, Simeon took him into his arms 8 and said: Now dismiss your servant, O Lord, according to your word. Because my eyes have seen your salvation, which you have prepared before the face of all peoples, a light to the revelation of the Gentiles and the glory of your people Israel. 9 And Simeon blessed them, and said to Mary his mother: Behold, this child is set for the fall and for the resurrection of many in Israel, and for a sign that shall be contradicted. 10 And a sword shall pierce your own soul, that the secret thoughts of many hearts shall be revealed.

LUKE 2:21–35

O Lord Jesus Christ, who condescended, together with your holy Mother, for our example to be obedient to the law for sin, grant us grace never to be ashamed of your law, but to labor to fulfill your commandments, to practice penance for our sins, and to approach your holy altar with those ardent desires with which holy Simeon received you into his arms. Amen.

THE FINDING OF THE CHILD JESUS IN THE TEMPLE

Let us contemplate in this mystery how the Blessed Virgin Mary, after having lost her beloved Son in Jerusalem, sought him for the space of three days, and at length found him the third day in the temple, in the midst of the doctors, discoursing with them, being at the age of twelve years.

Suggestions for intercession: for obedience to legitimate authority, trust in the Lord, knowledge and understanding of the Catholic faith, humility, patience, and diligence.

——— • ———

Most Blessed Virgin, more than a martyr in your sufferings, and yet the comfort of those who are afflicted: by that deep joy and relief that filled your soul at finding your beloved Son in the temple, obtain from him that we may so seek him and find him in the holy Catholic Church, as to be never more separated from him. Amen.

——— • ———

[1] The child grew, and waxed strong, full of wisdom, and the grace of God was in him. [2] And his parents went every year to Jerusalem at the solemn day of Passover. And they went up to Jerusalem according to the custom of the feast when he was twelve years old. [3] And having kept the days of the feast, the child Jesus remained in Jerusalem, and his parents did not know it. [4] And thinking that he was in their company, they went a day's journey, and then looked for him among their family and acquaintances. [5] Not finding him, they returned to Jerusalem, seeking him. [6] It came to pass that after three days they found him in the temple, sitting in the midst of the doctors, hearing them and asking them questions. [7] And all that heard him were astonished at his wisdom and his answers. And seeing him, they wondered. [8] And his mother said to him: Son, why have you behaved like this? Your father and I have searched for you in sorrow. [9] But he said to them: How is it that you looked for me? Did you not know that I must be about my Father's business? [10] And he went down with them and came to

Nazareth, and was subject to them. And his mother kept all these things in her heart.

LUKE 2:40–51

———•———

O Lord my God, the only good, you are the sea of sweetness and ocean of all perfection. We are confounded when we think how much our souls are moved at the loss of earthly goods, and yet feel so little trouble when we have lost you by sin. Grant, we beseech, that, despising all earthly things, we may sigh only to enjoy the vision of your glory and beauty in that kingdom, where, together with the Father and the Holy Spirit, you live and reign as God, world without end. Amen.

———•———

THE SORROWFUL MYSTERIES

THE AGONY IN THE GARDEN

Let us contemplate in this mystery how our Lord Jesus Christ was so afflicted for us in the garden of Gethsemane that his body was bathed in a sweat of blood, which ran down in great drops upon the ground.

Suggestions for intercession: for submission to the will of God, those agonized in mind, awareness of suffering in others, the gift of prayer.

———•———

Most holy Virgin, more than martyr, by that ardent prayer which your beloved Son poured forth to his Father in the garden, intercede for us, that our passions being reduced to the obedience of reason, we may always, and in all things, conform and subject ourselves to the will of God. Amen.

———•———

^{1} Jesus went out, according to his custom, to the Mount of Olives, and his disciples followed him. ^{2} And when he came to the place, he said to them: Pray, lest you enter into temptation. ^{3} And he drew away from them, about a stone's throw, and kneeling down, he prayed, saying: Father, if it be your will, remove this cup from me, but yet not my will but yours be done. ^{4} And there appeared to him an angel from heaven, strengthening him. ^{5} And in his agony he prayed the longer. And his sweat became as drops of blood, trickling down upon the ground. ^{6} And when he rose up from prayer and came to his disciples, he found them sleeping for sorrow. ^{7} And he said to them: Why are you asleep? Rise, pray, lest you enter into temptation. ^{8} While he was still speaking, a multitude came, and the one who was called Judas, one of the twelve, went to the front of them and drew near to Jesus in order to kiss him. And Jesus said to him: Judas, are you to betray the Son of man with a kiss? . . . ^{9} And Jesus said to the chief priests and magistrates of the temple and the elders that had come out against him: Why have you come out like this, carrying swords and clubs, as if I were a thief? While I was with you daily in the temple, you did not stretch out your hands against me; but this is your hour, and the hour of darkness. ^{10} And arresting him, they led him off to the high priest's house.

LUKE 22:39–54

O Lord Jesus Christ, who in the garden of Gethsemane taught us by word and example to overcome temptation by prayer, grant, we pray, that giving ourselves continually to prayer, we may obtain its abundant fruit, who lives and reigns forever and ever. Amen.

THE SCOURGING AT THE PILLAR

Let us contemplate in this mystery how our Lord Jesus Christ, being delivered up by Pilate to the fury of the Jews, was most cruelly scourged at a pillar.

Suggestions for intercession: think of each of your sins as being another stroke of the scourge, for those unjustly treated, cruelty and violence, abused children, the spirit of mortification.

— • —

O Mother of God, overflowing fountain of patience, through those blows that your only and most beloved Son suffered for us: obtain from him grace for us, that we may know how to mortify our rebellious senses, and cut off all occasions of sinning with the sword of grief and compassion that pierced your most gentle soul. Amen.

— • —

1 The chief priests accused Jesus of many things. 2 And Pilate interrogated him again, saying: Will you not answer at all? See how many accusations they make against you. But Jesus still said nothing, and Pilate was puzzled. 3 Now on the festival day he was accustomed to release for the Jews whichever of the prisoners they demanded. And there was one called Barabbas, who was in prison with some seditious men, who had committed murder in the uprising. 4 And when the crowd came up, they demanded that he would observe the custom as he had done before. 5 And Pilate answered them, saying: Shall I release for you the King of the Jews? For he knew that the chief priests had delivered Jesus up out of envy. 6 But the chief priests moved the people to release Barabbas for them. 7 And Pilate again said to them: What would you have me do, then, with the King of the Jews? And they again cried out:

Crucify him! [8] And Pilate said to them: Why? What evil has he done? But they cried out all the more: Crucify him! [9] And so Pilate, being willing to satisfy the people, released Barabbas for them, [10] and delivered up Jesus, when he had scourged him, to be crucified.

MARK 15:3–15

O Lord Jesus Christ who for our sakes took to yourself a human nature and suffered in your flesh for our example: grant that honoring your sacred Passion, we may imitate your blessed life of patience and penance, and attain at last to the glory of your resurrection, who lives and reigns forever and ever. Amen.

THE CROWNING WITH THORNS

Let us consider in this mystery how those cruel soldiers plaited a crown of sharp thorns and most painfully pressed it on the sacred head of our Lord Jesus Christ.

Suggestions for intercession: for earthy kings and rulers, governments, the right use of power, all who suffer, those who suffer mental illness, prayer for intellectual honesty, students and teachers, prayer to disregard what others think of us in the quest to do what is right.

O mother of our eternal Prince and King of Glory, by those sharp thorns with which his most holy head was pierced, we pray that through your intercession, we may be delivered from all notions of pride, and, in the day of judgment, from that condemnation that our sins deserve. Amen.

^{1} So then, Pilate took Jesus and scourged him. And the soldiers plaited a crown of thorns and put it on his head, and clothed him in a purple garment. ^{2} And they came to him and said: Hail, King of the Jews; and they struck him many blows. Pilate went out and said to the crowd: See I am bringing him out to you, that you may see that I find you have no case against him. ^{3} So Jesus came forth, wearing the crown of thorns and the purple garment. ^{4} And Pilate said to them: Behold the man. ^{5} So when the chief priests and servants had seen him, they cried out, saying: Crucify him, crucify him! Pilate said to them: Take him yourselves and crucify him, for I find no case against him. ^{6} The Jews answered: We have a law, and according to the law he ought to die, because he made himself the Son of God. So when Pilate heard this, he feared all the more. ^{7} And he entered the hall again and said to Jesus: From whence do you come? But Jesus made no answer. So Pilate said to him: Will you not speak to me? Are you unaware that I have power to crucify you, and power to release you? Jesus answered: You would not have any power against me unless it were given to you from above. Therefore, the one who delivered me to you has the greater sin. From that moment Pilate sought to release him. ^{8} But the Jews cried out, saying: If you release this man, you are not Caesar's friend. For whoever makes himself a king speaks against Caesar. ^{9} Now when Pilate heard these words, he brought Jesus forth and sat down in the judgment seat in the place that is called Lithostratos, and in Hebrew Gabbatha. And it was the preparation day of the Passover, about the sixth hour, when Pilate said to the Jews: Behold your king! But they cried out: Away with him, away with him. Crucify him! ^{10} Pilate said to them: Shall I crucify your king? The chief priests answered: We have no king but Caesar. So then he delivered Jesus to them to be crucified.

JOHN 19:1–16

O Lord Jesus Christ, immortal and invisible King: grant, we pray, that we who venerate your crown of thorns here upon earth may receive from you the crown of eternal glory in the life to come, who lives and reigns forever and ever. Amen.

THE CARRYING OF THE CROSS

Let us consider in this mystery how our Lord Jesus Christ, being sentenced to die, bore, with the greatest patience, the cross which was laid upon him for his greater torment and shame.

Suggestions for intercession: for the grace to carry our crosses cheerfully, those who come to the help of the afflicted, those who find life difficult, the spirit of meekness and patience.

O holy Virgin, example of patience, by the most painful carrying of the cross, in which your son bore the heavy weight of our sins, obtain for us from him courage and strength to follow his steps and bear our cross after him to the end of our lives. Amen.

1 They took Jesus and led him out, and bearing his own cross, he went forth to that place that is called Calvary, but in Hebrew Golgotha. 2 And as they led Jesus away, they laid hold of one Simon of Cyrene, coming in from the

country, and they laid the cross on him to carry behind Jesus. 3 And there followed him a great multitude of people, and of women who bewailed and lamented over him. 4 But Jesus turning to them, said: Daughters of Jerusalem, do not weep over me, but weep for yourselves and for your children. 5 For behold, the days shall come when they will say: Blessed are the barren, and the wombs that have not borne, and the breasts that have not given suck. 6 Then they shall begin to say to the mountains: Fall on us, and to the hills: Cover us. For if in the green wood they do these things, what shall be done in the dry? 7 And there were also two other criminals led with him to be put to death. 8 And when they had come to the place which is called Calvary, they crucified him there, 9 and also the robbers, one on the right hand and the other on the left. 10 And Jesus said: Father, forgive them, for they do not know what they are doing.

JOHN 19:16–17; LUKE 23:26–34

O Lord Jesus Christ, who has said, "No man can come to me, except he deny himself, and take up his cross and follow me": grant, we pray, that venerating your blessed patience in the carrying of the cross, we may bear all the crosses and trials of this valley of tears, that being purified by suffering, we may be admitted into your eternal rest, who lives and reigns forever and ever. Amen.

THE CRUCIFIXION AND DEATH OF OUR LORD
Let us contemplate in this mystery how our Lord Jesus Christ, being come to Mount Calvary, was stripped of his clothes, and his hands and feet were most cruelly nailed to

the cross on which he died, in the presence of his most afflicted Mother.

Suggestions for intercession: for the grace of final repentance, the dying, and those who care for them, gratitude to God for Jesus' sacrifice to save us.

— • —

O holy Mary, Mother of God, as the body of your beloved Son was for us stretched on the cross, so may our desires be daily more and more extended in his service, and our hearts wounded with compassion for his most bitter passion; and you, O most Blessed Virgin, grant by your powerful intercession that we may ever follow his example of love unto the end. Amen.

— • —

1 Now there stood by the cross of Jesus, his mother and his mother's sister, Mary of Cleophas, and Mary Magdalene. 2 When Jesus therefore had seen his mother and the disciple whom he loved standing near, he said to his mother: Woman, behold your son. 3 After that, he said to the disciple: Behold your mother. And from that hour the disciple took her as his own. 4 Afterwards, knowing that all things were now accomplished, in order that the Scriptures might be fulfilled, he said: I thirst. 5 Now there was a vessel set there full of vinegar. And they, putting a sponge full of vinegar on a hyssop stick, put it up to his mouth. 6 Jesus then, when he had taken the vinegar, said: It is consummated. 7 And bowing his head, he gave up his spirit. 8 Then the Jews, because it was Passover eve, not wishing the bodies to remain on the cross on the Sabbath—that Sabbath being a great Sabbath day—besought Pilate that their legs might be broken and that they might be taken away. 9 The soldiers came therefore, and they

broke the legs of the first, and of the other that was crucified with him. But afterwards they came to Jesus and they saw that he was already dead, so they did not break his legs. [10] Instead one of the soldiers with a lance opened his side, and immediately there came out blood and water.

JOHN 19:25–34

O Lord Jesus Christ, who for your infinite love became, for the sake of sinful man, the scorn of men and the outcast of the people, and died for us on the cross to obtain our relief from eternal shame: grant us, we pray, by the merits of thy most sorrowful crucifixion and by the glorious intercession of your most tender Mother, who stood by you at the cross, the spirit of perfect contrition for our sins, and of a holy death; who lives and reigns forever and ever. Amen.

THE GLORIOUS MYSTERIES

THE RESURRECTION

Let us contemplate in this mystery how our Lord Jesus Christ, triumphing gloriously over death, rose again on the third day, to die no more, to suffer no more.

Suggestions for intercession: for faith, confidence when we come to die, those whom we love that have died, the spirit of Christian joy and optimism, the victory of Jesus over our lesser natures.

O glorious Virgin Mary, by the great joy that you received in the resurrection of your only Son, we pray you to obtain from him that our hearts may never go astray after the false joys of this world, but may be ever and wholly employed in the pursuit of the only true and solid joys of heaven. Amen.

— • —

^{1} When the Sabbath was over, Mary Magdalene, Mary the mother of James, and Salome bought sweet spices that they might come and anoint Jesus. ^{2} And very early in the morning, the first day of the week, they came to the sepulchre, the sun being now risen. ^{3} And they said to one another: Who shall roll back the stone for us from the door of the tomb? ^{4} And when they looked, they saw that the stone had already been rolled back though the stone was very large. ^{5} They entered into the sepulchre, and they saw a young man sitting on the right side, clothed with a white robe, and they were astonished. ^{6} The young man said to them: Do not be afraid; you seek Jesus of Nazareth who was crucified. He is risen; he is not here: see the place where they had laid him. ^{7} But go, tell Peter and his disciples that he is going before you into Galilee; there you shall see him, as he told you. ^{8} And going back from the sepulchre, they told all these things to the eleven and to all the rest. ^{9} And it was Mary Magdalene and Joanna and Mary of James and the other women who were with them who told these things to the apostles. And these words seemed to them like foolish stories, and they did not believe them. ^{10} But Peter got up and ran to the sepulchre, and stooping down, he saw the linen cloths laid by themselves and went away wondering in himself at that which had come to pass.

MARK 16:1–7; LUKE 24:9–12

— • —

O Lord Jesus Christ, who sorrowfully descended to the dead and gloriously rose again on the third day: grant to the souls of the faithful departed your eternal light and peace; and to us your servants grace to die each day more and more to ourselves, that we may live wholly unto you; who lives and reigns forever and ever. Amen.

— • —

THE ASCENSION
Let us contemplate in this mystery how our Lord Jesus Christ, forty days after his resurrection, ascended into heaven, watched by his disciples, to their great wonder.

Suggestions for intercession: for faith in the unseen God, the coming of the Holy Spirit, trust in the God whom we cannot see but gives us his grace for every trial, the grace of great desire for heaven.

— • —

O Mother of God, comfort of the afflicted, as your beloved Son, when he ascended into heaven, lifted up his hands and blessed his apostles, so, blessed Mother, lift up your hands to him on our behalf, that we also may experience the effects of his blessing. Amen.

— • —

^{1} The former treatise I wrote, Theophilus, concerned all those things that Jesus began to do and teach until the day when, giving commands by the Holy Spirit to the apostles whom he had chosen, he was taken up. ^{2} To these he had showed himself alive after his passion by many proofs, for forty days appearing to them and speaking of the kingdom of God. ^{3} And eating together with them, he commanded them that they should not depart from Jerusalem, but should wait for the promise of the Father, which he had said they had heard about from his own mouth: 4 For John indeed baptized with water, but you shall be baptized with the Holy Spirit not many days from now. 5 So those who were present asked him: Lord, will you now restore the kingdom to Israel? But he said to them: It is not for you to know the times or moments that the Father has kept in his own power. 6 But you shall receive the power of the Holy Spirit coming upon you 7 and you shall be witnesses to me in Jerusalem, and in all Judea and Samaria, and even to the uttermost parts of the earth. 8 And when he had said these things, while they looked on, he was raised up, and a cloud took him out of their sight. 9 And while they gazed at him going into heaven, behold, two men stood beside them in white garments, who said: Men of Galilee; why do you stand looking up into heaven? This Jesus who is taken up from you into heaven shall come again in the same way as you have seen him go. 10 Then they returned to Jerusalem from the mount that is called Olivet, which is near Jerusalem, about a Sabbath journey.

ACTS 1:1–12

O Lord Jesus Christ, who descended upon earth to be our sacrifice, and ascended into heaven to be our eternal Priest and Advocate: grant us grace that, being detached from all earthly things, we may in heart and mind ascend to where you have already gone before us, who lives and reigns forever and ever. Amen.

THE COMING OF THE HOLY SPIRIT AT PENTECOST

Let us consider in this mystery how our Lord Jesus Christ, being seated at the right hand of God, sent, as he had promised, the Holy Spirit upon his apostles in the form of countless tongues of fire, and how the same apostles were inspired to begin the evangelization of the world.

Suggestions for intercession: for a renewal of the grace of our own confirmations, courage to share the gospel with others, people preparing for confirmation, missionaries, all the gifts of the Holy Spirit—wisdom, understanding, counsel, fortitude, knowledge, piety, and the fear of the Lord.

—— • ——

O sacred Virgin, spouse of the Holy Spirit, we beseech you to obtain that this same most sweet Comforter whom your beloved Son sent down on you and his apostles, causing such great joy, may teach us in this world the true way to salvation and make us to walk in the paths of virtue and good works. Amen.

—— • ——

1 And when the days of Pentecost came around, they were all together in one place. 2 And suddenly there came a sound from heaven, as of a mighty wind coming, and it filled the whole house where they were sitting. 3 And there appeared to them parted tongues as it were of fire, and these sat on every one of them. 4 And they were all filled with the Holy Spirit, and they began to speak with various languages, as the Holy Spirit directed them to speak. 5 Now there were Jews dwelling in Jerusalem, devout men out of every nation under heaven. 6 And when the news had spread, the crowd came together, and were astounded because every one heard them speak in his own tongue. 7 But others, mocking, said: These men are full of new wine. 8 But Peter lifted up his voice and spoke to them. 9 And with many words he exhorted them,

saying: Save yourselves from this perverse generation. Those, therefore, who received his words were baptized, and there were added about three thousand souls that day. [10] And they persevered in the doctrine of the apostles, in their communion, in the breaking of the bread and the prayers.

ACTS 2 (ADAPTED)

—•—

O Lord Jesus Christ, to whom is given all power in heaven and on earth: send down upon us the Holy Spirit the Comforter, that he may guide, support, and purify the souls of your servants and of your whole Church; who lives and reigns forever and ever. Amen.

—•—

THE ASSUMPTION OF OUR BLESSED LADY INTO HEAVEN

Let us contemplate in this mystery how the glorious Virgin, many years after the resurrection of her Son, herself passed body and soul out of this world to join him whom she had longed for, and for whom she lived.

Suggestions for intercession: for faith in the resurrection of the body on the last day, greater devotion to our Lady, devotion to the angels, the grace never to be satisfied with anything less than perfection in the spiritual life.

—•—

O most prudent Virgin, who, entering the heavenly palace filled the holy angels with joy and man with hope, intercede for us, we pray, at the hour of our death, that being delivered from the illusions and temptations of the devil, we may joyfully and securely pass out of this temporal state to enjoy the happiness of eternal life. Amen.

—•—

[1] My soul magnifies the Lord, my spirit rejoices in God who is my Savior, [2] who has looked upon the humility of his handmaiden. [3] Behold, all generations from now will acknowledge me blessed. [4] For the mighty one has done great things for me: Holy is his name! [5] His mercy is from one generation to the next on those who fear him. Mighty is his arm! [6] He has scattered the proud in the imagination of their hearts, [7] and has put down the powerful from their thrones, exalting those of humble degree. [8] The hungry he has filled with good things, [9] but the rich he has dismissed with nothing. [10] Remembering his mercy, he has helped his servant Israel as he promised to our fathers, to Abraham and to his posterity forevermore.

LUKE 1:46–55

O Lord Jesus Christ, who, when the work of her perfection was accomplished, called to yourself the soul of your most holy Mother, and did not suffer her body to see corruption: grant us, we beseech you, the desire of perfection, and daily to purify ourselves more and more from all our faults and imperfections, so that at the hour of death we may be found worthy to pass to the blessed vision of your glory, who lives and reigns forever and ever. Amen.

THE CORONATION OF OUR LADY AS QUEEN OF HEAVEN, AND THE GLORY OF THE SAINTS

Let us contemplate in this mystery how the glorious Virgin Mary was, to the great joy and exaltation of the whole court of heaven, crowned by her Son with the brightest diadem of glory, and how all the saints share with her the reward that awaits the righteous in heaven.

Suggestions for intercession: in honor of the saints, for God to make us among their number, the grace to imitate the virtues of the Blessed Virgin and the saints.

—— • ——

O glorious Queen of all the heavenly citizens, we beseech you to accept this rosary, which as a crown of roses we offer at your feet; and grant, most gracious Lady, that by your intercession our souls may be inflamed with so ardent a desire of seeing you so gloriously crowned, that it may never die in us until we shall be changed from glory into glory, casting down with you our golden crowns before the throne of divine majesty. Amen.

—— • ——

1 Blessed are you, O daughter, by the Lord the most high God, above all women upon the earth, 2 because he has so magnified your name this day that your praise shall not depart out of the lips of men who shall be mindful of the power of the Lord forever, 3 because you have not spared your life by reason of the tribulation of the people, but have prevented our ruin in the presence of our God. 4 And all the people said: So be it, so be it. 5 After this I saw a great multitude that no man could count, of all nations and tribes and peoples and tongues, standing before the throne and in sight of the Lamb, clothed with white robes and with palms in their hands. 6 And they cried out with a loud voice, saying: Salvation to our God, who sits upon the throne, and to the Lamb. 7 And all the angels stood round about the throne, and the elders, and the four living creatures, and they fell down before the throne upon their faces, and adored God saying: Amen. Benediction and glory and wisdom and thanksgiving, honor and power and strength to our God forever and

ever. Amen. ^{8} One of the elders said to me . . . These are those who have come out of the great tribulation and have washed their robes white in the blood of the Lamb. ^{9} Therefore they stand before the throne of God, and they serve him day and night in his temple, and he that sits on the throne shall dwell with them. ^{10} They shall hunger and thirst no more, nor shall the sun strike them, nor any heat. For the Lamb who sits on the throne shall rule them, and shall lead them to the fountains of life, and God shall wipe away all tears from their eyes.

JUDITH 13:18–20; REVELATION 7:9–17

O Lord Jesus Christ, who said, "In my Father's house there are many mansions, I go to prepare a place for you"; grant us, we pray, so to copy in our lives the holy virtues of your blessed Mother, that through her glorious intercession, we may attain the place prepared for us in your kingdom from the foundation of the world, who lives and reigns with God the Father and the Holy Spirit, one God, world without end. Amen.

VARIATIONS ON THE CLASSIC ROSARY

As recommended at Fatima, each decade may conclude with the following prayer, after the Glory be to the Father:

O my Jesus, forgive us our sins, save us from the fires of hell, and lead all souls to heaven, especially those who most need thy mercy.

———•———

Another way to pray the rosary, valuable for those who find their minds wandering, is to interpose a reminder of the current mystery into each Hail Mary.

. . . and blessed is the fruit of thy womb . . .

The Annunciation . . . Jesus, incarnate.
The Visitation . . . Jesus, bringer of joy.
The Nativity . . . Jesus, born in poverty.
The Presentation . . . Jesus, light of the nations.
The Finding . . . Jesus, our teacher.

The Agony . . . Jesus, agonized.
The Scourging . . . Jesus, scourged.
The Crowning . . . Jesus, crowned with thorns.
The Carrying . . . Jesus, who bore his cross.
The Crucifixion . . . Jesus, crucified for our sins.

The Resurrection . . . Jesus, risen from the dead.
The Ascension . . . Jesus, ascended into heaven.
Pentecost . . . Jesus, who sends the Holy Spirit.
The Assumption . . . Jesus, receiving thee into heaven.
The Coronation . . . Jesus, crowning thee.

Holy Mary, mother of God . . .

OTHER TYPES OF ROSARY

THE DIVINE MERCY DEVOTION

One Our Father
One Hail Mary
One Apostles' Creed

—•—

On each single "Our Father" bead:

Eternal Father, I offer you the Body and Blood, Soul and Divinity of your dearly beloved Son, our Lord Jesus Christ, in atonement for our sins and those of the whole world.

—•—

On each "Hail Mary" bead:

For the sake of his sorrowful Passion
have mercy on us and on the whole world.

—•—

At the end of each decade, say the following prayer three times:

Holy God,
Holy Mighty One,
Holy Immortal One,
have mercy on us and on the whole world.

—•—

THE ROSARY OF OUR LADY OF SORROWS

This devotion is a modified form of the rosary focusing on the spiritual martyrdom of Mary, particularly in the passion and death of Jesus. A rosary specially designed for this devotion consists of seven "decades" of seven beads. The rosary is prayed in the ordinary way while meditation focuses on Mary's seven sorrows.

1. Simeon foretells that the sword of sorrow shall pierce the soul of Mary, when Jesus is presented in the temple.
2. Mary and Joseph are forced to flee into Egypt with the infant Jesus, and live there in exile.
3. The child Jesus is lost for three days in Jerusalem and is eventually found in the temple.
4. Mary meets her Son on the way to execution on Calvary.
5. Mary stands under the cross as her Son dies.
6. Mary receives the body of her dead Son into her arms.
7. Mary sees the body of her Son laid in the tomb.

THE ROSARY OF ST. PHILIP NERI

On each bead, say:

Virgin mother of God, pray to Jesus for me.

Or simply say:

Virgin and Mother!

Some people like to think of a different person in need at each invocation.

THE JESUS PRAYER

This prayer is a form of rosary used widely among Byzantine Catholics and Orthodox Christians, though the construction of the rosary beads differs. There is no reason why it cannot be used on ordinary (Western) beads.

On each bead, say:

Lord Jesus Christ, Son of the living God,
have mercy on me, a sinner!

STATIONS OF THE CROSS

The Stations of the Cross is a popular devotion in which participants focus their prayer on pictorial representations of fourteen scenes of Christ's passion. The practice originated in pilgrims' visits to the scenes of the Passion in Jerusalem. The devotion became widely popular in Europe in the Middle Ages among those not able to travel to the Holy Land. In this century, a fifteenth station commemorating the Resurrection is often added, acknowledging that devotion to the Passion is incomplete without it.

A number of prayers and devotions are offered for each of the stations that follow. It is not recommended that all be prayed, but that a selection be made to suit the occasion of the prayers and the time available. At each station, an act of love, such as this one, is usually prayed at some point:

I love thee, Jesus, my love above all things. I repent with my whole heart for having offended thee. Never permit me to separate myself from thee again; grant that I may love thee always, and then do with me as thou wilt.

—— • ——

449

At the High Altar

In the name of the Father, the Son, ✠ and the Holy Spirit. Amen.

A reading from the first letter of St. John

That which we have seen and have heard, we declare to you, that you too may have fellowship with us, and our fellowship may be with the Father and with his Son Jesus Christ. And these things we write to you that you may rejoice, and your joy may be full. And this is the declaration which we have heard from him and now we declare it to you: God is light, and in him is no darkness at all.

If we say that we have fellowship with him, and walk in darkness, we lie, and do not do the truth. But if we walk in the light, as he also is in the light, we have fellowship with one another, and the blood of Jesus Christ cleanses us from all sin.

If we say that we have no sin, we deceive ourselves, and the truth is not in us. If we confess our sins, he is faithful and just, to forgive our sins, and to cleanse us from all iniquity. If we say that we have not sinned, we make him a liar, and his word is not in us. My little children, I write these things to you, that you may not sin. But if anyone does sin, we have an advocate with the Father: Jesus Christ the just. He is the propitiation for our sins; and not for ours only, but also for those of the whole world.

1 John 1:3–2:2

Heavenly Father, who did not spare your only Son, but freely gave him up for the life of the world, be present with us here as we prepare to remember your Son's terrible sufferings, undergone for our salvation. Do not let such labor go in vain, but touch our hearts, that we may be moved to sincere repentance for those sins that made our redeemer undergo such a sorrowful sacrifice.

—— • ——

O Jesus, our adorable Savior, behold us prostrate at thy feet, imploring thy mercy for ourselves and for the souls of all the faithful departed. Vouchsafe to apply to us the infinite merits of thy Passion, on which we are about to meditate. Grant that while we trace this path of sighs and tears, our hearts may be so touched with contrition and repentance that we may be ready to embrace with joy all the crosses and sufferings and humiliations of this our life and pilgrimage.

CHALLONER

—— • ——

O Jesus Christ, my Lord, with what great love didst thou pass over the painful road which led thee to death; and I, how often have I abandoned thee! But now I love thee with my whole soul, and because I love thee, I am sincerely sorry for having offended thee. My Jesus, pardon me, and permit me to accompany thee in this journey. Thou art going to die for love of me, and it is my wish also, O my dearest Redeemer, to die for love of thee. O yes, my Jesus, in thy love I wish to live; in thy love I wish to die.

ST. ALPHONSUS LIGUORI

—— • ——

THE FIRST STATION
Jesus is condemned to death

CALL: We adore thee, O Christ,
and we bless thee,

RESPONSE: Because by thy holy cross thou
hast redeemed the world.

Consider how Jesus, after having been scourged and crowned with thorns, was unjustly condemned by Pilate to die on the cross.

———•———

A reading from the Gospel according to St. Matthew
Pilate saw that he was achieving nothing, but rather that a riot was breaking out, so taking water, he washed his hands before the people, saying: "I am innocent of the blood of this just man: you do what you wish." And all the people answered, saying: "His blood be upon us and upon our

children." Then he released Barabbas to them, and having scourged Jesus, gave him to them to be crucified.

MATTHEW 27:24–26

Leaving the house of Caiaphas, and dragged before Pilate and Herod, mocked, beaten, and spat upon, his back torn with scourges, his head crowned with thorns, Jesus, who on the last day will judge the world, is himself condemned by unjust judges to a death of ignominy and torture.

Jesus is condemned to death. His death-warrant is signed, and who signed it but I, when I committed my first mortal sins? My first mortal sins, when I fell away from the state of grace into which thou didst place me by baptism; these it was that were thy death-warrant, O Lord. The Innocent suffered for the guilty. Those sins of mine were the voices which cried out, "let him be crucified." That willingness and delight of heart with which I committed them was the consent which Pilate gave to this clamorous multitude. And the hardness of heart which followed upon them, my disgust, my despair, my proud impatience, my obstinate resolve to sin on, the love of sin which took possession of me—what were these contrary and impetuous feelings but the blows and the blasphemies with which the fierce soldiers and the populace received thee, thus carrying out the sentence which Pilate had pronounced?

J. H. NEWMAN

Iudas, mercator pessimus	Judas, wretched trader,
osculo petiit Dominum:	betrayed the Lord with
ille ut agnus innocens non	a kiss. The Lord, as an
negavit Iudae osculum:	innocent lamb, would
Denariorum numero	not refuse Judas' kiss.

Christum Iudaeis tradidit.	He betrayed Christ for a few miserable coins.
CALL: Melius illi erat, si natus non fuisset. Denariorum numero Christum Iudaeis tradidit.	*CALL:* Would that he had never been born! He betrayed Christ for a few miserable coins.

TENEBRAE RESPONSE

— • —

Behold our Lord and our God, mocked, scourged, crowned with thorns, and condemned to death for the sins that we have committed!

Holy God!
Holy, mighty one!
Holy, immortal one!
Have mercy on us!

— • —

It was for us that thou didst suffer, O blessed Jesus; it was for our sins thou wast condemned to die. Oh, grant that we may detest them from the bottom of our hearts, and by this repentance obtain thy mercy and pardon.

CHALLONER

— • —

Stabat Mater dolorosa Iuxta crucem lacrymosa Dum pendebat Filius.	At the cross her station keeping Stood the mournful Mother weeping Close to Jesus to the last.

— • —

THE SECOND STATION
Jesus is made to bear his cross

CALL: We adore thee, O Christ,
and we bless thee,
RESPONSE: Because by thy holy cross thou
hast redeemed the world.

Consider how Jesus, in making this journey with the cross on his shoulders, thought of us and offered for us to his Father the death he was about to undergo.

———•———

A reading from the Gospel according to St. Matthew
Then the soldiers of the governor, taking Jesus into the hall, gathered around him, stripped him, dressed him in a scarlet cloak, plaited a crown out of thorns and placed it on his head, with a reed in his right hand. They knelt before him and mocked him, saying: "Hail, King of the Jews." And spitting upon him, they took the reed and struck him

about the head with it. And after they had mocked him, they took off the cloak from him, and made him put on his own garments, and led him away to crucify him.

MATTHEW 27:27–31

A strong, and therefore heavy Cross, for it is strong enough to bear him on it when he arrives at Calvary, is placed upon his torn shoulders. He receives it gently and meekly, nay, with gladness of heart, for it is to be the salvation of mankind.

True; but recollect, that heavy Cross is the weight of our sins. As it fell upon his neck and shoulders, it came down with a shock. Alas! what a sudden, heavy weight have I laid upon thee, O Jesus. And, though in the calm and clear foresight of thy mind—for thou seest all things— thou wast fully prepared for it, yet thy feeble frame tottered under it when it dropped down upon thee. Ah! how great a misery is it that I have lifted up my hand against my God. How could I ever fancy he would forgive me, unless he had himself told us that he underwent his bitter passion in order that he might forgive us. I acknowledge, O Jesus, in the anguish and agony of my heart, that it was my sins that struck thee on the face, that bruised thy sacred arms, that tore thy flesh with iron rods, that nailed thee to the Cross, and let thee slowly die upon it.

J. H. NEWMAN

Tamquam ad latronem existis cum gladiis et fustibus comprehendere me: Cotidie apud vos eram in templo docens et non	As if I were a criminal, you surround me with swords and clubs. Day by day I taught in the temple and you never laid hands on me:

me tenuistis: et ecce
flagellatum ducitis ad
crucifigendum.

CALL: Cumque iniecissent
manus in Iesum, et
tenuissent eum, dixit ad
eos: Cotidie apud vos eram
in templo docens et non
me tenuistis: et ecce
flagellatum ducitis ad
crucifigendum.

yet now you scourge me
and lead me out to my
crucifixion.

CALL: And when they laid
hands on Jesus and held
him, he said to them:
Day by day I taught in the
temple and you never laid
hands on me: yet now you
scourge me and lead me
out to my crucifixion.

———•———

Dear Lord, the thought that you have commanded me to
take up my cross and follow in your footsteps frightens me
when I consider just where those footsteps led. Give me
courage, I beg, and a cheerful spirit just when the road
seems darkest.

———•———

Behold our Lord and our God, led willingly to a cruel
death for the sins that we have committed!

Holy God!
Holy, mighty one!
Holy, immortal one!
Have mercy on us!

———•———

O Jesus, grant us, by virtue of thy cross, to embrace with
meekness and cheerful submission the difficulties of our
state, and to be ever ready to take up our cross and follow
thee.

CHALLONER

———•———

Cuius animam gementem	Through her heart his sorrow sharing
Contristatam et dolentem	All his bitter anguish bearing
Pertransivit gladius.	Now at length the sword had passed.

THE THIRD STATION
Jesus falls the first time under his cross

CALL:	We adore thee, O Christ, and we bless thee,
RESPONSE:	Because by thy holy cross thou hast redeemed the world.

Consider this first fall of Jesus under his cross. His flesh was torn by the scourges, his head was crowned with thorns, and he had lost a great quantity of blood. He was so weakened he could scarcely walk, yet he had to carry this great load upon his shoulders. The soldiers struck him rudely, and he fell several times.

—•—

A reading from the prophet Isaiah

Surely it is our sins that he has carried: our sorrows that he has borne, and we have thought of him as if he were a leper, as though he had been struck by God and afflicted.

But he was wounded for our iniquities, he was bruised for our sins: the chastisement of our peace was upon him, and by his bruises we are healed. All we like sheep have gone astray, every one has turned aside into his own way; and the Lord has laid on him the iniquity of us all. He was offered because it was his own will, and he did not even open his mouth; he was led as a sheep to the slaughter and as a lamb to the shearer: not even opening his mouth.

ISAIAH 53:4–7

Satan fell from heaven in the beginning; by the just sentence of his Creator he fell, against whom he had rebelled. And when he had succeeded in gaining man to join him in his rebellion, and his Maker came to save him, then his brief hour of triumph came, and he made the most of it. When the Holiest had taken flesh, and was in his power, then in his revenge and malice he determined, as he himself had been struck down by the almighty arm, to strike in turn a heavy blow at him who struck him. Therefore it was that Jesus fell down so suddenly.

O dear Lord, by this thy first fall raise us all out of sin, who have so miserably fallen under its power.

J. H. NEWMAN

Animam meam dilectam tradidi in manus iniquorum, et facta est mihi hereditas mea sicut leo in silva: dedit contra me voces adversarius, dicens: Congregamini, et properate ad devorandum	The soul that I loved I betrayed into the hands of the wicked, and my inheritance has turned on me like a lion in the jungle; my adversary cries against me: "Let us band together and destroy him"; they have

illum: posuerunt me in
deserto solitudinis, et luxit
super me omnis terra:
Quia non est inventus
qui me agnosceret, et
faceret bene.

abandoned me as if in a
lonely desert, and the whole
world mourns. And there is
not one who recognizes me,
or who will show me
kindness.

CALL: Insurrexerunt in me
viri absque misericordia,
et non pepercerunt
animae meae: Quia non
est inventus qui me
agnosceret, et faceret bene.

CALL: Merciless men have
risen against me, they will
not spare me: And there is
not one who recognizes me,
or who will show me
kindness.

———•———

Behold our Lord and our God, crushed to the ground for
the sins that we have committed!

Holy God!
Holy, mighty one!
Holy, immortal one!
Have mercy on us!

———•———

O Jesus, who for our sins didst bear the heavy burden of
the cross, and fall under its weight, may the thoughts of thy
sufferings make us watchful over ourselves, and save us
from any grievous fall into sin.

CHALLONER

———•———

O quam tristis et afflicta
Fuit illa benedicta
Mater Unigeniti!

Oh, how sad and sore distressed
Was that Mother highly blessed,
Of the sole-begotten One!

———•———

THE FOURTH STATION
Jesus meets his afflicted mother

CALL: We adore thee, O Christ,
and we bless thee,
RESPONSE: Because by thy holy cross thou
hast redeemed the world.

Consider the meeting of the Son and the mother that took place on this journey. Their looks became like so many arrows, to wound those hearts that loved each other so tenderly.

A reading from the Gospel according to St. Luke
And Simeon . . . said to Mary: Behold, this child is set for the fall and for the resurrection of many in Israel, and for

a sign that shall be contradicted; and a sword shall pierce your own soul, that out of many hearts thoughts may be revealed.

LUKE 2:34–35

A reading from the book of Lamentations
To what can I compare you, or to what can I liken you, daughter of Jerusalem? How am I to understand you, that I may comfort you, O Virgin daughter of Zion? For great as the sea is your sorrow: who, then, can heal you?

LAMENTATIONS 2:13

There is no part of the history of Jesus but Mary has her part in it. There are those who profess to be his servants, who think that her work was ended when she bore him, and after that she had nothing to do but disappear and be forgotten. But we, O Lord, thy children of the Catholic Church, do not think so of thy Mother. She brought the tender infant into the temple, she lifted him up in her arms when the wise men came to adore him. She fled with him to Egypt, she took him up to Jerusalem when he was twelve years old. He lived with her at Nazareth for thirty years. She was with him at the marriage-feast. Even when he had left her to preach, she hovered about him. And now she shows herself as he toils along the Sacred Way with his Cross on his shoulders.

Sweet Mother, let us ever think of thee when we think of Jesus; and when we pray to him, ever aid us by thy powerful intercession.

J. H. NEWMAN

Caligaverunt oculi mei a fletu meo: quia elongatus est a me, qui consolabatur me: Videte, omnes populi, Si est dolor similis sicu dolor meus.	My eyes are worn out with weeping: those who could console me are far away: Look, everybody: Is there any sorrow like to my sorrow?
CALL: O vos omnes, qui transitis per viam, attendite, et videte. Si est dolor similis sicut dolor meus.	*CALL:* O all you passersby: look, then, and see: Is there any sorrow like to my sorrow?

Behold our Lord and our God suffering, and see the sorrow that our sins have given his holy mother!

Holy God!
Holy, mighty one!
Holy, immortal one!
Have mercy on us!

O Jesus, by the compassion which thou didst feel for thy Mother, have compassion on us, and give us a share in her intercession. O Mary, most afflicted Mother! intercede for us, that, through the sufferings of thy Son, we may be delivered from the wrath to come.

CHALLONER

Quae moerebat et dolebat Pia Mater, dum videbat Nati poenas inclyti.	Christ above in torment hangs; She beneath beholds the pangs Of her dying glorious Son.

THE FIFTH STATION
Simon of Cyrene helps Jesus to carry his cross

CALL: We adore thee, O Christ,
             and we bless thee,
RESPONSE: Because by thy holy cross thou
             hast redeemed the world.

Consider how his executioners, seeing that at each step Jesus was on the point of expiring, and fearing that he would die on the way, whereas they wished him to die the ignominious death of the cross, constrained Simon the Cyrenian to carry the cross behind our Lord.

—•—

A reading from the Gospel according to St. Mark
And they forced one Simon, a Cyrenian, who passed by, coming in from the country, the father of Alexander and Rufus, to take up his cross.

MARK 15:21

—•—

A reading from the Gospel according to St. Luke

Jesus said to all: If anyone will come after me, let him deny himself, and take up his cross daily, and follow me. For whoever wishes to save his life shall lose it, whereas he that loses his life for my sake shall save it. How is it an advantage for a man to gain the whole world and yet lose himself: throw himself away?

LUKE 9:23–25

Jesus could bear his cross alone, did he so will; but he permits Simon to help him, in order to remind us that we must take part in his sufferings, and have a fellowship in his work. His merit is infinite, yet he condescends to let his people add their merit to it. The sanctity of the Blessed Virgin, the blood of the martyrs, the prayers and penances of the saints, the good deeds of all the faithful take part in that work which, nevertheless, is perfect without them. He saves us by his blood, but it is through and with ourselves that he saves us. Dear Lord, teach us to suffer with thee, make it pleasant to us to suffer for thy sake, and sanctify all our sufferings by the merits of thy own.

J. H. NEWMAN

Sicut ovis ad occisionem ductus est, et dum male tracteretur, non aperuit os suum: traditus est ad mortem, Ut vivificaret populum suum.	He was led as a lamb before his killers, and when he was badly treated he did not open his mouth: he was betrayed unto death, that he might give life to his people.
CALL: Tradidit in mortem animam suam, et inter	*CALL:* He was betrayed unto death, and reputed among

sceleratos reputatus est. Ut vivificaret populum suum.	the wicked, that he might give life to his people.

———•———

Behold our Lord and our God, exhausted and able no more to carry his cross, and all for the sins that we have committed!

Holy God!
Holy, mighty one!
Holy, immortal one!
Have mercy on us!

———•———

O Lord Jesus, may it be our privilege also to bear thy cross; may we glory in nothing else. By it may the world be crucified unto us, and we unto the world; may we never shrink from sufferings, but rather rejoice if we may be counted worthy to suffer for thy name's sake.

CHALLONER

———•———

Quis est homo qui non fleret, Matrem Christi si videret In tanto supplicio?	Is there one who would not weep, Whelmed in miseries so deep Christ's dear Mother to behold?

———•———

THE SIXTH STATION
Veronica wipes the face of Jesus

CALL: We adore thee, O Christ,
and we bless thee,

RESPONSE: Because by thy holy cross thou
hast redeemed the world.

Consider how the holy woman named Veronica, seeing Jesus so ill-used, and his face bathed in sweat and blood, presented him with a towel, with which he wiped his adorable face, leaving on it the impression of his holy countenance.

———•———

A reading from the prophet Isaiah
There is no beauty in him, nor comeliness; we have seen him, and there was no sightliness, that we should desire him: despised, and the most abject of men, a man of sorrows, and acquainted with grief, and his look was as if it were hidden away and despised, so we esteemed him

worthless. But surely it is our infirmities that he has borne; our sorrows that he has carried, and we have thought of him as we would a leper, and as one struck by God and afflicted. But it was for our iniquities that he was wounded, and it was for our sins that he was bruised, and by his bruises we are healed.

ISAIAH 53:2–5

A reading from the second letter of St. Paul to the Corinthians But we all, beholding the glory of the Lord with open face, are transformed into the same image from glory to glory as by the Spirit of the Lord.

2 CORINTHIANS 3:18

My most beloved Jesus! Thy face was beautiful before, but in this journey it has lost all its beauty, and wounds and blood have disfigured it. Alas! my soul also was once beautiful, when it received thy grace in baptism; but I have disfigured it since by my sins. Thou alone, my Redeemer, canst restore it to its former beauty. Do this by thy passion, O Jesus.

ST. ALPHONSUS LIGUORI

Tradiderunt me in manus impiorum, et inter iniquos proiecerunt me, et non pepercerunt animae meae: congregati sunt adversum me fortes: Et icut gigantes steterunt giants contra me.

They betrayed me into the hands of the unholy, and cast me down among the wicked: they would not even spare my soul: I am surrounded by violent men who seek to harm me: like giants they threaten me.

CALL: Alieni insurrexerunt   *CALL:* Strange men have
adversum me, et fortes   risen against me, and
quaesierunt animam meam.   the violent seek to take
Et sicut gigantes steterunt   my life: like giants they
contra me.   threaten me.

——— • ———

Behold the face of the Lord, wounded and made repulsive
for the sins that we have committed!

Holy God!
Holy, mighty one!
Holy, immortal one!
Have mercy on us!

——— • ———

O sacred Head, surrounded
By crown of piercing thorn!
O bleeding head, so wounded,
Reviled, and put to scorn!
Death's pallid hue comes o'er thee,
The glow of life decays;
Yet angel hosts adore thee,
And tremble as they gaze.

——— • ———

O my Jesus, look upon us with mercy; turn your face toward each of us as you turned to Veronica, not that we may
see your face with our earthly eyes, for surely we cannot
deserve this privilege; but turn toward our hearts, we pray,
so that keeping you in our remembrance, we may forever
draw from you, the source of power, strength for our daily
battles. Amen.

POPE PIUS IX

——— • ———

Quis non posset contristari,	Can the human heart refrain
Christi Matrem	From partaking in her pain
contemplari	In that Mother's pain
Dolentem cum Filio?	untold?

THE SEVENTH STATION
Jesus falls the second time

CALL: We adore thee, O Christ,
and we bless thee,

RESPONSE: Because by thy holy cross thou
hast redeemed the world.

Consider the second fall of Jesus under the cross, a fall that renews the pain of his head and members.

———•———

A reading from the prophet Isaiah

For the wickedness of my people have I struck him; he has done no iniquity, neither was there any deceit in his mouth. And the Lord was pleased to crush him in weakness.

Because his soul has labored, he shall see and be filled: by his knowledge shall this my servant justify many, and he shall bear their iniquities. Therefore I will distribute to him whole armies, and he shall divide the spoils of the strong, because he handed over his soul to death, and was reputed with the wicked, and he has borne the sins of many, and he has prayed for transgressors.

ISAIAH 53:9–12 (ADAPTED)

What streams of precious blood poured forth from the veins of our Blessed Lord when laden with the heavy cross on the sad way to Calvary! The very streets and ways of Jerusalem, through which he passed, were watered with it. This he did for the scandals, literally, the stumbling blocks, which his own followers had laid in the path of others by their own bad example, their infidelities. How many people have I led astray by my lukewarmness, my thoughtlessness, my lack of devotion? My God, may I henceforth make smooth your path before you into people's hearts by my fidelity.

Lord God, so awful are the crimes of the world that even after receiving supernatural help and Simon's assistance, you fell again because of the weight of sin. Dear Lord, my falls will be for quite a different reason—where you did fall from weakness of the body, my failures are from weakness of the flesh; but whether through laziness or malice, I pray that your example may encourage me to rise. Lord, I mean to go on; I seem to have shaken off the cross as being quite beyond my strength, but, Lord, I want to take it up again and go ahead with you.

DOM HUBERT VAN ZELLER

Omnes amici mei
dereliquerunt me, et
praevaluerunt insidiantes
mihi: tradidit me quam
diligebam: Et terribilibus
oculis plaga crudeli
percutientes, aceto
potabant me.

All my friends abandoned
me, and those who laid a
snare for me have triumphed
over me: the one whom I
loved has betrayed me: And
glaring at me, wounding me
with cruel blows, they gave
me vinegar to drink.

CALL: Inter iniquos
proiecerunt me, et non
pepercerunt animae meae.
Et terribilibus oculis plaga
crudeli percutientes, aceto
potabant me.

CALL: They cast me down
among the wicked, and they
did not spare my soul. And
glaring at me, wounding me
with cruel blows, they gave
me vinegar to drink.

Behold our Lord and our God, crushed to the ground a
second time for the sins that we have committed!

Holy God!
Holy, mighty one!
Holy, immortal one!
Have mercy on us!

O Jesus! falling again under the burden of our sins, and of
thy sufferings for our sins, how often have we grieved thee
by our repeated falls into sin! Oh, may we rather die than
ever offend thee again!

CHALLONER

Pro peccatis suae gentis
Vidit Iesum in tormentis
Et flagellis subditum

Bruised, derided, cursed, defiled,
She beheld her tender Child
All with bloody scourges rent.

THE EIGHTH STATION
Jesus speaks to the daughters of Jerusalem

CALL: We adore thee, O Christ,
and we bless thee,

RESPONSE: Because by thy holy cross thou
hast redeemed the world.

Consider how these women wept with compassion at seeing Jesus in such a pitiable state, streaming with blood as he walked along. "My children," said he, "weep not for me, but for yourselves and for your children."

A reading from the Gospel according to St. Luke

There followed Jesus a great multitude of people, and women who wailed and lamented for him. But Jesus, turning to them, said: "Daughters of Jerusalem, do not weep over me, but weep for yourselves and for your children; for behold, the days shall come when they will say: Blessed are the barren, and the wombs that have not borne, and the breasts that have not given suck. Then they shall begin to say to the mountains: Fall upon us, and to the hills: Cover us."

LUKE 23:27–30

A reading from the book of Lamentations
My eyes have failed with weeping, my soul is in torment, my heart is poured out upon the earth for the destruction of the daughter of my people, when the children and the infants faint away in the streets of the city.

LAMENTATIONS 2:11

Ever since the prophecy of old time, that the Savior of man was to be born of a woman of the stock of Abraham, the Jewish women had desired to bear him. Yet, now that he was really come, how different, as the Gospel tells us, was the event from what they had expected. He said to them "that the days were coming when they should say Blessed are the barren, and the wombs that have not borne, and the breasts which have not given suck."

Ah, Lord, we know not what is good for us, and what is bad. We cannot foretell the future, nor do we know when thou comest to visit us, in what form thou wilt come. And therefore we leave it all to thee. Do thou thy good pleasure to us and in us. Let us ever look at thee, and do thou look upon us, and give us the grace of thy bitter cross and Passion, and console us in thy own way and at thy own time.

J. H. NEWMAN

Plange quasi virgo,
plebs mea: ululate,
pastores, in cinere et
cilicio, Quia venit dies
Domini magna, et
amara valde.

CALL: Accingite vos,
sacerdotes, et plangite
ministri altaris,
aspergite vos cinere.
Quia venit dies
Domini magna,
et amara valde.

Cry like a virgin, my people:
grieve, you shepherds, in
sackcloth and ashes, For the
great day of the Lord is
coming, and it will be very
bitter.

CALL: Gird yourselves up,
you priests, and weep,
you that serve at the altar;
sprinkle yourselves with ashes.
For the great day of
the Lord is coming, and
it will be very bitter.

— • —

Behold our Lord and our God, suffering bitterly for the
sins that we have committed, yet placing his children first!

Holy God!
Holy, mighty one!
Holy, immortal one!
Have mercy on us!

— • —

O Lord Jesus, we mourn, and we will mourn both for thee
and for ourselves; for thy suffering, and for our sins which
caused them. Oh, teach us so to mourn that we may be
comforted, and escape those dreadful judgments prepared
for all who reject or neglect thee in this life.

CHALLONER

— • —

Vidit suum dulcem	For the sins of his own
Natum	nation,
Moriendo desolatum,	Saw him hang in desolation
Dum emisit spiritum.	Till his spirit forth he sent.

THE NINTH STATION
Jesus falls the third time

CALL: We adore thee, O Christ,
and we bless thee,

RESPONSE: Because by thy holy cross thou
hast redeemed the world.

Consider the third fall of Jesus Christ. His weakness was extreme, and the cruelty of his executioners excessive, who tried to hasten his steps when he could scarcely move.

———•———

A reading from the book of Psalms
I lie fallen to the pavement: give me life according to your word. I have declared my ways, and you have heard me: teach me your justifications, and I will contemplate your wondrous works. My soul lies leaden through heaviness: give me strength according to your word.

PSALM 119:25–28

———•———

Jesus had now arrived almost at the summit of Calvary, but before he reached the spot where he was to be crucified, his strength again fails him, and he falls the third time, to be again dragged up and goaded onward by the brutal soldiers.

CHALLONER

My dearest Jesus: how often have I, too, fallen again and again. How often have I thought that I could never arise and carry on. And here I see before me a reminder that in the greatest extremes, you persevered, urged on by your desire to let the will of your heavenly Father be done. Give me, dearest Lord, some share of this same perseverance: to labor on despite the wounds, to toil and not to seek for rest until I, too, have done the will of him who is my Father, thanks to your heroic sacrifice.

Dixerunt impii apud se, non recte cogitantes: Circum-veniamus iustum, quoniam contrarius est operibus nostris: promittit se scientiam Dei habere, Filium Dei se nominat, et gloriatur patrem se habere Deum: Videamus si sermones illius veri sunt: et si est vere Filius Dei, liberet eum de manibus nostris: mortis turpissima condemnemus eum.

The wicked say among themselves, not thinking rightly: Let us surround the just man, for he is opposed to what we want to do: he claims to have knowledge of God. He calls himself the Son of God, and glories in pretending that he has God for his Father: Let us see if his words are true, for if he truly is the Son of God, God will free him from our hands: we will condemn him to a most horrible death.

CALL: Tamquam nugaces aestimati sumus ab illo, et abstinet se a viis nostris tamquam ab immunditiis: et praefert novissima iustorum. Videamus si sermones illius veri sunt: et si est vere Filius Dei, liberet eum de manibus nostris: mortis turpissima condemnemus eum.

CALL: He reckons us as worthless, and keeps away from us as though we were unclean, and behaves as if the final end of the just were happy. Let us see if his words are true, for if he truly is the Son of God, God will free him from our hands: we will condemn him to a most horrible death.

———•———

Lord and our God, crushed to the ground yet a third time for the sins that we have committed!

Holy God!
Holy, mighty one!
Holy, immortal one!
Have mercy on us!

———•———

O Lord Jesus, we entreat thee, by the merits of this thy third most painful fall, to pardon our frequent relapses and our long continuance in sin; and may the thought of these thy sufferings make us to hate our sins more and more.

CHALLONER

———•———

Eia Mater,
 fons amoris,
Me sentire vim doloris
Fac, ut tecum
 lugeam

O thou Mother!
 fount of love!
Touch my spirit from above,
Make my heart with
 thine accord.

———•———

THE TENTH STATION
Jesus is stripped of his garments

CALL: We adore thee, O Christ,
and we bless thee,

RESPONSE: Because by thy holy cross thou
hast redeemed the world.

Consider the violence with which Jesus was stripped by his executioners. His inner garments adhered to his torn flesh and were dragged off so roughly that the skin came with them. Thus your compassionate Savior was cruelly treated.

———•———

A reading from the Gospel according to St. Matthew
And they came to the place that is called Golgotha, which is the place of Calvary. And they gave him wine to drink mingled with gall. And when he had tasted, he would not drink. And after they had crucified him, they divided his

garments, casting lots, that what the prophet had spoken might be fulfilled: They divided my garments among them, and upon my vesture they cast lots. And they sat and watched him.

MATTHEW 27:33–36

Lord, I see in this Station the complete offering of yourself. I see this offering as an invitation to me: "Give me yourself," you say, "not only what you have, but what you are." Lord God, I am nearing Calvary with you: teach me to strip myself of all that is not of God, until at last I stand beside your cross offered entirely to you. Only in this way can I be worthy of the final sacrifice of my own life to you.

DOM HUBERT VAN ZELLER

Jesus would give up everything of this world before he left it. He exercised the most perfect poverty. Even when he left the holy house of Nazareth and went out to preach, he had nowhere to lay his head. He lived on the poorest food, and on what was given to him by those who loved and served him. And therefore he chose a death in which not even his clothes were left to him. He parted with what seemed most necessary, and even a part of him, by the law of human nature since the fall.

Grant us in like manner, O dear Lord, to care nothing for anything on earth, and to bear the loss of all things, and to endure even shame, reproach, contempt and mockery, rather than that you shall be ashamed of us at the last day.

J. H. NEWMAN

Ierusalem, surge, et exue te vestibus iucunditatis: induere cinere et cilicio, Quia in te occisus est Salvator Israel.	Jerusalem, arise, and cast off your garments of joy: put on sackcloth and ashes, For in your midst has been killed the Savior of Israel.
CALL: Deduc quasi torrentem lacrimas per diem et noctem, et non taceat pupilla oculi tui. Quia in te occisus est Salvator Israel.	*CALL:* Let your tears run down by day and night, and give your eyes no rest, For in your midst has been killed the Savior of Israel.

— • —

Behold our Lord and our God, publicly stripped naked and humiliated for the sins that we have committed!

Holy God!
Holy, mighty one!
Holy, immortal one!
Have mercy on us!

— • —

O Lord Jesus, thou didst endure this shame for our most shameful deeds. Strip us, we beseech thee, of all false shame, conceit, and pride, and make us so to humble ourselves voluntarily in this life, that we may escape everlasting ignominy in the world to come.

CHALLONER

— • —

Fac ut ardeat cor meum	Make me feel as thou hast felt,

In amando Christum
  Deum
Ut sibi
  complaceam.

Make my soul to glow
  and melt
With the love of Christ
  my Lord.

THE ELEVENTH STATION
Jesus is nailed to the cross

CALL: We adore thee, O Christ,
and we bless thee,

RESPONSE: Because by thy holy cross thou
hast redeemed the world.

Consider how Jesus, having been placed upon the cross, extended his hands and offered to his eternal Father the sacrifice of his life for our salvation. Those barbarians fastened him with nails and then, securing the cross, allowed him to die with anguish on that infamous gibbet.

—·—

A reading from the Gospel according to St. Mark
It was the third hour when they crucified him. And the inscription of his crime was written: "The King of the

Jews." With him they crucified two thieves, one on his right hand and the other on his left. Thus the Scripture was fulfilled that says: And with the wicked he was reputed. And those who passed by blasphemed at him, saying: Ha! It was you that was going to destroy the temple in three days and build it up again! Save yourself and come down from the cross, then! In the same manner, the chief priests and scribes also mocked him to each other: He saved others, but he cannot save himself.

MARK 15:25–31

O Christ Jesus, I adore you, because you were lifted up from the earth in order to draw all things to yourself. For with your arms outstretched on the cross, I see you as though you were reaching out to embrace us, and I hear you cry: Come to me, all you who labor and are burdened and I will receive and refresh you. O Lord, if I am too sluggish in coming to you, draw me, O Jesus, with the cords of your love which you have shown in being willingly nailed to a cross. Let it be my supreme and only delight to know and seek Jesus, and him crucified. Far be it from me to glory, save in the cross of my Lord Jesus Christ.

O eternal Father, behold, this is your beloved Son in whom you are well pleased. Look upon the face of your anointed one, and turn away your face from my sins, for which your only-begotten Son humbled himself, being made obedient even to the death of the cross. Behold: he is our advocate with you, and the propitiation for our sins, for he has himself borne our sins in his body on the tree, and by his stripes we are healed. The voice of the blood of your Son cries to you from the earth, not for vengeance, but for pardon. Let his passion and death be to us a remedy for and remission of our sins, we beg. Let the pains and wounds of his body become medicine to heal our souls' infirmity.

— • —

Tenebrae factae sunt, dum crucifixissent Jesum Judaei, et circa horam nonam exclamavit Jesus voce magna: Deus meus, ut quid me derelequisti? Et inclinato capite, emisit spiritum.	And there was darkness when the Jews crucified Jesus, and around the ninth hour, Jesus cried out with a loud voice: My God, why have you deserted me? And with bowed head, he gave up his spirit.
CALL: Exclamans Jesus voce magna, ait: Pater, in manus tuas commendo spiritum meum. Et inclinato capite, emisit spiritum.	CALL: Jesus cried out with a loud voice: Father, into your hands I commend my spirit. And with bowed head, he gave up his spirit.

— • —

Behold our Lord and our God, cruelly nailed to a cross for the sins that we have committed!

Holy God!
Holy, mighty one!
Holy, immortal one!
Have mercy on us!

— • —

O Jesus, nailed to the cross, fasten our hearts there also, that they may be united to thee until death shall strike us with its fatal blow, and with our last breath we shall have yielded up our souls to thee.

CHALLONER

— • —

Sancta Mater,	Holy Mother,
istud agas,	pierce me through;
Crucifixi	In my heart each
fige plagas	wound renew,
Cordi meo valide.	Of my Savior crucified.

THE TWELFTH STATION

Jesus dies upon the cross for our salvation

CALL: We adore thee, O Christ,
and we bless thee,

RESPONSE: Because by thy holy cross thou
hast redeemed the world.

Consider how Jesus, after three hours' agony on the cross, being consumed with anguish, abandoned himself to the weight of his body, bowed his head, and died.

———•———

A reading from the Gospel according to St. Mark
And when the sixth hour came, there was darkness over the whole earth until the ninth hour. And at the ninth hour, Jesus cried out with a loud voice, saying Eloi, Eloi,

lama sabacthani? Which is, interpreted: My God, my God, why have you forsaken me? Some of the bystanders, hearing this, said: Listen: he is calling on Elijah. One ran and filled a sponge with vinegar, and putting it on a reed, gave it to him to drink, saying: let us see if Elijah will come to take him down. But Jesus, having cried out with a loud voice, gave up the spirit. And the veil of the temple was torn in two, from top to bottom. The centurion who stood beside him, seeing that having cried out in this manner he had given up the spirit, said: Indeed this man was the Son of God.

MARK 15:33–39

— • —

Consummatum est. It is completed: it has come to a full end. The mystery of God's love toward us is accomplished. The price is paid, and we are redeemed. The eternal Father determined not to pardon us without a price, in order to show especial favor. He condescended to make us valuable to him, as we set a price for what we buy. He might have saved us without a price—by the mere *fiat* of his will. But to show his love for us he took a price which, if there was to be a price set upon us at all, if there was any price at all to be taken for the guilt of our sins, could be nothing short of the death of his Son in our nature.

O my God and Father: you have valued us so much as to pay the highest of all possible prices for our sinful souls—help us to love and choose you above all things as the one necessary and one only good.

J. H. NEWMAN

— • —

Ecce quomodo moritur iustus, et nemo percipit

Behold how the righteous dies, and nobody notices:

corde: et viri iusti
tolluntur, et nemo
considerat; a facie
iniquitatis sublatus est
iustus: Et erit in pace
memoria eius.

the just man is taken
away, and nobody cares:
the righteous is taken
away by iniquity and
his memory will be
in peace.

CALL: Tamquam agnus
coram tondente se
obmutuit, et non aperuit
os suum: de angustia, et
de iudicio sublatus est.
Et erit in pace
memoria eius.

CALL: Like a lamb before
its shearers he was silent,
and he did not open his
mouth: in violence and by
force of law was he taken
and his memory will be
in peace.

———•———

Behold our Lord and our God, willingly butchered in our
place for the sins that we have committed!

Holy God!
Holy, mighty one!
Holy, immortal one!
Have mercy on us!

———•———

O Jesus, we devoutly embrace that honored cross where
thou didst love us even unto death. In that death we place
all our confidence. Henceforth let us live only for thee;
and in dying for thee let us die loving thee, and in thy
sacred arms.

CHALLONER

———•———

Tui nati vulnerati
Tam dignati pro me pati
Poenas mecum divide.

Let me share with thee his pain
Who for all my sins was slain
Who for me in torments died.

———•———

THE THIRTEENTH STATION
Jesus is taken down from the cross

CALL: We adore thee, O Christ,
         and we bless thee,
RESPONSE: Because by thy holy cross thou
         hast redeemed the world.

Consider how, after our Lord had expired, two of his disciples, Joseph and Nicodemus, took him down from the cross and placed him in the arms of his afflicted mother, who received him with unutterable tenderness and pressed him to her bosom.

A reading from the Gospel according to St. John

The Jews, because it was the Passover, being unwilling that the bodies should remain on the cross during the Sabbath day—for that was a great Sabbath day—requested of Pilate that their legs might be broken and that they might be taken away. The soldiers therefore came and they broke the legs of the first, and of the other that was crucified with him. But after they came to Jesus, when they saw that he was already dead, they did not break his legs. Instead, one of the soldiers with a spear opened his side, and immediately there came out blood and water. And he that saw it has given testimony, and his testimony is true. And he knows that he speaks the truth, that you also may believe. For these things were done so that the Scripture might be fulfilled: you shall not break a bone of him. And again, another Scripture says: they shall look on him whom they pierced. After these things, Joseph of Arimathea, who was a disciple of Jesus, but secretly for fear of the Jews, made a request of Pilate that he might take away the body of Jesus. And Pilate gave him leave. He came therefore and took away the body of Jesus.

JOHN 19:31–38

He is your property now, O Virgin Mother, once again, for he and the world have met and parted. He went out from you to do his Father's work—and he has done and suffered it. Satan and bad men have no longer any claim upon him—too long has he been in their arms. He has not been in your arms, O Mother of God, since he was a child—but now, you have a claim upon him, when the world has done its worst. We rejoice in this great mystery. He has been hidden in your womb, he has lain on your bosom, he has been carried in your arms—and now that he is dead, he is placed upon your lap. Virgin Mother of God, pray for us.

J. H. NEWMAN

Recessit pastor noster,
fons aquae vivae, ad cuius
transitum sol obscuratus
est: Nam et ille captus est,
qui captivum tenebat
primum hominem: hodie
portas mortis et seras
pariter Salvator noster
disrupit

Our shepherd is gone, the
fount of living waters, at
whose passing the very sun
was darkened: For the one
who held the first man
prisoner is himself taken:
our Savior has broken the
gates of death and
its portals.

CALL: Destruxit quidem
claustra inferni, et subvertit
potentias diaboli. Nam et
ille captus est, qui
captivum tenebat primum
hominem: hodie portas
mortis et seras pariter
Salvator noster disrupit.

CALL: He has destroyed the
eternal prison, and
undermined the power of
the devil; for the one who
held the first man prisoner
is himself taken: today our
Savior has broken the gates
of death and its portals.

Behold our Lord and our God, dead in the arms of his
grieving mother for the sins that we have committed!

Holy God!
Holy, mighty one!
Holy, immortal one!
Have mercy on us!

O thou whose grief was boundless as an ocean that hath
no limits, Mary, Mother of God, grant us a share in thy
most holy sorrow for the sufferings of thy Son, and have
compassion on our infirmities. Accept us as thy children
with thy beloved disciple. Show thyself a mother unto us;

and may he, through thee, receive our prayer, who for us
vouchsafed to be thy Son.

CHALLONER

—•—

Fac me tecum pie flere	Let me mingle tears with thee
Crucifixo	Mourning him who
condolere	mourn'd for me
Donec ego vixero	All the days that I may live.

—•—

THE FOURTEENTH STATION

Jesus is laid in the tomb

CALL: We adore thee, O Christ,
and we bless thee,
RESPONSE: Because by thy holy cross thou
hast redeemed the world.

Consider how the disciples carried the body of Jesus to bury it, accompanied by his holy mother, who arranged it in the sepulchre with her own hands. Then they closed the tomb, and all withdrew.

A reading from the Gospel according to St. John
Joseph of Arimathea . . . took away the body of Jesus, and Nicodemus also came—he was the one who first came to Jesus at night, secretly, for fear of the Jews—bringing a

mixture of myrrh and aloes, about a hundred pounds' weight. So they took the body of Jesus and bound it in linen cloths with the spices, according to the manner that Jews observe at a burial. Now there was a garden in the place where he was crucified, and in the garden a new sepulchre where no one had yet been laid. Since it was the Jewish Passover, and because the sepulchre was near at hand, they laid Jesus there.

JOHN 19:38–42

Jesus, when he was nearest to his everlasting triumph, seemed to be farthest from triumphing. When he was nearest to entering upon his kingdom, and exercising all power in heaven and earth, he was lying dead in a cave of the rock. He was wrapped round in burying clothes, and confined within a sepulchre of stone, where he was soon to have a glorified spiritual body, which could penetrate all substances, go to and fro quicker than thought, and was about to ascend on high.

Make us to trust in you, O Jesus, that you will display in us a similar providence. Make us sure, O Lord, that the greater is our distress, the nearer we are to you. The more men scorn us, the more you honor us. The more men insult us, the higher you will exalt us. The more they forget us, the more you keep us in mind. The more they abandon us, the closer you will bring us to yourself.

J. H. NEWMAN

Sepulto Domino, signatum est monumentum, volventes lapidem ad ostium monumenti:

When the Lord was buried, they sealed the place, rolling a stone over the doorway: And they posted

Ponentes milites, qui custodirent illum.	soldiers who kept watch over him.
CALL: Accedentes principes sacerdotum ad Pilatum, petierunt illum. Ponentes milites, qui custodirent illum.	*CALL:* The high priests went to Pilate to petition him: And they posted soldiers who kept watch over him.

—— • ——

Behold our Lord and our God, laid in the tomb for the sins that we have committed!

Holy God!
Holy, mighty one!
Holy, immortal one!
Have mercy on us!

—— • ——

We too, O God, shall descend into the grave whenever it shall please thee, as it shall please thee, and wheresoever it shall please thee. Let thy just decrees be fulfilled; let our sinful bodies return to their parent dust, but do thou, in thy great mercy, receive our immortal souls, and when our bodies have risen again place them likewise in thy kingdom, that we may love and bless thee forever. Amen.

CHALLONER

—— • ——

Iuxta crucem tecum stare	By the cross with thee to stay
Et me tibi sociare	There with thee to weep and pray
In planctu desidero.	Is all I ask of thee to give.

—— • ——

THE FIFTEENTH STATION
Jesus rises gloriously from the tomb

CALL: We adore thee, O Christ,
and we bless thee,
RESPONSE: Because by thy holy cross thou
hast redeemed the world.

Consider how on the third day our Blessed Savior, treading death underfoot, rose gloriously from the sepulchre where he had been laid and appeared to his mother and his beloved disciples.

A reading from the Gospel according to St. Matthew
And at the end of the Sabbath, when it began to dawn, beginning the first day of the week, Mary Magdalene and the other Mary came to see the sepulchre. And behold,

there was a great earthquake, for an angel of the Lord had descended from heaven, and as he came, he rolled back the stone, and sat upon it. His countenance was like lightning and his garments as snow. And for fear of him, the guards were struck with terror, and became like dead men. And the angel spoke, and said to the women: Do not fear: for I know that you seek Jesus who was crucified. He is not here, for he is risen, as he had said. Come, and see the place where the Lord was laid. And go quickly: tell his disciples that he is risen; and behold he will go before you into Galilee; there you shall see him. So, I have foretold it to you. And they went out quickly from the sepulchre with fear but great joy, running to tell his disciples. And behold, Jesus met them saying: Hail! And they came up and took hold of his feet and adored him. Then Jesus said to them: Fear not. Go, tell my brethren that they should go into Galilee; there they shall see me.

MATTHEW 28:1–10

The longed-for redemption is come; the end to which we have looked forward is here. What greater and better thing can we do than to proclaim the power of the risen Lord? This Jesus bursting the bolts of hell, has raised for us the glorious banner of his Resurrection, and returning from the grave, he bears mankind aloft to the wondering stars, mankind which of old was overthrown by the enemy's malice. O mystical and worshipful transactions of this wonderful mystery! What holy and eternal blessings are showered upon holy mother Church! She has no desire for the things that perish; all her longing is to find that which may redeem. Even as Mary joyed in holy child-bearing, so the Church exults in the beauty of her children's rebirth. That blessed fount which poured from the side of our Lord has washed away the mass of our sins, and those reborn find at the sacred altars the bread of eternal life.

———•———

Paschal triumph, Paschal joy,
Only sin can this destroy;
From sin's death do thou set free,
Souls re-born, dear Lord, in thee,
Hymns of glory, songs of praise,
Father, unto thee we raise.
Risen Lord, all praise to thee,
Ever with the Spirit be.

Outside Lent, the Regina Caeli could be sung (see p. 580).

———•———

Holy Lord, Light and true salvation of the faithful, illumine our hearts with the brightness of our Lord's resurrection, so that through knowledge of God's trinity and unity we may become worthy to be numbered with the children of light, as members of Christ and temples of the Holy Spirit.

———•———

Quando corpus morietur	While my body here decays
Fac ut animae donetur	May my soul thy goodness praise
Paradisi gloria.	Safe in paradise with thee.
Amen.	Amen.

———•———

AT THE HIGH ALTAR AGAIN

A reading from the letter of St. Paul to the Romans
If God is for us, who is against us? He who did not spare even his own Son, but delivered him up for us all: has he not also, with him, given us everything? Who shall accuse the elect of God, whom God has justified? Who is it that can condemn? Christ Jesus who died, and who is risen again, who is at the right hand of God and who makes intercession for us? Who then shall separate us from the love of Christ? Shall tribulation, or distress, or famine, or nakedness, or danger, or persecution, or the sword? In all these things we have overcome because of him who has loved us. For I am sure that neither death, nor life, nor angels, nor principalities, nor powers, nor things present, nor things to come, nor might, nor height, nor depth, nor any other creature shall be able to separate us from the love of God, which is in Christ Jesus our Lord.

ROMANS 8:31–35, 37–39

A reading from the letter of St. Paul to the Philippians
Christ humbled himself, becoming obedient unto death, even to the death of the cross. For which cause God also has exalted him, and gave him the name that is above all names, that at the name of Jesus every knee should bow, of those who are in heaven, on earth, and under the earth, and that every tongue should confess that the Lord Jesus Christ is in the glory of God the Father.

PHILIPPIANS 2:8–11

Let us pray.

Look down, O Lord, we beg, upon this family of yours, for which our Lord Jesus Christ did not refuse to be delivered into the hands of wicked men and to endure the torments of the cross, and who lives and reigns forever and ever. Amen.

— • —

The following prayer may be used instead:

Almighty God, who by the precious blood of thine only-begotten Son didst sanctify the standard of the cross: grant, we beseech thee, that all those who rejoice in the glory of the same holy cross may at all times and places feel the gladness of thy protection. Through the same Christ our Lord. Amen.

— • —

Ave verum corpus natum	Hail to thee, true body sprung
Ex Maria Virgine.	From the Virgin Mary's womb!
Vere passum, immolatum	The same that on the cross was hung,
In cruce pro homine.	And bore for man the bitter doom!
Cuius latus perforatum	Thou, whose side was pierced, and flowed
Unda fluxit et sanguine:	Both with water and with blood;
Esto nobis praegustatum	Suffer us to taste of thee,
Mortis in examine.	In our life's last agony.

O Iesu dulcis,   Son of Mary, Jesu blest,
O Iesu pie,   Sweetest, gentlest,
O Iesu, Fili Mariae   holiest.

TRANSLATED BY E. CASWALL

VARIATION ON THE STATIONS OF THE CROSS

When you do not have a lot of time, spend only a moment before each station. The following are suggestions for prayers you might like to use at each pause:

Eternal Father, I offer you the blood, the passion, the death of Jesus, and the sorrows of the Blessed Virgin, for the remission of my sins, the deliverance of the souls in Purgatory, the wants of our Holy Mother the Church, and the conversion of sinners.

POPE PIUS IX

Eternal Father, I offer you the precious blood of Jesus in reparation for my sins, and for the needs of the holy Church. My Jesus, mercy!

POPE PIUS VII

My sweetest Jesus, be not to me a Judge but a Savior!

ST. JEROME EMILIANI

Viva! Viva! Gesù

Glory be to Jesus,
Who, in bitter pains,
Poured for me the life-blood
From his sacred veins.

O Lord Jesus Christ, holy, immortal God, have mercy upon us all, and upon all people; purify us with your holy blood, forgive us with your holy blood, save us with your holy blood now and forever. Amen.

— • —

To what excess, O my Savior, hast thou loved me! O Jesus, crucified for my salvation, save me!

— • —

Quaerens me sedisti lassus, Redemisti crucem passus; Tantus labor non sit cassus.	You sought me to exhaustion, And redeemed me with your cross; Let not such a labor be in vain!

FROM THE DIES IRAE

— • —

DEVOTIONS FOR THE MASS

BEFORE MASS

A prayer of St. Ambrose

Lord Jesus Christ, I approach your banquet table in fear and trembling, for I am a sinner, and dare not rely on my own worth but only on your goodness and mercy. I am defiled by many sins in body and soul, and by my unguarded thoughts and words. Gracious God of majesty and awe, I seek your protection, I look for your healing; poor troubled sinner that I am, I appeal to you, the fountain of all mercy. I cannot bear your judgment, but I trust in your salvation. Lord, I show my wounds to you and uncover my shame before you. I know my sins are many and great, and they fill me with fear, but I hope in your mercies, for they cannot be numbered. Lord Jesus Christ, eternal king, God and man, crucified for mankind, look upon me with mercy and hear my prayer, for I trust in you. Have mercy on me, full of sorrow and sin, for the depth of your compassion never ends. Praise to you, saving sacrifice, offered on the wood of the cross for me and for all mankind. Praise to the noble and precious blood, flowing from the wounds of my crucified Lord Jesus Christ and washing away the sins of the whole world. Remember, Lord, your creature, whom you have redeemed with your blood. I repent my sins, and I long to put right what I have done. Merciful Father, take away all my offenses and sins; purify me in body and soul, and make me worthy to taste the holy of holies. May your body and blood, which I intend to receive, although I am unworthy, be for me the remission of my sins, the washing away of my guilt, the end of my evil thoughts, and the rebirth of my better instincts. May it incite me to do the works pleasing to you and profitable to my health in body and soul, and be a firm defense against the wiles of my enemies. Amen.

—— • ——

Jesus, my God and my all, my soul longs for you. My heart yearns to receive you in Holy Communion. Come, bread of heaven and food of angels, to nourish my soul and to rejoice my heart. Come, most lovable friend of my soul, to inflame me with such love that I may never again be separated from you.

—— • ——

A prayer of St. Thomas Aquinas

Almighty and ever-living God, I approach the sacrament of your only-begotten Son, our Lord Jesus Christ. I come sick to the doctor of life, unclean to the fountain of mercy, blind to the radiance of eternal light, and poor and needy to the Lord of heaven and earth. Lord, in your great generosity, heal my sickness, wash away my defilement, enlighten my blindness, enrich my poverty, and clothe my nakedness. May I receive the bread of angels, the King of kings and Lord of lords, with humble reverence, with the purity and faith, the repentance and love, and the determined purpose that will help to bring me to salvation. May I receive the sacrament of the Lord's body and blood, and its reality and power. Kind God, may I receive the body of your only-begotten Son, our Lord Jesus Christ, born from the womb of the Virgin Mary, and so be received into his mystical body and numbered among his members. Loving Father, as on my earthly pilgrimage I now receive your beloved Son under the veil of a sacrament, may I one day see him face-to-face in glory, who lives and reigns with you forever. Amen.

——•——

A collect for purity

O God, to whom all hearts are open, and from whom nothing lies hidden, cleanse, we pray, the thoughts of our hearts by the inspiration of your Holy Spirit, that we may come to love you perfectly and worthily praise your holy name. Through Christ our Lord. Amen.

——•——

Behold, O my loving Savior, I present myself before your holy altar, to assist at the divine sacrifice. Give me all the grace you wish me to derive from it, and take away, I beg, all that impedes that grace. Fill my heart with love for you who have not hesitated to give yourself for me on the altar of the cross.

——•——

Grant me, O God, a warm heart, an open ear, and a ready tongue to assist at this holy Mass. May my participation be wholehearted, and may my humble prayer ascend like incense in your sight, O Most High, and be joined with the worship of your angels.

——•——

THE BIDDING OF THE BEDES

This prayer, here somewhat modernized, comes from the ancient rites used in England before the Reformation and is sometimes read at the sermon time before High Mass.

Let us offer now a special prayer to God Almighty, and to the Glorious Virgin, his Mother, our Lady Saint Mary, and to all saints, for the peace and welfare of holy Church; for our Holy Father, the Pope, for our Right Reverend Father, the Bishop of this diocese; for the clergy of this church and all that have the charge of souls, as well as for all religious men and women, that God grant them each in their degree so well to do that it may bring glory to God and salvation to souls.

We pray for our Sovereign, and for all that rule in the land, that God may give them counsel so to do, that it may be to his praise and the welfare of the realm.

We pray now especially for all the faithful of this diocese; for all toilers both on land and sea, that God keep them safe in soul and in body and also in goods; for all of good life, that God maintain them therein and give them an increase of goodness; and for all those that are bound in debt, or in deadly sin, that God of his great mercy soon lead them out.

And that these prayers may be heard and brought about the sooner, let everyone here present now say one *Pater Noster* and an *Ave Maria*.

Now let us offer a prayer to our Blessed Lady, Saint Mary, and to all the saints in heaven for all the people of this parish, wherever they may be, especially for all those that are sick, that God of his goodness send them release of pain and turn them to the way that is most to his pleasure and the welfare of their souls.

Let us pray especially for all those that have made the celebration of this Mass possible, through their offerings and contributions to God and to this holy church, that God reward them with everlasting bliss, and we pray for those that do not do so, that God soon bring them to amendment.

Let us likewise pray for all those that serve or sing in this church; for those that give or bequeath of their goods to it; for those that find any ornament, vestment or vessel, candle or lamp, for the worship of God, or of any of his saints in this place, for those who founded this church, and for those who have maintained it.

For all these people, and for all here present, and for all that have need of prayer, let everyone now hail our Lady with an *Ave*.

And now let us pray for all the souls that await God's mercy in the purification of Purgatory, especially for the souls of our parents, kinsfolk and friends; for all those whose bones are buried in this parish, and for all souls for whom we are bound to pray, that God of his great mercy release them from their pain, if it be his blessed will.

And that our prayers may somewhat stand them in stead, every one of your charity help them heartily with a *Pater Noster* and an *Ave Maria*.

—·—

Let us, who mystically represent the Cherubim, singing the thrice-holy hymn to the life-giving Trinity, cast away from us all earthly care; that we may receive the King of all, surrounded by the angelic hosts. Alleluia, Alleluia, Alleluia. Lift up your hands to the Sanctuary, and bless the Lord.

LITURGY OF ST. JOHN CHRYSOSTOM

—·—

PREPARATION FOR COMMUNION

I believe, O Lord, and acknowledge, that you are Christ, the Son of the living God, who came into the world to save sinners, of whom I am the greatest. I believe that what I receive is indeed your very own pure Body and precious Blood. So I pray you: have mercy on me, and forgive my sins, intentional and unintentional, which I have committed whether by word or by deed, knowingly and unknowingly: and so make me worthy without condemnation to partake of your most pure Mysteries, that my sins may be forgiven, and bring eternal life. Amen.

LITURGY OF ST. JOHN CHRYSOSTOM

My father and my God, help me to make a worthy communion: restore in me the image of Jesus your Son which I have lost, that, with Thomas the doubter, I too may acknowledge him as my Lord and my God, whom I am about to receive today.

O Son of God, take me today as a partaker at your mystical banquet: for I will not tell your enemies your secrets, nor will I kiss you as Judas did, but like the just thief I appeal to you: *Remember me, O Lord, when you come into your kingdom.*

LITURGY OF ST. JOHN CHRYSOSTOM

O holy Lord, almighty Father, eternal God, grant me worthily to receive this most holy Body and Blood of your Son our Lord Jesus Christ that I may thereby receive forgiveness of all my sins, and be filled with your Holy Spirit, and possess your peace; for you are the only God, and there is no other beside you, whose kingdom and glorious reign lasts forever and ever. Amen.

SARUM PRIMER

O God, weaken, cast away, and forgive my sins, as many as I have committed, knowingly and unknowingly, whether by word or by deed: O forgive them all, kind lover of man; and by the prayers of your most pure and ever Virgin Mother, make me worthy, without condemnation, to receive your blessed and most pure Body, for the healing of soul and body alike. For yours is the kingdom, the power, and the glory: Father, and Son, and Holy Spirit, now, and always, and forever and ever. Amen.

Let the partaking of your holy Mysteries be to me not for judgment or condemnation, O Lord, but for the healing of both soul and body.

LITURGY OF ST. JOHN CHRYSOSTOM

O God the Father, fount and source of all goodness, who, moved by your loving-kindness, willed your only-begotten Son to descend for us to this base world and to take flesh, that same which I, unworthy one, will soon receive: I worship you, I glorify you, I praise you with utter dedication of my mind and heart, and beg you not to abandon us your servants, but rather forgive us our sins, that so we may be enabled to serve you, the only living and true God with a clean heart and a chaste body. Through the same Christ our Lord. Amen.

SARUM PRIMER

Hail forevermore, most holy flesh of Christ, to me before all and above all the highest source of joy. The body of our Lord Jesus Christ be to me, a sinner, the way and the life. In the name of the Father, Son, and Holy Spirit. Amen.

And hail forevermore, heavenly drink, to me before all and above all the highest source of joy. The body and blood of our Lord Jesus Christ be to me a perpetual healing to everlasting life. Amen. In the name of the Father, Son, and Holy Spirit. Amen.

SARUM PRIMER

THANKSGIVING AFTER COMMUNION

I thank you, Holy Lord, almighty Father, eternal God, for refreshing me with the most sacred Body and Blood of your Son our Lord Jesus Christ, and I pray that this Sacrament of our salvation of which I, an unworthy sinner, have partaken, does not judge or condemn me as I deserve, but be beneficial to the preservation of my body, and the keeping of my soul unto everlasting life. Amen.

SARUM PRIMER

—•—

Welcome to my heart, Lord Jesus. Take me and renew me, transform and mold me into your image. Let the memory and grace of this communion remain with me for today and throughout life. Amen.

—•—

O divine Lord! Thou hast at length satisfied the earnest desires of my heart. I possess thee, I embrace thee; O make me entirely thine. Indeed I am not worthy to receive thee under my roof: say but the word and I shall truly be healed.

—•—

AFTER MASS

Placeat Tibi Sancta Trinitas

May this Mass be pleasing to you, O Holy Trinity; may it be a source of grace to the priest who has said it, to us who have heard it and to all those for whom we have offered it. Amen.

A prayer of St. Thomas Aquinas after Mass

Lord, Father, all-powerful and ever-living God, I thank you, for even though I am a sinner, your unprofitable servant, not because of my worth but in the kindness of your mercy, you have fed me with the precious body and blood of your Son, our Lord Jesus Christ. I pray that this holy communion may bring me not condemnation and punishment, but forgiveness and salvation. May it be a helmet of faith and a shield of good will. May it purify me from evil ways and put an end to my evil passions. May it bring me charity and patience, humility and obedience, and growth in the power to do good. May it be my strong defense against all my enemies, visible and invisible, and the perfect calming of all my evil impulses, bodily and spiritual. May it unite me more closely to you, the one true God, and lead me safely through death to everlasting happiness with you. And I pray that you will lead me, a sinner, to the banquet where you, with your Son and Holy Spirit, are true and perfect light, total fulfillment, everlasting joy, gladness without end, and perfect happiness to your saints. Grant this through Christ our Lord. Amen.

A prayer of St. Bonaventure

Pierce, O most sweet Lord Jesus, my inmost soul with the most joyous and healthful wound of your love, with true, serene, and most holy apostolic charity, that my soul may ever languish and melt with love and longing for you, that it may yearn for you and faint for your courts, and long to be dissolved and to be with you. Grant that my soul may hunger after you, the bread of angels, the refreshment of holy souls, our daily and supersubstantial bread, having all sweetness and savor and every delight of taste, upon whom the angels desire to look, and may my inmost soul be filled with the sweetness of your savor; may it ever thirst after you, the fountain of life, the fountain of wisdom and knowledge, the fountain of eternal light, the torrent of pleasure, the richness of the house of God; may it ever compass you, seek you, find you, run to you, attain you, meditate upon you, speak of you, and do all things to the praise and glory of your name, with humility and discretion, with love and delight, with ease and affection, and with perseverance unto the end; may you alone be ever my hope, my entire assurance, my riches, my delight, my pleasure, my joy, my rest and tranquillity, my peace, my sweetness, my fragrance, my sweet savor, my food, my refreshment, my refuge, my help, my wisdom, my portion, my possession and my treasure, in whom may my mind and my heart be fixed and firm and rooted immovably henceforth and forever. Amen.

—— • ——

We thank you, Lord, lover of humanity, benefactor of our souls, that you have made us worthy today to partake of your heavenly and undying Sacraments. Straighten out our path; strengthen us in your devotion; protect us; give strength to our steps, through the prayers and intercession of the glorious Mother of God and ever-virgin Mary, and of all your Saints.

LITURGY OF ST. JOHN CHRYSOSTOM

—— • ——

Anima Christi

Soul of Christ, be my sanctification;
Body of Christ, be my salvation;
Blood of Christ, fill all my veins;
Water of Christ's side, wash out my stains;
Passion of Christ, my comfort be;
O good Jesu, listen to me;
In thy wounds I fain would hide,
Ne'er to be parted from Thy side;
Guard me, should the foe assail me;
Call me when my life shall fail me;
Bid me come to Thee above,
With Thy saints to sing Thy love,
World without end.

TRANSLATED BY J. H. NEWMAN

BENEDICTION OF THE BLESSED SACRAMENT

Benediction is a service of exposition and adoration of the Blessed Sacrament, concluding with a blessing of the congregation with the sacrament. The devotion, which celebrates the real presence of Christ in the Eucharist, became a regular feature of Catholic devotional life after the Council of Trent. Benediction is less common today, but it remains an established feature of communal Catholic devotions.

O salutaris
  Hostia
Quae Caeli
  pandis ostium
Bella praemunt
  hostilia,
Da robur,
  fer auxilium.
Uni, trinoque
Domino
Sit sempiterna gloria,
Qui vitam sine
  termino
Nobis donet
  in patria.
Amen.
	O saving victim,
	  opening wide
	The gate of heav'n to
	  man below,
	Our foes press on from
	  every side,
	Thine aid supply, thy
	  strength bestow.
	To thy great name be
	  endless praise,
	Immortal Godhead,
	  one in three,
	O grant us endless length
	  of days
	In our true native land
	  with thee. Amen.

At this point there may be prayers or readings.

Tantum ergo Sacramentum	Down in adoration falling, Lo! the sacred Host we hail.

520

Veneremur cernui.
(All bow.)
Et antiquum
 documentum
Novo cedat ritui.
Praestet fides
 supplementum
Sensuum defectui.
Genitori, genitoque
Laus et iubilatio:
Salus, honor, virtus
 quoque
Sit et benedictio:
Procedenti ab
 utroque
Compar sit
 laudatio.
Amen.

CALL: Panem de caelis
praestitisti eis.
RESPONSE: Omne
delectamentum in se
habentem.

(All bow.)
Lo, o'er ancient forms
 departing,
Newer rites of grace prevail;
Faith, for all defects
 supplying
Where the feeble
 senses fail.
To the everlasting Father,
And the Son who reigns
 on high
With the Holy Ghost
 proceeding
Forth from each eternally,
Be salvation, honor,
 blessing.
Might and endless majesty.
Amen.

CALL: You gave them
manna from heaven.
RESPONSE: And very sweet
it was to the taste.

The following prayer or another collect in English is now sung or said:

Oremus.

Deus, qui nobis sub
sacramento mirabili
passionis tuae memoriam
reliquisti: tribue
quaesumus, ita nos

Let us pray.

O God, who in this
wonderful sacrament left us
a memorial of your passion,
grant that as we venerate
this holy mystery of your

corporis et sanguinis tui	body and blood, we may
sacra mysteria venerari;	come to experience the
ut redemptionis tuae	effects of your redemption,
fructum in nobis iugiter	who live and reign forever
sentiamus. Qui vivis et	and ever. Amen.
regnas in saecula	
saeculorum. Amen.	

The priest raises the Sacred Host in blessing. The following Divine Praises may at some point be said:

Blessed be God
Blessed be his holy name
Blessed be Jesus Christ, true God and true Man
Blessed be the name of Jesus
Blessed be his most Sacred Heart
Blessed be his most Precious Blood
Blessed be Jesus in the most holy Sacrament of the altar
Blessed be the Holy Spirit, the Paraclete
Blessed be the great Mother of God, Mary most holy
Blessed be her holy and immaculate conception
Blessed be her glorious assumption
Blessed be the name of Mary, Virgin and Mother
Blessed be St. Joseph, her spouse most chaste
Blessed be God in his angels and in his saints

Finally, as the Blessed Sacrament is returned to the tabernacle, the following hymn or another hymn is sung:

ANTIPHON: Adoremus in aeternum sanctissimum Sacramentum.	**ANTIPHON:** Let us adore forever the most holy Sacrament.
Laudate Dominum, omnes gentes, Laudate eum, omnes	Praise the Lord, all you nations, Praise him, all you peoples.

populi.
Quoniam confirmata
est super nos
misericordia eius,
Et veritas Domini manet
in aeternum.
Gloria Patri et Filio
et Spiritui Sancto.
Sicut erat in principio
et nunc et semper, et in
saecula saeculorum. Amen.

For his mercy has been
shown forth toward us,
And the Lord keeps his
word forever.
Glory be to the Father,
and to the Son, and to
the Holy Spirit.
As it was in the beginning,
is now and ever shall be,
world without end.
Amen.

ANTIPHON: Adoremus in
aeternum sanctissimum
Sacramentum.

ANTIPHON: Let us adore
forever the most holy
Sacrament.

In some places the following is sung three times instead:

O Sacrament most holy,
O Sacrament divine!
All praise and all thanksgiving
be every moment thine!

DEVOTIONS BEFORE THE BLESSED SACRAMENT

An act of spiritual communion

I believe in you, O my Jesus, present in the most holy Sacrament of the Altar; I love you above all things; and I desire to receive you into my soul. Since I cannot now receive you sacramentally, come at least spiritually into my heart. I embrace you and I unite myself to you, as if you were already there. Permit me never to be separated from you.

—— • ——

O most loving Jesus, to what an excess thy love has gone! Of thy own flesh and most precious blood thou hast prepared for me a divine banquet, in which thou givest me thy whole self. What could have moved thee to this transport of love? Nothing else, surely, than thy most loving heart. O adorable heart of my Jesus, furnace of divine love, receive into thy sacred wound my soul, that I may learn in that school of charity how to love my God, who has given me such wonderful proofs of his love. Amen.

—— • ——

A morning prayer before the Blessed Sacrament

Lord Jesus, present before me in the Sacrament of the Altar, help me to cast out from my mind all thoughts of which you do not approve and from my heart all emotions which you do not encourage. Enable me to spend my entire day as a coworker with you, carrying out the tasks that you have entrusted to me.

Be with me at every moment of this day: during the long hours of work, that I may never tire or slacken from your service; during my conversations, that they not become for me occasions of meanness toward others; during the moments of worry and stress, that I may remain patient and spiritually calm; during periods of fatigue and illness, that I may avoid self-pity and think of others; during times of temptation, and that I may take refuge in your grace.

Help me to remain generous and loyal to you this day, and so be able to offer it all up to you with its successes which I have achieved by your help and its failures which have occurred through my own fault. Let me come to the wonderful realization that life is most real when it is lived with you as the guest of my soul.

—•—

Our most dear Savior Christ, which after the finishing of the old paschal sacrifice hast instituted the new sacrament of thine own blessed body and blood for a memorial of thy bitter passion, give us such true faith therein, and such fervent devotion thereto, that our souls may take fruitful spiritual food thereby.

ST. THOMAS MORE

—•—

A prayer for a quarter of an hour before the Blessed Sacrament
To please me, my dear child, it is not necessary to know much; all that is required is to love me much, to be deeply sorry for ever having offended me, and desirous of being ever faithful to me in future.

Speak to me now as you would to your dearest friend. Tell me all that now fills your mind and heart. Are there any you wish to commend to me? Tell me their names, and tell me what you would wish me to do for them. Do not fear, ask for much; I love generous hearts, which, forgetting themselves, wish well to others.

Speak to me of the poor you wish to comfort; tell me of the sick that you would wish to see relieved. Ask of me something for those who have been unkind to you, or who have crossed you. Ask much for them all; commend them with all your heart to me.

And ask me many graces for yourself. Are there not many and many you would wish to name, that would make you happier to yourself, more useful and pleasing to others, more worthy of the love of me, the dearest Lord, Master and Spouse of your soul? Tell me the whole list of the favors you want of me. Tell me them with humility, knowing how poor you are without them, how unable to gain them by yourself; ask for them with much love, that they may make you more pleasing to me.

With all a child's simplicity, tell me how self-seeking you are, how proud, vain, irritable, how cowardly in sacrifice, how lazy in work, uncertain in your good resolutions, and then ask me to bless and crown your efforts. Poor child, fear not, blush not at the sight of so many failings; there are Saints in Heaven who had the faults you have; they came to me lovingly, they prayed earnestly to me, and my grace has made them good and holy in my sight.

You should be mine, body and soul: fear not, therefore, to ask of me gifts of body and mind, health, judgment, memory, and success—ask for them for my sake: that God may be glorified in all things. I can grant everything, and never refuse to give what may make a soul dearer to me and better able to fulfill the will of God.

Have you no plans for the future which occupy

perhaps distress, your mind? Tell me your hopes, your fears. Is it about your future state? your position among my creatures? some good you wish to bring to others? In what shall I help and bless your good will?

And for me you must have—have you not? some zeal, some wish to do good to the souls of others. Some, perhaps, who love and care for you, have ceased, almost, to know or care for me. Shall I give you strength, wisdom and tact, to bring these poor ones close to my Heart again? Have you failed in the past? tell me how you acted; I will show you why you did not gain all you expected; rely on me, I will help you, and will guide you to lead others to me.

And what crosses have you, my dear child? Have they been many and heavy ones? Has someone caused you pain? someone wounded your self-love? slighted you? injured you? Lay your head upon my breast, and tell me how you suffered. Have you felt that some have been ungrateful to you, and unfeeling toward you? Tell me all, and in the warmth of my Heart you will find strength to forgive and even to forget that they have ever wished to pain you.

And what fears have you, my child? My providence shall comfort you; my love sustain you. I am never away from you, never can abandon you. Are some growing cold in the interest and love they had for you? Pray to me for them; I will restore them to you if it be better for you and your sanctification.

Have you not some happiness to make known to me? What has happened, since you came to me last, to console you, to gladden and give you joy? What was it? a mark of true friendship you received? a success unexpected and almost unhoped for? a fear suddenly taken away from you? and did you remember the while, that in all it was my will, my love, that brought all that your heart has been so glad to have? It was my hand, my dear child, that guided and prepared all for you. Look to me now, my child, and say, 'Dear Jesus, I thank you.'

You will soon leave me now; what promises can you make me? Let them be sincere ones, humble ones, full of love and desire to please me. Tell me how carefully you will avoid every occasion of sin, drive from you all that leads to harm, and shun the world—the great deceiver of souls.

Promise me to be kind to the poor; loving for my sake, to friends; forgiving to your enemies, and charitable to all, not in word alone and actions, but in your very thoughts. When you have little love for your neighbor, whom you see, you are forgetting me who am hidden from you.

Love all my saints; seek the help of your holy patrons. I love to glorify them by giving you much through them. Love, above all, my own sweet glorious Mother—she is your mother; O love her, speak to her often, and she will bring you to me, and for her sake I will love and bless you more each day.

Return soon to me again, but come with your heart empty of the world, for I have many more favors to give, more than you can know of; bring your heart so that I may fill it with many gifts of my love.

My peace be with you.

FROM *A SIMPLE PRAYER BOOK*

A prayer to the five wounds

The anonymous writer plays on the old word for beloved—leman—and the lemon, that bitter fruit.

Jesus Christ, my Leman sweet,
That diedest on the bitter tree,

With all my might I thee beseech
For thy deep woundès two and three,
That as firmly may thy love
Into mine heart fixèd be
As was the spear into thine Heart
When thou sufferedst death for me.
My Jesu sweet, who died on Rood,
For the love of me,—
And boughtest me with thy Blood,
Have then mercy upon me;
And should me hinder any thing
From my love of thee,
Should it be dear, it shall be loathed;
So take it away from me. Amen.

VERNON MANUSCRIPT

O Godhead Hid

How infinitely, indescribably, wonderful
is your presence, O Lord, in the Sacred Host.
What I see looks just like a white disc.
I feel it, smooth and so very ordinary:
I taste it and experience the flavor of bread.
Yet, you Lord, Truth itself, have said
"This is my Body."
Never once in my life have I doubted that.
I thank you for the gift of faith.
"Than Truth's own word there is no truer token."
Those standing beneath the cross to
  which you were nailed
saw your human Body; poor, weak, suffering.
But your Godhead remained so hidden.
Now, even your Body is concealed too.
I believe, Lord; help my unbelief.

I bow down in wonder before your humility.
Immeasurable greatness hidden under the semblance of
  the commonest of foods.
Your human Body is here, Jesus,
glorified but still bearing the wounds of your Passion,
wounds you endured for love of me.
Yes, Lord, you died for me.
You continue to offer yourself for me.
Through your dying I am able to live.
But you also give me yourself to feed my soul.
I believe that when I was baptized I was born again.
I received a wonderful new life,
a sharing in the life of the Divine Trinity,
a life that is indeed divine.
You, Lord, in your wonderful providence
feed everything according to its nature.
You feed the divine life of my soul
with divine food, your own very Self.
O mystery of mysteries, O mystery of faith.
I need your own gift to begin to understand it all.
How I long to cry out to the whole wide world,
"Why are you starving?
Why do you refuse the food that is God?"
Lord, I do believe.
Increase my faith. Move me to share it.

FRANCIS CANON RIPLEY

It seems white, and is red;
It is quick, and seems dead;
It is flesh, and seems bread;
It is one and seems two;
It is God's body and no more.

EARLY ENGLISH POEM

O divine Jesus, alone in so many tabernacles throughout the world without visitor or worshiper: I offer you my own heart. May its every beat be a prayer of love for you. In your love you are ever watching me: you never sleep, and like the father of the prodigal son, you are always looking out for returning sinners. O loving Jesus, O lonely Jesus, may my heart be a lamp, the light of which shall burn and comfort you alone in time and in eternity. Amen.

The Adorable Presence

With peeping pace and silent step
They pass the sleepy nest of books
Imprisoned under lock and key
Beneath the ever-watchful gaze
 Of two-faced time.

Soon touched with holy awe they cross
Themselves and see with wakened eyes
Christ himself gazing lovingly
Surrounded by his Mother blest
 And the heavenly company.

They yearn to utter the splendor
Of heaven's everlasting joy
They yearn to quench their thirsty souls
Upon the tears of Christ divine.
 Such yearning is also mine.

T. J. RHIDIAN JONES

A prayer before a crucifix

O most kind and sweet Jesus: behold, I cast myself on my knees in your sight, and with all the fervor that is in me, I beg you to plant deeply in my heart the virtues of faith, hope, and charity, together with a true sorrow for my sins and a firm purpose of amendment, as I have before my eyes and I contemplate with the utmost sorrow of soul the image of your five wounds, and I remember the words of the prophet David: They have pierced my hands and feet: they have even counted my bones (Psalm 22:17).

LITANIES

THE GREAT LITANY OF SAINTS

The Great Litany of Saints is customarily prayed at solemn occasions, particularly the Forty Hours devotion, the Easter Vigil, priestly ordinations, and processions. It can also be prayed at other suitable times. The litany is actually composed of two parts. The first part invokes the prayers of a series of saints and holy people; the second part is a series of petitions. The Catholic practice of calling on the saints for assistance is ancient, dating from the earliest Christian times.

KYRIE ELEISON.
Kyrie eleison.
CHRISTE ELEISON.
Christe eleison.
KYRIE ELEISON.
Kyrie eleison.

LORD, HAVE MERCY.
Lord, have mercy.
CHRIST, HAVE MERCY.
Christ, have mercy.
LORD, HAVE MERCY.
Lord, have mercy.

PATER DE CAELIS
  DEUS,
miserere nobis.
FILI REDEMPTOR MUNDI
  DEUS,
miserere nobis.
SPIRITUS SANCTE DEUS,
miserere nobis.
SANCTA TRINITAS, UNUS
  DEUS,
miserere nobis.

GOD THE FATHER OF
  HEAVEN,
have mercy on us.
GOD THE SON, REDEEMER
  OF THE WORLD,
have mercy on us.
GOD THE HOLY SPIRIT,
have mercy on us.
HOLY TRINITY, ONE
  GOD,
have mercy on us.

SANCTA MARIA,	HOLY MARY,
ora pro nobis.	*pray for us.*
SANCTA DEI GENITRIX,	HOLY MOTHER OF GOD,
ora pro nobis.	*pray for us.*
SANCTA VIRGO VIRGINUM,	HOLY VIRGIN OF VIRGINS,
ora pro nobis.	*pray for us.*
SANCTI MICHAEL, GABRIEL ET RAPHAEL,	SAINTS MICHAEL, GABRIEL, AND RAPHAEL,
orate pro nobis.	*pray for us.*
OMNES SANCTI ANGELI,	ALL HOLY ANGELS,
orate pro nobis.	*pray for us.*
SANCTE ABRAHAM,	HOLY ABRAHAM,
ora	*pray*
SANCTE MOYSES,	HOLY MOSES,
ora	*pray*
SANCTE ELIA,	HOLY ELIJAH,
ora	*pray*
SANCTE IOANNES BAPTISTA,	SAINT JOHN THE BAPTIST,
ora	*pray*
SANCTE IOSEPH,	SAINT JOSEPH,
ora	*pray*
OMNES SANCTI PATRIARCHAE ET PROPHETAE,	ALL HOLY PATRIARCHS AND PROPHETS,
orate	*pray*
SANCTI PETRE ET PAULE,	SAINTS PETER AND PAUL,
orate	*pray*
SANCTE ANDREA,	SAINT ANDREW,
ora	*pray*
SANCTI IOANNES ET IACOBE,	SAINTS JAMES AND JOHN,
orate	*pray*

SANCTE THOMA,	SAINT THOMAS,
ora	*pray*
SANCTE MATTHAEE,	SAINT MATTHEW,
ora	*pray*
OMNES SANCTI APOSTOLI,	ALL HOLY APOSTLES,
orate	*pray*
SANCTE LUCA,	SAINT LUKE,
ora	*pray*
SANCTE MARCE,	SAINT MARK,
ora	*pray*
SANCTE BARNABA,	SAINT BARNABAS,
ora	*pray*
SANCTA MARIA MAGDALENA,	SAINT MARY MAGDALENE,
ora	*pray*
OMNES SANCTI DISCIPULI DOMINI,	ALL HOLY DISCIPLES OF THE LORD,
orate	*pray*
SANCTE STEPHANE,	SAINT STEPHEN,
ora	*pray*
SANCTE IGNATI ANTIOCHENE,	SAINT IGNATIUS OF ANTIOCH,
ora	*pray*
SANCTE POLYCARPE,	SAINT POLYCARP,
ora	*pray*
SANCTE IUSTINE,	SAINT JUSTIN,
ora	*pray*
SANCTE LAURENTI,	SAINT LAURENCE,
ora	*pray*
SANCTE CYPRIANE,	SAINT CYPRIAN,
ora	*pray*
SANCTE BONIFATI,	SAINT BONIFACE,
ora	*pray*

SANCTE STANISLAE,	SAINT STANISLAUS,
ora	*pray*
SANCTE THOMA BECKET,	SAINT THOMAS BECKET,
ora	*pray*
SANCTI IOANNES FISHER ET THOMA MORE,	SAINTS JOHN FISHER AND THOMAS MORE,
orate	*pray*
SANCTE PAULE MIKI,	SAINT PAUL MIKI,
ora	*pray*
SANCTI IOANNES DE BREBEUF ET ISAAC JOGUES,	SAINTS JOHN DE BREBEUF AND ISAAC JOGUES,
orate	*pray*
SANCTE PETRE CHANEL,	SAINT PETER CHANEL,
ora	*pray*
SANCTE CAROLE LWANGA,	SAINT CHARLES LWANGA,
ora	*pray*
SANCTAE PERPETUA ET FELICITAS,	SAINTS PERPETUA AND FELICITY,
orate	*pray*
SANCTA AGNES,	SAINT AGNES,
ora	*pray*
SANCTA MARIA GORETTI,	SAINT MARIA GORETTI,
ora	*pray*
OMNES SANCTI MARTYRES,	ALL HOLY MARTYRS,
orate	*pray*
SANCTI LEO ET GREGORI,	SAINTS LEO AND GREGORY,
orate	*pray*
SANCTE AMBROSI,	SAINT AMBROSE,
ora	*pray*
SANCTE HIERONYME,	SAINT JEROME,
ora	*pray*
SANCTE AUGUSTINE,	SAINT AUGUSTINE,
ora	*pray*

SANCTE ATHANASI,	SAINT ATHANASIUS
ora	pray
SANCTI BASILI ET	SAINTS BASIL AND
GREGORI NAZIANZENE,	GREGORY NAZIENZEN,
orate	pray
SANCTE IOANNES	SAINT JOHN
CHRYSOSTOME,	CHRYSOSTOM,
ora	pray
SANCTE MARTINE,	SAINT MARTIN,
ora	pray
SANCTE PATRICI,	SAINT PATRICK,
ora	pray
SANCTI CYRILLE ET	SAINTS CYRIL AND
METHODI,	METHODIUS,
orate	pray
SANCTE CAROLE	SAINT CHARLES
BORROMEO,	BORROMEO,
ora	pray
SANCTE FRANCISCE	SAINT FRANCIS
DE SALES,	DE SALES,
ora	pray
SANCTE PIE DECIME,	SAINT PIUS X,
ora	pray
SANCTE ANTONI,	SAINT ANTHONY,
ora	pray
SANCTE BENEDICTE,	SAINT BENEDICT,
ora	pray
SANCTE BERNARDE,	SAINT BERNARD,
ora	pray
SANCTI FRANCISCE	SAINTS FRANCIS
ET DOMINICE,	AND DOMINIC,
orate	pray

SANCTE THOMA DE AQUINO,	SAINT THOMAS AQUINAS,
ora	*pray*
SANCTE IGNATI DE LOYOLA,	SAINT IGNATIUS OF LOYOLA,
ora	*pray*
SANCTE FRANCISCE XAVIER,	SAINT FRANCIS XAVIER,
ora	*pray*
SANCTE VINCENTI DE PAUL,	SAINT VINCENT DE PAUL,
ora	*pray*
SANCTE IOANNES MARIA VIANNEY,	SAINT JOHN MARY VIANNEY,
ora	*pray*
SANCTE IOANNES BOSCO,	SAINT JOHN BOSCO,
ora	*pray*
SANCTA CATHARINA SENENSIS,	SAINT CATHERINE OF SIENA,
ora	*pray*
SANCTA TERESIA DE AVILA,	SAINT TERESA OF AVILA,
ora	*pray*
SANCTA ROSA DE LIMA,	SAINT ROSE OF LIMA,
ora	*pray*
SANCTE LUDOVICE,	SAINT LOUIS,
ora	*pray*
SANCTA MONICA,	SAINT MONICA
ora	*pray*
SANCTA ELISABETHA HUNGARIAE,	SAINT ELIZABETH OF HUNGARY,
ora	*pray*
OMNES SANCTI ET SANCTAE DEI,	ALL HOLY SAINTS OF GOD,
orate	*pray*

PROPITIUS ESTO,	BE MERCIFUL,
libera nos, Domine.	*Lord, deliver us.*
AB OMNI MALO,	FROM ALL EVIL,
libera nos, Domine.	*Lord, deliver us.*
AB OMNI PECCATO,	FROM ALL SIN,
libera	*Lord, deliver us.*
AB INSIDIIS	FROM THE SNARES
DIABOLI,	OF THE DEVIL,
libera	*Lord, deliver us.*
AB IRA ET ODIO ET OMNI	FROM ANGER, HATE AND
MALA VOLUNTATE,	ALL ILL-WILL,
libera	*Lord, deliver us.*
A MORTE PERPETUA,	FROM EVERLASTING DEATH,
libera	*Lord, deliver us.*
PER INCARNATIONEM TUAM,	BY YOUR INCARNATION,
libera	*Lord, deliver us.*
PER NATIVITATEM TUAM,	BY YOUR NATIVITY,
libera	*Lord, deliver us.*
PER BAPTISMUM ET	BY YOUR BAPTISM AND
SANCTUM IEIUNIUM TUUM,	HOLY FAST,
libera	*Lord, deliver us.*
PER CRUCEM ET	BY YOUR CROSS
PASSIONEM TUAM,	AND PASSION,
libera	*Lord, deliver us.*
PER MORTEM ET	BY YOUR DEATH AND
SEPULTURAM TUAM,	BURIAL,
libera	*Lord, deliver us.*
PER SANCTAM	BY YOUR HOLY
RESURRECTIONEM TUAM,	RESURRECTION,
libera	*Lord, deliver us.*
PER ADMIRABILEM	BY YOUR WONDERFUL
ASCENSIONEM TUAM,	ASCENSION,
libera	*Lord, deliver us.*

PER EFFUSIONEM SPIRITUS SANCTI, *libera*	BY YOUR POURING OUT OF THE HOLY SPIRIT, *Lord, deliver us.*
PER GLORIOSUM ADVENTUM TUUM, *libera*	BY YOUR GLORIOUS SECOND COMING, *Lord, deliver us.*
CHRISTE, FILI DEI VIVI, *miserere nobis.*	CHRIST, SON OF THE LIVING GOD, *have mercy on us.*
QUI IN HUNC MUNDUM VENISTI, *miserere*	WHO CAME INTO THIS WORLD, *have mercy on us.*
QUI IN CRUCE PEPENDISTI, *miserere*	WHO HUNG UPON THE CROSS, *have mercy on us.*
QUI MORTEM PROPTER NOS ACCEPISTI, *miserere*	WHO ACCEPTED DEATH FOR OUR SAKES, *have mercy on us.*
QUI IN SEPULCRO IACUISTI, *miserere*	WHO LAY BURIED IN THE TOMB, *have mercy on us.*
QUI A MORTUIS RESURREXISTI, *miserere*	WHO AROSE FROM DEATH, *have mercy on us.*
QUI IN CAELOS ASCENDISTI, *miserere*	WHO ASCENDED TO HEAVEN, *have mercy on us.*
QUI SPIRITUM SANCTUM IN APOSTOLOS MISISTI, *miserere*	WHO SENT THE HOLY SPIRIT UPON THE APOSTLES, *have mercy on us.*
QUI SEDES	WHO ARE SEATED AT THE

AD DEXTERAM PATRIS, *miserere*	RIGHT HAND OF THE FATHER, *have mercy on us.*
QUI VENTURUS ES IUDICARE VIVOS ET MORTUOS, *miserere*	WHO WILL COME TO JUDGE THE LIVING AND THE DEAD, *have mercy on us.*
UT NOBIS PARCAS, *te rogamus, audi nos.*	THAT YOU MIGHT SPARE US, *we beseech you to hear us.*
UT AD VERAM PAENITENTIAM NOS PERDUCERE DIGNERIS, *te rogamus*	THAT YOU MIGHT DRAW US TO TRUE PENITENCE, *we beseech*
UT NOSMETIPSOS IN TUO SANCTO SERVITIO CONFORTARE ET CONSERVARE DIGNERIS, *te rogamus*	THAT YOU MIGHT CONFIRM US IN YOUR HOLY SERVICE, *we beseech*
UT OMNIBUS BENEFACTORIBUS NOSTRIS SEMPITERNA BONA RETRIBUAS, *te rogamus*	THAT YOU MIGHT GRANT ALL OUR BENEFACTORS ETERNAL REWARD, *we beseech*
UT FRUCTUS TERRAE DARE ET CONSERVARE DIGNERIS, *te rogamus*	THAT YOU MIGHT GRANT US THE FRUITS OF THE EARTH, *we beseech*
UT NOBIS INDULGEAS, *te rogamus*	THAT YOU MIGHT BE PATIENT WITH US, *we beseech*
UT MENTES NOSTRAS AD CAELESTIA DESIDERIA ERIGAS, *te rogamus*	THAT YOU MIGHT LIFT OUR MINDS TO HEAVENLY THINGS, *we beseech*

UT ANIMAS NOSTRAS, FRATRUM, PROPINQUORUM ET BENEFACTORUM NOSTRORUM AB AETERNA DAMNATIONE ERIPIAS, *te rogamus*	THAT YOU MIGHT FREE OUR SOULS, AND THOSE OF OUR NEIGHBORS AND BENEFACTORS FROM ETERNAL DAMNATION, *we beseech*
UT OMNIBUS FIDELIBUS DEFUNCTIS REQUIEM AETERNAM DONARE DIGNERIS, *te rogamus*	THAT YOU MIGHT GIVE REST TO ALL THE FAITHFUL DEPARTED, *we beseech*
UT MUNDUM A PESTE, FAME ET BELLO SERVARE DIGNERIS, *te rogamus*	THAT YOU MIGHT KEEP THE WORLD FROM DISEASE, FAMINE, AND WAR, *we beseech*
UT CUNCTIS POPULIS PACEM ET VERAM CONCORDIAM DONARE DIGNERIS, *te rogamus*	THAT YOU MIGHT GRANT TO ALL PEOPLE PEACE AND TRUE CONCORD, *we beseech*
UT ECCLESIAM TUAM SANCTAM REGERE ET CONSERVARE DIGNERIS, *te rogamus*	THAT YOU MIGHT BE PLEASED TO GOVERN AND KEEP YOUR HOLY CHURCH, *we beseech*
UT DOMNUM APOSTOLICUM ET OMNES ECCLESIASTICOS ORDINES IN SANCTA RELIGIONE CONSERVARE DIGNERIS, *te rogamus*	THAT YOU MIGHT BE PLEASED TO KEEP THE POPE AND ALL IN HOLY ORDERS TRUE IN HOLY RELIGION, *we beseech*
UT OMNIBUS IN CHRISTUM CREDENTIBUS	THAT YOU MIGHT GRANT UNITY TO

UNITATEM LARGIRI
DIGNERIS,
te rogamus
UT OMNES HOMINES AD
EVANGELII LUMEN
PERDUCERE DIGNERIS,
te rogamus, audi nos.

AGNUS DEI,
  QUI TOLLIS
  PECCATA MUNDI,
miserere nobis.
AGNUS DEI,
  QUI TOLLIS
  PECCATA MUNDI,
miserere nobis.
AGNUS DEI,
  QUI TOLLIS
  PECCATA MUNDI,
miserere nobis.

CHRISTE, AUDI NOS.
Christe, audi nos.
CHRISTE, EXAUDI
  NOS.
Christe, exaudi nos.

KYRIE ELEISON.
CHRISTE ELEISON.
KYRIE ELEISON.

Oremus.

Deus, refugium nostrum et
virtus, adesto piis Ecclesiae
tuae precibus, auctor ipse

ALL WHO BELIEVE
IN CHRIST,
we beseech
THAT YOU MIGHT LEAD
ALL PEOPLE TO THE LIGHT
OF THE GOSPEL,
we beseech you to hear us.

LAMB OF GOD,
  YOU TAKE AWAY THE SINS
  OF THE WORLD;
have mercy on us.
LAMB OF GOD,
  YOU TAKE AWAY THE SINS
  OF THE WORLD;
have mercy on us.
LAMB OF GOD,
  YOU TAKE AWAY THE SINS
  OF THE WORLD;
have mercy on us.

CHRIST, HEAR US.
Christ, hear us.
CHRIST, GRACIOUSLY
  HEAR US.
Christ, graciously hear us.

LORD, HAVE MERCY.
CHRIST, HAVE MERCY.
LORD, HAVE MERCY.

Let us pray.

O God, our refuge and
strength, author of all
holiness, hear the holy

pietatis, et praesta, ut,	prayers of your Church,
quod fideliter petimus,	and grant what we
effcaciter consequamur.	faithfully ask. Through
Per Christum Dominum	Christ our Lord.
nostrum. Amen.	Amen.

THE LITANY OF LORETO

The Litany of Loreto, the best-known litany in honor of Mary, is associated with the House of Loreto, a Marian pilgrimage site in Italy. The litany borrows many images from the Old Testament, particularly those involving the manisfestations of God, and applies them to Mary, who is *Theotokos*, the "God-bearer."

KYRIE ELEISON.	LORD, HAVE MERCY.
Kyrie eleison.	*Lord, have mercy.*
CHRISTE ELEISON.	CHRIST, HAVE MERCY.
Christe eleison.	*Christ, have mercy.*
KYRIE ELEISON.	LORD, HAVE MERCY.
Kyrie eleison.	*Lord, have mercy.*

PATER DE CAELIS DEUS,	GOD THE FATHER OF HEAVEN,
miserere nobis.	*have mercy on us.*
FILI REDEMPTOR MUNDI DEUS,	GOD THE SON, REDEEMER OF THE WORLD,
miserere nobis.	*have mercy on us.*
SPIRITUS SANCTE DEUS,	GOD THE HOLY SPIRIT,
miserere nobis.	*have mercy on us.*
SANCTA TRINITAS, UNUS DEUS,	HOLY TRINITY, ONE GOD,
miserere nobis.	*have mercy on us.*

SANCTA MARIA,	HOLY MARY,
ora pro nobis.	*pray for us.*
SANCTA DEI GENITRIX,	HOLY MOTHER OF GOD,
ora pro nobis.	*pray for us.*
SANCTA VIRGO VIRGINUM,	HOLY VIRGIN OF VIRGINS,
ora	*pray*
MATER CHRISTI,	MOTHER OF CHRIST,
ora	*pray*

MATER DIVINAE GRATIAE, *ora*	MOTHER OF DIVINE GRACE, *pray*
MATER PURISSIMA, *ora*	MOTHER MOST PURE, *pray*
MATER CASTISSIMA, *ora*	MOTHER MOST CHASTE, *pray*
MATER INVIOLATA, *ora*	MOTHER INVIOLATE, *pray*
MATER INTEMERATA, *ora*	MOTHER UNDEFILED, *pray*
MATER AMABILIS, *ora*	MOTHER MOST AMIABLE, *pray*
MATER ADMIRABILIS, *ora*	MOTHER MOST ADMIRABLE, *pray*
MATER BONI CONSILII, *ora*	MOTHER OF GOOD COUNSEL, *pray*
MATER CREATORIS, *ora*	MOTHER OF OUR CREATOR, *pray*
MATER SALVATORIS, *ora*	MOTHER OF OUR SAVIOR, *pray*
MATER ECCLESIAE, *ora*	MOTHER OF THE CHURCH, *pray*
MATER FAMILIAE, *ora*	MOTHER OF THE FAMILY, *pray*
VIRGO PRUDENTISSIMA, *ora*	VIRGIN MOST PRUDENT, *pray*
VIRGO VENERANDA, *ora*	VIRGIN MOST VENERABLE, *pray*
VIRGO PRAEDICANDA, *ora*	VIRGIN MOST RENOWNED, *pray*

VIRGO POTENS,	VIRGIN MOST POWERFUL,
ora	*pray*
VIRGO CLEMENS,	VIRGIN MOST MERCIFUL,
ora	*pray*
VIRGO FIDELIS,	VIRGIN MOST FAITHFUL,
ora	*pray*
SPECULUM IUSTITIAE,	MIRROR OF JUSTICE,
ora	*pray*
SEDES SAPIENTIAE,	SEAT OF WISDOM,
ora	*pray*
CAUSA NOSTRAE LAETITIAE,	CAUSE OF OUR JOY,
ora	*pray*
VAS SPIRITUALE,	SPIRITUAL VESSEL,
ora	*pray*
VAS HONORABILE,	VESSEL OF HONOR,
ora	*pray*
VAS INSIGNE DEVOTIONIS,	VESSEL OF SINGULAR DEVOTION,
ora	*pray*
ROSA MYSTICA,	MYSTICAL ROSE,
ora	*pray*
TURRIS DAVIDICA,	TOWER OF DAVID,
ora	*pray*
TURRIS EBURNEA,	TOWER OF IVORY,
ora	*pray*
DOMUS AUREA,	HOUSE OF GOLD,
ora	*pray*
FOEDERIS ARCA,	ARK OF THE COVENANT,
ora	*pray*
IANUA CAELI,	GATE OF HEAVEN,
ora	*pray*
STELLA MATUTINA,	MORNING STAR,
ora	*pray*

SALUS INFIRMORUM,	HEALTH OF THE SICK,
ora	*pray*
REFUGIUM PECCATORUM,	REFUGE OF SINNERS,
ora	*pray*
CONSOLATRIX AFFLICTORUM,	COMFORTER OF THE AFFLICTED,
ora	*pray*
AUXILIUM CHRISTIANORUM,	HELP OF CHRISTIANS,
ora	*pray*
REGINA ANGELORUM,	QUEEN OF ANGELS,
ora	*pray*
REGINA PATRIARCHARUM,	QUEEN OF PATRIARCHS,
ora	*pray*
REGINA PROPHETARUM,	QUEEN OF PROPHETS,
ora	*pray*
REGINA APOSTOLORUM,	QUEEN OF APOSTLES,
ora	*pray*
REGINA MARTYRUM,	QUEEN OF MARTYRS,
ora	*pray*
REGINA CONFESSORUM,	QUEEN OF CONFESSORS,
ora	*pray*
REGINA VIRGINUM,	QUEEN OF VIRGINS,
ora	*pray*
REGINA SANCTORUM OMNIUM,	QUEEN OF ALL SAINTS,
ora	*pray*
REGINA SINE LABE ORIGINALI CONCEPTA,	QUEEN CONCEIVED WITHOUT ORIGINAL SIN,
ora	*pray*
REGINA SACRATISSIMI ROSARII,	QUEEN OF THE MOST HOLY ROSARY,
ora	*pray*

REGINA PACIS,
ora

AGNUS DEI,
QUI TOLLIS
PECCATA MUNDI,
parce nobis, Domine.
AGNUS DEI,
QUI TOLLIS
PECCATA MUNDI,
exaudi nos, Domine.
AGNUS DEI,
QUI TOLLIS
PECCATA MUNDI,
miserere nobis.

CHRISTE, AUDI NOS.
Christe, audi nos.
CHRISTE, EXAUDI
NOS.
Christe, exaudi nos.

CALL: Ora pro nobis,
sancta Dei Genitrix.
RESPONSE: Ut digni
effciamur promissionibus
Christi.

Oremus.

Gratiam tuam, quaesumus,
Domine, mentibus nostris
in-funde: ut qui, Angelo
nuntiante, Christi Filii
tui incarnationem
cognovimus, per

QUEEN OF PEACE,
pray

LAMB OF GOD,
YOU TAKE AWAY THE SINS
OF THE WORLD,
spare us, O Lord.
LAMB OF GOD,
YOU TAKE AWAY THE SINS
OF THE WORLD,
graciously hear us, O Lord.
LAMB OF GOD,
YOU TAKE AWAY THE SINS
OF THE WORLD,
have mercy on us.

CHRIST, HEAR US.
Christ, hear us.
CHRIST, GRACIOUSLY
HEAR US.
Christ, graciously hear us.

CALL: Pray for us, O
holy mother of God.
RESPONSE: That we may
be made worthy of the
promises of Christ.

Let us pray.

Pour forth, we beseech
thee, O Lord, thy grace
into our hearts; that we,
to whom the incarnation
of Christ, thy Son, was made
known by the message of an

passionem eius et crucem ad resurrectionis gloriam perducamur. Per eundem Christum Dominum nostrum. Amen.	angel, may, by his passion and cross, be brought to the glory of his resurrection. Through the same Christ our Lord. Amen.

THE LITANY OF THE SACRED HEART

The Litany of the Sacred Heart is a popular expression of devotion to the Sacred Heart of Jesus (see pp. 573–76). The essence of this devotion is reverence for Jesus' heart as a symbol of God's redemptive love.

LORD, HAVE MERCY.

Lord, have mercy.

CHRIST, HAVE MERCY.

Christ, have mercy.

LORD, HAVE MERCY.

Lord, have mercy.

CHRIST, HEAR US.

Christ, graciously hear us.

GOD THE FATHER OF HEAVEN,

Have mercy on us.

GOD THE SON, REDEEMER OF THE WORLD,

Have mercy on us.

GOD THE HOLY GHOST,

Have mercy on us.

HOLY TRINITY, ONE GOD,

Have mercy on us.

HEART OF JESUS, SON OF THE ETERNAL FATHER,

Have mercy on us.

HEART OF JESUS, FORMED BY THE HOLY GHOST IN THE WOMB OF THE VIRGIN MOTHER,

Have mercy on us.

HEART OF JESUS, UNITED HYPOSTATICALLY TO THE WORD OF GOD,

Have mercy on us.

HEART OF JESUS, INFINITE IN MAJESTY,

Have mercy on us.

HEART OF JESUS, HOLY TEMPLE OF GOD,
Have mercy on us.
HEART OF JESUS, TABERNACLE OF THE MOST HIGH,
Have mercy on us.
HEART OF JESUS, HOUSE OF GOD, AND GATE OF HEAVEN,
Have mercy on us.
HEART OF JESUS, GLOWING FURNACE OF CHARITY,
Have mercy on us.
HEART OF JESUS, ABODE OF JUSTICE AND LOVE,
Have mercy on us.
HEART OF JESUS, FULL OF KINDNESS AND LOVE,
Have mercy on us.
HEART OF JESUS, ABYSS OF ALL VIRTUES,
Have mercy on us.
HEART OF JESUS, MOST WORTHY OF ALL PRAISE,
Have mercy on us.
HEART OF JESUS, KING AND CENTER OF ALL HEARTS,
Have mercy on us.
HEART OF JESUS, WHEREIN ARE ALL THE TREASURE OF
WISDOM AND KNOWLEDGE,
Have mercy on us.
HEART OF JESUS, WHEREIN ABIDES THE FULLNESS OF
THE GODHEAD,
Have mercy on us.
HEART OF JESUS, IN WHICH THE FATHER WAS WELL
PLEASED,
Have mercy on us.
HEART OF JESUS, OF WHOSE FULLNESS WE HAVE ALL
RECEIVED,
Have mercy on us.
HEART OF JESUS, DESIRE OF THE ETERNAL HILLS,
Have mercy on us.

HEART OF JESUS, PATIENT AND ABOUNDING IN MERCY,
Have mercy on us.
HEART OF JESUS, RICH UNTO ALL THAT CALL UPON THEE,
Have mercy on us.
HEART OF JESUS, SOURCE OF LIFE AND HOLINESS,
Have mercy on us.
HEART OF JESUS, ATONEMENT FOR OUR INIQUITIES,
Have mercy on us.
HEART OF JESUS, GLUTTED WITH REPROACHES,
Have mercy on us.
HEART OF JESUS, BRUISED FOR OUR SINS,
Have mercy on us.
HEART OF JESUS, MADE OBEDIENT UNTO DEATH,
Have mercy on us.
HEART OF JESUS, PIERCED BY THE LANCE,
Have mercy on us.
HEART OF JESUS, SOURCE OF ALL CONSOLATION,
Have mercy on us.
HEART OF JESUS, OUR LIFE AND RESURRECTION,
Have mercy on us.
HEART OF JESUS, OUR PEACE AND RECONCILIATION,
Have mercy on us.
HEART OF JESUS, VICTIM OF SIN,
Have mercy on us.
HEART OF JESUS, SALVATION OF ALL WHO TRUST IN THEE,
Have mercy on us.
HEART OF JESUS, HOPE OF ALL WHO DIE IN THEE,
Have mercy on us.
HEART OF JESUS, DELIGHT OF ALL THE SAINTS,
Have mercy on us.

LAMB OF GOD, WHO TAKEST AWAY THE SINS OF
  THE WORLD,
Spare us, O Lord.

LAMB OF GOD, WHO TAKEST AWAY THE SINS OF
THE WORLD,
Graciously hear us, O Lord.
LAMB OF GOD, WHO TAKEST AWAY THE SINS OF
THE WORLD,
Have mercy on us.

CALL: Jesus, meek and humble of heart,
RESPONSE: Make our hearts like unto thy heart.

Let us pray.

Almighty and everlasting God, look upon the heart of thy well-beloved Son, and upon the praise and satisfaction that he rendered to thee on behalf of sinners; and, being thus appeased, grant them the pardon that they seek from thy mercy, in the name of the same Jesus Christ, thy Son, who lives and reigns with thee forever and ever. Amen.

THE GREAT CREEDS

The Apostles' Creed

The Apostles' Creed, with theological roots in the first decades of the Church, expresses basic Christian beliefs in a trinitarian structure. It is widely used in liturgical settings and personal prayers.

I believe in God the Father Almighty, Creator of heaven and earth; and in Jesus Christ his only Son our Lord; who was conceived by the Holy Spirit, born of the Virgin Mary, suffered under Pontius Pilate, was crucified, dead, and buried; he descended into hell; the third day he rose again from the dead; he ascended into heaven, is seated at the right hand of God the Father Almighty; from thence he shall come to judge the living and the dead. I believe in the Holy Spirit; the holy Catholic Church; the communion of saints; the forgiveness of sins; the resurrection of the body; and life everlasting. Amen.

The Nicene Creed

The Nicene Creed was originally formulated by the Council of Nicaea in 325 and affirmed, with modifications, by the Council of Constantinople in 381. It is the basic statement of belief used by both Western and Eastern churches.

I believe in one God, the Father Almighty, Maker of heaven and earth, and of all things visible and invisible. And in one Lord Jesus Christ, the only-begotten Son of God, born of the Father before all ages; God of God; Light of Light; true God; begotten, not made, consubstantial with the Father, by whom all things were made. Who, for us men, and for our salvation, came down from heaven; and was incarnate by the Holy Ghost, of the Virgin Mary; and was made man. He was crucified also for us, suffered under Pontius Pilate, and was buried. And the third day he rose again, according to the scriptures, and ascended into heaven, sitting at the right hand of the Father; and he shall come again with glory, to judge both the living and the dead; of whose kingdom there shall be no end. And I believe in the Holy Ghost, the Lord and giver of life, who proceedeth from the Father and the Son; who together with the Father and the Son is adored and glorified; who spake by the Prophets. And one holy Catholic and Apostolic Church. I confess one baptism for the remission of sins. And I look for the resurrection of the dead, and the life of the world to come. Amen.

The Athanasian Creed

The Athanasian Creed was fashioned in the fifth century in response to controversies about the Incarnation and the relationship between the human and divine natures of Christ. It consists of forty declarations and is divided into two parts. The first part concerns the doctrine of the triune God; the second part addresses the doctrine of the Incarnation and redemption. The condemnation that begins the creed should not be misunderstood. The Church teaches that it applies only to those who willfully and knowingly reject what is contained in the creed. It does not condemn anyone who honestly seeks the truth or has not been taught the faith.

Whosoever will be saved, before all things it is necessary that he hold the Catholic faith. Which faith, except every one do keep entire and inviolate, without doubt he shall perish everlastingly.

Now the Catholic faith is this: that we worship one God in Trinity, and Trinity in Unity. Neither confounding the Persons, nor dividing the Substance. For one is the Person of the Father; another of the Son, another of the Holy Ghost.

But the Godhead of the Father, and of the Son, and of the Holy Ghost, is all one, the glory equal, the majesty coeternal.

Such as the Father is, such is the Son, and such is the Holy Ghost. The Father is uncreated, the Son is uncreated, and the Holy Ghost is uncreated. The Father is incomprehensible, the Son is incomprehensible, and the Holy Ghost is incomprehensible. The Father is eternal, the Son is eternal, and the Holy Ghost is eternal.

And yet they are not three Eternals, but one Eternal. As also they are not three Uncreateds, nor three Incomprehensibles; but one Uncreated and one Incomprehensible. In like manner the Father is Almighty, the Son is Almighty, and the Holy Ghost is Almighty.

And yet they are not three Almighties, but one Almighty. So the Father is God, the Son is God, and the Holy Ghost is God; and yet they are not three Gods, but one God. So likewise the Father is Lord, the Son is Lord, and the Holy Ghost is Lord; and yet they are not three Lords, but one Lord.

For as we are compelled by Christian truth to acknowledge each Person by Himself to be God and Lord: We are forbidden by the Catholic religion to say there are three Gods, or three Lords.

The Father is made of no one, neither created nor begotten. The Son is from the Father alone, neither made nor created, but begotten. The Holy Ghost is from the Father and the Son, not made, nor created, nor begotten, but proceeding.

So there is one Father, not three Fathers; one Son, not three Sons; and one Holy Ghost, not three Holy Ghosts.

And in this Trinity there is nothing before or after, nothing greater or less; but the whole three Persons are coeternal to one another, and coequal. So that in all things, as it hath been already said above, the Unity is to be worshiped in Trinity, and the Trinity in Unity. He, therefore, that would be saved, must thus think of the Trinity.

Furthermore, it is necessary to everlasting salvation, that he also believe rightly the Incarnation of our Lord Jesus Christ. Now the right faith is, that we believe and confess that our Lord Jesus Christ, the Son of God, is both God and Man. He is God of the substance of His Father, begotten before the world; and He is man of the substance of His Mother, born in the world; Perfect God, and perfect man, subsisting of a rational soul and human flesh. Equal to the Father according to His Godhead, and less than the Father according to His manhood. Who, although He be both God and Man, yet He is not two but one Christ. One, not by the conversion of the Godhead into flesh, but by the taking of the manhood unto God. One altogether, not by confusion of substance, but by unity of person. For as the rational soul and the flesh is one man, so God and Man is one Christ.

Who suffered for our salvation, descended to hell, rose again the third day from the dead. He ascended into heaven: He sitteth at the right hand of God the Father Almighty; from thence He shall come to judge the living and the dead. At whose coming all men have to rise again in their bodies, and shall give an account of their own works. And they that have done good shall go into life everlasting; and they that have done evil, into everlasting fire.

This is the Catholic faith, which, except a man believe faithfully and steadfastly, he cannot be saved.

Glory be to the Father, and to the Son, and the Holy Ghost.

As it was in the beginning, is now, and ever shall be, world without end. Amen.

OUR SAVIOR JESUS CHRIST

THE JESUS PSALTER

This prayer is believed to have been composed in the fifteenth century by Richard Whytford, who was a diocesan priest before joining the highly influential Brigittine double monastery of Syon, Middlesex. The Jesus Psalter is featured in many of the early printed primers and was revised by Bishop Challoner (1691–1781).

> *There is no other name under heaven given to men whereby we must be saved.*
>
> *(Acts 4:12)*

FIRST PART

You must begin with a devout kneeling, or bowing, at the adorable name of Jesus, saying:

At the name of Jesus let every knee bow, both in heaven,

560

on earth, and under the earth; and let every tongue acknowledge that the Lord Jesus Christ is in the glory of God the Father.

PHILIPPIANS 2:10–11

—.—

THE FIRST PETITION

Jesus! (repeated ten times) thou God of compassion, have mercy on me, and forgive the many and great offenses I have committed in thy sight. Many have been the follies of my life, and great are the miseries I have deserved for my ingratitude. Have mercy on me, dear Jesus, for I am weak; heal me, O Lord, for I am unable to help myself. Deliver me from an inordinate affection for any of thy creatures, which may divert my eyes from incessantly looking up to thee. For the love of thee, grant me henceforth the grace to hate sin, and, out of a just esteem of thee, to despise all worldly vanities.

Have mercy on all sinners, I beseech thee, dear Jesus: turn their vices into virtues; and making them sincere lovers of thee, and observers of thy law, conduct them to bliss in everlasting glory. For the sake of thy glorious name, Jesus, and through the merits of thy bitter passion, have mercy also on the souls in purgatory. O blessed Trinity, one eternal God, have mercy on me.

Our Father . . .

Hail Mary . . .

—.—

THE SECOND PETITION

Jesus! *(repeated ten times)* help me to overcome all temptations to sin, and the malice of my ghostly enemy. Help me to spend my time in virtuous actions, and in such labors as are acceptable to thee. Enable me to resist and repel every inordinate emotion of sloth, gluttony, and carnality. Render my heart enamored of virtue, and inflamed with desires of thy glorious presence. Help me to merit and preserve a good name by a peaceable and pious life, to thy honor, O Jesus, to my own comfort, and the edification of others.

Have mercy on all sinners . . . *(as in the first petition)*

Our Father . . .

Hail Mary . . .

———•———

THE THIRD PETITION

Jesus! *(repeated ten times)* grant me effectual strength of soul and body, to please thee in the performance of such virtuous actions as may bring me to thy everlasting joy and felicity. Grant me, O merciful Savior, a firm purpose to amend my life, and to make atonement for the years past; those years, which I have lavished, to thy displeasure, in vain or wicked thoughts, evil words, deeds, and habits. Make my heart obedient to thy will, and ready, for thy love, to perform all the works of mercy. Grant me the gifts of the Holy Ghost, which, through a virtuous life, and devout frequenting of thy most holy sacraments, may at length conduct me to thy heavenly kingdom.

Have mercy on all sinners . . .

Our Father . . .

Hail Mary . . .

———•———

THE FOURTH PETITION

Jesus! *(repeated ten times)* comfort me, and grant me grace to fix in thee my chief joy and only felicity; inspire me with heavenly meditations, spiritual sweetness, and fervent desires of thy glory; ravish my soul with the contemplation of heaven, where I hope to dwell everlastingly with thee. Bring thy unspeakable goodness to my frequent recollection, and let me always, with gratitude, remember thy gifts; but when thou bringest the multitude of the sins whereby I have so ungratefully offended thee to sad remembrance, comfort me with the assurance of pardon; and by the spirit of true penance, purging away my guilt, prepare me for the possession of thy heavenly kingdom.

Have mercy on all sinners . . .

Our Father . . .

Hail Mary . . .

THE FIFTH PETITION

Jesus! *(repeated ten times)* make me constant in faith, hope, and charity. Grant me perseverance in virtue, and a resolution never to offend thee. May the memory of thy passion, and of those bitter pains thou didst suffer for my sake, fortify my patience, and refresh my soul under every tribulation and adversity. Render me a strenuous professor of the Catholic faith, and a diligent frequenter of my religious duties. Let me not be blinded by the delights of a deceitful world, nor my fortitude shaken by internal frauds or carnal temptations. My heart has forever fixed its repose in thee, and resolved to have contempt for all things in order to gain thine eternal reward.

Have mercy on all sinners . . .

Our Father . . .

Hail Mary . . .

———•———

*The Lord Jesus Christ, for our sakes, became obedient
unto death, even the death of the cross.*
(Philippians 2:8)

———•———

Hear these petitions, O most merciful Savior, and grant me
the grace frequently to repeat and consider them, that they
may serve as so many easy steps, whereby my soul may
ascend to thy knowledge and love, and to a diligent performance of my duty to thee and my neighbor, through
the whole course of my life. Amen.

Our Father . . .

Hail Mary . . .

I believe in God . . .

———•———

SECOND PART
Begin as before, saying:

At the name of Jesus let every knee bow, both in heaven,
on earth, and under the earth; and let every tongue acknowledge that the Lord Jesus Christ is in the glory of
God the Father.

PHILIPPIANS 2:10–11

———•———

THE SIXTH PETITION
Jesus! *(repeated ten times)* enlighten me with spiritual wisdom, whereby I may arrive at a knowledge of thy good-

ness, and of everything which is most acceptable to thee. Grant me a perfect apprehension of my only good, and a discretion to regulate my life accordingly. Grant me wisely to proceed from virtue to virtue, till at length I enjoy a clear sight of thy glory. Forbid, dear Lord, that I return to the sins of which I accused myself at the tribunal of confession. Let others be edified by my pious example, and my enemies mollified by my good counsel.

Have mercy on all sinners . . .

Our Father . . .

Hail Mary . . .

———•———

THE SEVENTH PETITION

Jesus! *(repeated ten times)* grant me grace inwardly to fear thee, and avoid every occasion whatsoever of offending thee. Let the threats of the torments prepared for sinners, the dread of the loss of thy love, and of thy heavenly inheritance, always keep me in awe. Suffer me not to slumber in sin, but rather rouse me to repentance, lest through thine anger I may be overtaken by the sentence of eternal wrath and endless damnation. Let the powerful intercession of thy blessed Mother and all thy saints, but above all thine own merits and mercy, serve as a rampart between my poor soul and thine avenging justice. Enable me, O my God, to work out my salvation with fear and trembling, and the apprehension of thy sacred judgments. Make me a more humble and diligent suitor to the throne of thy mercy.

Have mercy on all sinners . . .

Our Father . . .

Hail Mary . . .

———•———

THE EIGHTH PETITION

Jesus! *(repeated ten times)* grant me the grace truly to love thee, for thine infinite goodness and those excessive bounties I have received, or shall ever hope to receive from thee. Let the recollection of thy benignity and patience conquer the malice and wretched propensity of my perverse nature. May the consideration of the many deliverances, frequent calls, and continual helps I have received from thee during the course of my life, make me blush at my ingratitude. Ah, what return dost thou require of me for all thy mercies, but that I love thee! And why dost thou require it? Because thou art my only good! thou art my dear Lord! the sole object of my life; and I will diligently keep thy commandments, because I truly love thee.

Have mercy on all sinners . . .

Our Father . . .

Hail Mary . . .

THE NINTH PETITION

Jesus! *(repeated ten times)* grant me the grace always to remember my latter end, and the account I am to give after death; that my soul may be always well disposed, and ready to depart out of this life in thy grace and favor. At that hour, by the powerful intercession of thy blessed Mother, the glorious assistance of St. Michael, and my good angel, rescue my poor soul, O Lord, from the snares of the enemy of my salvation. Remember, then, thy mercy, O dear Jesus, and hide not thy face from me on account of my offenses. Secure me against the terrors of that awful period, by causing me now to die daily to all earthly things, and to have my conversation continually in heaven. Let the remembrance of thy death teach me to set a just value on life, and the memory of thy resurrection encourage me to descend cheerfully to the grave.

Have mercy on all sinners . . .

Our Father . . .

Hail Mary . . .

———•———

THE TENTH PETITION

Jesus! *(repeated ten times)* send me my purgatory in this life, and thus prevent me from being tormented in the cleansing fire, which awaits those souls who have not been suffciently purified in this world. Vouchsafe to grant me those merciful crosses and afflictions which thou seest necessary for weaning my affections from things here below. Suffer not my heart to find any repose but in sighing after thee, since no one can see thee who loves anything which is not for thy sake. Too bitter, alas, will be the anguish of the soul that desires to be united to thee, and whose separation is retarded by the heavy chains of sin. Keep me, then, O my Savior, continually mortified in this world, that being purified thoroughly with the fire of thy love, I may pass from hence to the immediate possession of thee in everlasting glory.

Have mercy on all sinners . . .

Our Father . . .

Hail Mary . . .

———•———

The Lord Jesus Christ, for our sakes, became obedient unto death, even the death of the cross.

(Philippians 2:8)

———•———

Hear these petitions, O most merciful Savior, and grant me the grace frequently to repeat and consider them, that they may serve as so many easy steps, whereby my soul may ascend to thy knowledge and love, and to a diligent performance of my duty to thee and my neighbor, through the whole course of my life. Amen.

Our Father . . .

Hail Mary . . .

I believe in God . . .

———•———

THIRD PART
Begin as before, saying:

At the name of Jesus let every knee bow, both in heaven, on earth, and under the earth; and let every tongue acknowledge that the Lord Jesus Christ is in the glory of God the Father.

PHILIPPIANS 2:10–11

———•———

THE ELEVENTH PETITION

Jesus! *(repeated ten times)* grant me grace to avoid bad company; or, if I should chance to come in the midst of such, preserve me from being infected with the least temptation to mortal sin, through the merits of thine uncorrupt conversation among sinners. Art thou not always present, O Lord? And wilt thou not take an exact account of all our words and actions, and judge us accordingly? How then dare I converse with liars, slanderers, drunkards, or blasphemers; or with those whose discourse is either vain, quarrelsome, or dissolute. Repress in me, dear Jesus, every inordinate affection to carnal pleasures and to delights of taste; and strengthen me by thy grace to avoid such company as would enkindle the flames of those unruly appetites. May thy power, thy wisdom, and thy fatherly compassion defend, direct, and chastise me; and cause me to lead such a life that I may be fit hereafter for the conversation of angels.

Have mercy on all sinners . . .

Our Father . . .

Hail Mary . . .

THE TWELFTH PETITION

Jesus! *(repeated ten times)* grant me the grace to call on thee for help in all my necessities, and frequently to remember thy death and resurrection. Wilt thou be deaf to my cries, Who hast laid down thy life for my ransom? Or canst thou not save me who took it up again for my crown? "Call on me in the day of trouble, and I will deliver thee." Whom have I in heaven but thee, O my Jesus, from whose blessed mouth issued such sweet words? Thou art my sure rock of defense against all my enemies, and my gracious assistant in every good work. I will then invoke thee with confidence in all trials and afflictions, and when thou hearest me, O Jesus, thou wilt have mercy on me.

Have mercy on all sinners . . .

Our Father . . .

Hail Mary . . .

THE THIRTEENTH PETITION

Jesus! *(repeated ten times)* enable me to persevere in a virtuous life, and never to grow weary in thy service till thou rewardest me in thy kingdom. In pious customs, holy duties, and in all honest and necessary employments, continue, O Lord, to strengthen me both in soul and body. My life is nothing on earth but a pilgrimage toward the heavenly Jerusalem, to which he that sits down or turns out of the way can never arrive. May I always, O Jesus, follow thy blessed example. With how much pain and how little pleasure didst thou press on to a bitter death—the assured way to a glorious resurrection. Let me frequently meditate on those severe words of thine: He only that perseveres to the end shall be saved.

Have mercy on all sinners . . .

Our Father . . .

Hail Mary . . .

THE FOURTEENTH PETITION

Jesus! *(repeated ten times)* grant me grace to fix my mind on thee, especially while I converse with thee in time of prayer. Check the wanderings of my fanciful brain, put a stop to the desires of my fickle heart, and suppress the power of my spiritual enemies, who at that time endeavor to withdraw my mind from heavenly thoughts to vain imaginations. Thus shall I joyfully look on thee as my deliverer from all evil, and thank thee as my benefactor, for all the good I have received, or hope to obtain. I shall be convinced that thou art my chief good, and that all other things were ordained by thee only as the means of engaging me to fix my affections on thee alone that by persevering till death in thy love and service, I might be eternally happy. Let all my thoughts, O beloved of my soul, be absorbed in thee, that my eyes being shut to all vain and sinful objects may become worthy to behold thee, face-to-face, in thy everlasting glory.

Have mercy on all sinners . . .

Our Father . . .

Hail Mary . . .

———•———

THE FIFTEENTH PETITION

Jesus! *(repeated ten times)* grant me the grace to order my life with reference to my eternal welfare, sincerely intending, and wisely referring all the operations of my soul and body toward obtaining the reward of thy infinite bliss and eternal felicity. For what use is this world, but a school for the tutoring of souls, created for eternal happiness in the next? And how are they educated but by an anxious desire of enjoying God, their only end? Break my froward spirit, Jesus, by the reins of humility and obedience. Grant me grace to depart hence with the most sovereign contempt for this world, and with a heart overflowing with joy at the thought of going to thee. Let the memory of thy passion make me cheerfully undergo every temptation or suffering in this state of probation, for love of thee; whilst my soul, in the meantime, languishes after that life of consummate bliss and immortal glory, which thou hast prepared for thy servants in heaven. O Jesus, let me frequently and attentively consider, that whatsoever I may gain, if I lose thee, all is lost; and that whatever I may lose, if I obtain thee, all is gained.

Have mercy on all sinners . . .

Our Father . . .

Hail Mary . . .

———•———

The Lord Jesus Christ, for our sakes, became obedient unto death, even the death of the cross.

(Philippians 2:8)

———•———

Hear these petitions, O most merciful Savior, and grant me the grace frequently to repeat and consider them, that they may serve as so many easy steps, whereby my soul may ascend to thy knowledge and love, and to a diligent performance of my duty to thee and my neighbor, through the whole course of my life. Amen.

Our Father . . .

Hail Mary . . .

I believe in God . . .

———•———

THE SACRED HEART OF JESUS

The modern form of devotion to the Sacred Heart of Jesus was developed by St. Margaret Mary Alacoque at Paray-le-Monial, France, in the seventeenth century. Jesus appeared to the nun, showing her his heart and saying, "Behold the heart which has loved mankind so much." This devotion to Christ's mercy and love was in contrast to Jansenism, which emphasized God's terrible wrath and promoted a legalistic code of conduct. Devotion to the Sacred Heart of Jesus remains a popular form of Catholic piety.

Most Holy Heart of Jesus, fountain of every blessing, I adore you, I love you, and with a lively sorrow for my sins, I offer you this poor heart of mine. Make me humble, patient, pure and wholly obedient to your will. Grant, good Jesus, that I may live *in* you and *for* you. Protect me in the midst of danger: comfort me in my afflictions: give me health of body, assistance in my temporal needs, your blessing on all that I do, and the grace of a holy death. Amen.

—— • ——

Stay with me, and then I shall begin to shine as you shine, so to shine as to be a light to others. The light, O Jesus, will be all from you. It will be you who shines through me upon others. Give light to them as well as to me; light them with me, through me. Make me preach you without preaching—not by words, but by my example and by the sympathetic influence, of what I do—by my visible resemblance to your saints, and the evident fullness of the love which my heart bears to yours.

J. H. NEWMAN

—— • ——

Grant, O Sweet Jesus, that in honoring your Sacred Heart, we may learn to practice meekness and humility, obtain the peace you have promised, and find rest for our souls. We beg of you this grace. Amen.

— • —

O heart of Jesus, grant me an increase of faith in you, strong faith to realize you, a loving faith to appreciate you, a trusting faith to turn to you in every want and sorrow. O loving Heart, I commend to you my thoughts, words, and works that you may inspire and guide them, my affections, intentions and desires that you may purify and direct them; my dearly bought soul that you may sanctify and save it; my last sigh that you may receive it united to your own. Amen.

— • —

A prayer of St. Bernard

How good and sweet it is, Jesus, to dwell in your heart! All my thoughts and affections will I sink in the Heart of Jesus, my Lord. I have found the Heart of my king, my brother, my friend, the Heart of my beloved Jesus. And now that I have found your Heart, which is also mine, dear Jesus, I will pray to you. Grant that my prayer may reach you, may find entrance to your Heart. Draw me to yourself. O Jesus, who are infinitely above all beauty and every charm, wash me clean from my defilement; wipe out even the smallest trace of sin. If you, who are all-pure, will purify me, I will be able to make my way into your Heart and dwell there all my life long. There I will learn to know your will, and find the grace to fulfill it. Amen.

— • —

For the pope

O most Sacred Heart of Jesus, pour down abundantly your blessings upon your Church, upon the supreme Pontiff, Pope [N.], and upon all the clergy: give perseverance to the just, convert sinners, enlighten unbelievers, bless our parents, friends and benefactors, help the dying, free the souls in Purgatory, and extend over all hearts the sweet empire of your love. Amen.

To the heart of Jesus in the Eucharist

O most Sacred, most loving Heart of Jesus, thou art concealed in the Holy Eucharist, and thou beatest for us still. Now as then thou sayest, Desiderio desideravi—"With desire I have desired." I worship thee then with all my best love and awe, with my fervent affection, with my most subdued, most resolved will. O my God, when thou dost condescend to allow me to receive thee, to eat and drink thee, and thou for a while dost take up thy abode within me, O make my heart beat with thy Heart. Purify it of all that is earthly, all that is proud and sensual, all that is hard and cruel, of all perversity, of all disorder, of all deadness. So fill it with thee that neither the events of the day nor the circumstances of the time may have power to ruffle it, but that in thy love and thy fear it may have peace.

J. H. NEWMAN

Act of Consecration to the Sacred Heart of Jesus

I, [N.], give myself and consecrate to the Sacred Heart of our Lord Jesus Christ, my person and my life, my actions, pains and sufferings, so that I may be unwilling to make use of any part of my being save to honor, love, and glorify the Sacred Heart. This is my unchanging purpose, namely, to be all his, and to do all things for the love of him, at the same time renouncing with all my heart whatever is displeasing to him. I therefore take you, O Sacred Heart, to be the only object of my love, the guardian of my life, my assurance of salvation, the remedy of my weakness and inconstancy, the atonement for all the faults of my life, and my sure refuge at the hour of death. Be then, O Heart of goodness, my justification before God our Father, and turn away from me his justified anger. O Heart of love, I put all my confidence in you, for I fear everything from my own wickedness and frailty, but I hope for all things from your goodness and bounty. Consume in me all that displeases you or resists your holy will; let your pure love imprint itself so deeply on my heart, that I shall never be able to forget or to be separated from you. May I obtain from your loving kindness the grace of having my name written on your heart, for in you I desire to place all my happiness and all my glory, living and dying in your true service.

ST. MARGARET MARY ALACOQUE

—— • ——

Love of the heart of Jesus, inflame my heart.
Charity of the heart of Jesus, flow into my heart.
Strength of the heart of Jesus, support my heart.
Mercy of the heart of Jesus, pardon my heart.
Patience of the heart of Jesus, grow not weary of my heart.
Kingdom of the heart of Jesus, be in my heart.
Wisdom of the heart of Jesus, teach my heart.
Will of the heart of Jesus, guide my heart.
Zeal of the heart of Jesus, consume my heart.
Immaculate Virgin Mary, pray for me to the heart of Jesus.

ELIZABETH RUTH OBBARD

—— • ——

OUR BLESSED LADY

THE GREAT ANTIPHONS TO OUR LADY

One of these antiphons to our Lady is sung after compline each evening. They are given here with their traditional seasonal applications, together with the appropriate versicles and collects.

From the First Sunday of Advent until February 2

Alma Redemptoris Mater,	Mother of Christ! hear
quae pervia caeli	thou thy people's cry,
Porta manes, et stella	Star of the deep, and portal
maris, succurre cadenti,	of the sky!
Surgere qui curat, populo:	Mother of him who thee
tu quae genuisti,	from nothing made,
Natura mirante, tuum	Sinking we strive, and call
sanctum Genitorem,	to thee for aid.

Virgo prius ac posterius,
  Gabrielis ab ore
Sumens illud Ave,
  peccatorum miserere.

Oh, by that joy which
  Gabriel brought to thee,
Thou Virgin first and last,
  let us thy mercy see.

— • —

Versicle and collect from Advent until Christmas Eve

CALL: Angelus Domini
nuntiavit Mariae.
RESPONSE: Et concepit de
Spiritu Sancto.

CALL: The Angel of the
Lord declared unto Mary.
RESPONSE: And she con-
ceived by the Holy Spirit.

Oremus.

Let us pray.

Gratiam tuam, quaesumus,
Domine, mentibus nostris
infunde: ut qui, Angelo
nuntiante, Christi Filii
tui incarnationem
cognovimus; per passionem
eius et crucem, ad
resurrectionis gloriam
perducamur. Per eundem
Christum Dominum
nostrum. Amen.

Pour forth, we beseech
thee, O Lord, thy grace into
our hearts, that we, to
whom the incarnation of
Christ, thy Son, was made
known by the message of an
angel, may, by his passion
and cross, be brought to
the glory of his resurrection.
Through the same Christ
our Lord. Amen.

— • —

Versicle and collect from Christmas Eve until February 2

CALL: Post partum, Virgo,
inviolata permansisti.
RESPONSE: Dei Genetrix,
intercede pro nobis.

CALL: After childbirth, thou
didst remain a pure virgin.
RESPONSE: O mother of
God, intercede for us.

Oremus.

Let us pray.

Deus, qui salutis aeterne,
beatae Mariae virginitate

O God, who by the fruitful
virginity of Blessed Mary

fecunda, humano generi
praemia praestitisti: tribue,
quaesumus; ut ipsam
pro nobis intercedere
sentiamus,per quam
meruimus auctorem
vitae suscipere, Dominum
nostrum Iesum Christum,
Filium tuum. Amen.

hast given to mankind the
rewards of eternal salvation,
grant, we besech thee, that
we may experience her
intercession for us, by
whom we deserved to
receive the Author of life,
our Lord Jesus Christ, thy
Son. Amen.

Versicle and collect from February 2 until Easter

Ave, Regina caelorum,
Ave, Domina Angelorum:
Salve, radix, salve, porta,
Ex qua mundo lux
est orta:
Gaude,Virgo gloriosa,
Super omnes speciosa,
Vale, o valde decora,
Et pro nobis
Christum
exora.

Hail, O Queen of heaven,
Hail, mistress of the angels,
Hail, root of Jesse,
heaven's gate,
From whom light
dawned on us.
Joy to thee, glorious Virgin,
More beautiful than any other,
Good-night, surpassing
beauty!
Pray for us to Christ.

CALL: Dignare me laudare
te,Virgo sacrata.
RESPONSE: Da mihi
virtutem contra hostes
tuos.

CALL: Grant that I may
praise thee, O Sacred
Virgin.
RESPONSE: Give me
strength against thy foes.

Oremus.

Let us pray.

Concede, misericors Deus,
fragilitati nostrae
praesidium: ut, qui sanctae
Dei Genetricis memoriam

Grant to our weakness,
O merciful God, the help
of thy protection, that we
who commemorate the

agimus; intercessionis eius auxilio, a nostris iniquitatibus resurgamus. Per eundem Christum Dominum nostrum. Amen.	holy mother of God may, aided by her intercession, arise from all our iniquities. Through the same Christ our Lord. Amen.

— • —

Versicle and collect throughout Eastertide

Regina caeli, laetare, alleluia;	Rejoice, O Queen of heaven, alleluia,
Quia quem meruisti portare, alleluia	The Son thou wast found worthy to bear, alleluia,
Resurrexit, sicut dixit, alleluia	Has risen as he said, alleluia.
Ora pro nobis Deum, alleluia.	Pray for us to God, alleluia.
CALL: Gaude et laetare, Virgo Maria, alleluia.	CALL: Rejoice, and be glad, O Virgin Mary, alleluia.
RESPONSE: Quia surrexit Dominus vere, alleluia.	RESPONSE: For the Lord hath risen indeed, alleluia.
Oremus.	Let us pray.
Deus, qui per resurrectionem Filii tui, Domini nostri Iesu Christi, mundum laetificare dignatus es: praesta, quaesumus; ut, per eius Genetricem Virginem Mariam, perpetuae capiamus gaudia vitae. Per eundem Christum Dominum nostrum. Amen.	God who hast brought gladness to the world through the resurrection of thy Son our Lord Jesus Christ, we beseech thee that through his virgin mother Mary we may obtain the joys of everlasting life. Through the same Christ our Lord. Amen.

— • —

Versicle and collect from Trinity Sunday until Advent

Salve, Regina, mater misericordiae; vita, dulcedo, et spes nostra, salve. Ad te clamamus exsules filii Hevae. Ad te suspiramus gementes et flentes in hac lacrimarum valle. Eia ergo, advocata nostra, illos tuos misericordes oculos ad nos converte. Et Iesum, benedictum fructum ventris tui nobis post hoc exsilium ostende. O clemens, o pia, o dulcis Virgo Maria.

CALL: Ora pro nobis, sancta Dei Genetrix.
RESPONSE: Ut digni effciamur promissionibus Christi.

Oremus.

Omnipotens sempiterne Deus, qui gloriosae Virginis Matris Mariae corpus et animam, ut dignum Filii tui habitaculum effci mereretur, Spiritu Sancto cooperante, praeparasti: da, ut, cuius

Hail, holy Queen, mother of mercy; hail, our life, our sweetness and our hope! To thee do we cry, poor banished children of Eve. To thee do we send up our sighs, mourning and weeping in this vale of tears. Turn, then, most gracious advocate, thine eyes of mercy toward us, and after this exile show unto us the blessed fruit of thy womb, Jesus. O clement, O loving, O sweet Virgin Mary!

CALL: Pray for us, holy mother of God.
RESPONSE: That we may be made worthy of the promises of Christ.

Let us pray.

Almighty, everlasting God, who by the cooperation of the Holy Spirit didst prepare the body and soul of the glorious Virgin Mother Mary to become a habitation fit for thy Son, grant that as we rejoice in her commemoration, we

commemoratione	may by her loving
laetamur, eius pia	intercession be delivered
intercessione, ab	from present evils and
instantibus malis et a	from eternal death.
morte perpetua liberemur.	Through the same
Per eundem Christum	Christ our Lord.
Dominum nostrum. Amen.	Amen.

OTHER DEVOTIONS TO OUR LADY

The Memorare

Remember, O most loving Virgin Mary, that it is a thing unheard of that anyone ever had recourse to thy protection, implored thy help, or sought thy intercession, and was left forsaken. Filled, therefore, with confidence in thy goodness, I fly to thee, O Mother, Virgin of Virgins; to thee I come, before thee I stand, a sorrowful sinner. Despise not my words, O Mother of the Word incarnate, but graciously hear and grant my prayer. Amen.

ST. BERNARD

---•---

O Blessed Virgin Mary, unspotted Mother of my God and Savior Jesus Christ, be a mother to me, since your adorable Son has been pleased to call us all his brethren, and to recommend us all to thee in the person of his beloved disciple. Take me and mine under your holy protection, and continually represent to the eternal Father, on our behalf, the merits of the death and passion of your Son, our Savior.

---•---

It is truly right that we bless you, O Theotokos, God-bearer, the ever blessed and most pure Mother of our God: more honored than the Cherubim, and more glorious beyond compare than the Seraphim, for you, undefiled, gave birth to God the Word: therefore we praise you, O true Mother of God.

LITURGY OF ST. JOHN CHRYSOSTOM

---•---

A prayer of St. Aloysius

To thee, O holy Mary, my sovereign Mistress, to thy blessed trust and special charge, and to the bosom of thy mercy, this day and every day, and at the hour of my death I commend myself, my soul and my body: to thee I commit all my hope and all my consolation, my distresses and my miseries, my life and the end thereof; that through thy most holy intercession, and through thy merits, all my works may be directed and disposed, according to thy will and the will of thy Son. Amen.

———— • ————

Blessed art thou, O Mary, for in thee have been accomplished the mysteries and enigmas of the prophets. Thou wast prefigured for Moses in the burning bush, and in the cloud; for Jacob in the heavenly ladder; for David in the ark of the covenant; for Ezekiel in the gate closed and sealed. And now, their mysterious words are realized. Glory be to the Father, who sent his only Son to manifest himself through Mary, deliver us from error and to glorify his memory in heaven and on earth.

BALAI THE CHOREPISCOPOS (FIFTH CENTURY)

———— • ————

Verses in Passiontide

Lady Mary, thy bright crown
    Is no mere crown of majesty;
For with the reflex of his own
    Resplendent thorns Christ circled thee.

The red rose of this Passion-tide
    Doth take a deeper hue from thee,
In the five wounds of Jesus dyed,
    And in thy bleeding thoughts, Mary!

The soldier struck a triple stroke,
    That smote thy Jesus on the tree:
He broke the Heart of Hearts, and broke
    The Saint's and Mother's hearts in thee.

Thy Son went up the angels' ways,
    His passion ended; but, ah me!
Thou found'st the road of further days
    A longer way of Calvary:

On the hard cross of hope deferred
    Thou hung'st in loving agony,
Until the mortal-dreaded word
    Which chills *our* mirth, spake mirth to thee.

The angel Death from this cold tomb
    Of life did roll the stone away;
And he thou barest in thy womb
    Caught thee at last into the day,
Before the living throne of whom
    The lights of Heaven burning pray.

FRANCIS THOMPSON

Hail Mary, daughter of God the Father! Hail Mary, mother of God the Son! Hail Mary, spouse of the Holy Ghost! Hail Mary, temple of the Most Holy Trinity! Hail Mary, my Mistress, my wealth, my mystic rose, Queen of my heart my Mother, my life, my sweetness and my dearest hope! I am all thine, and all that I have is thine, O Virgin blessed above all things. May thy soul be in me to magnify the Lord; may thy spirit be in me to rejoice in God. Place thyself, O faithful Virgin, as a seal upon my heart, that in thee and through thee I may be found faithful to God. Grant, most gracious Virgin, that I may be numbered among those whom thou art pleased to love, to teach and to guide, to favor and to protect as thy children. Grant that with the help of thy love I may despise all earthly consolation and cling to heavenly things, till through the Holy Spirit, thy faithful spouse, and through thee, his faithful spouse, Jesus Christ thy Son be formed within me for the glory of the Father. Amen.

ST. LOUIS MARIE GRIGNION DE MONTFORT

For the assistance of the Blessed Virgin

O rod of Jesse, holy flower of David, most blessed Virgin Mary: thou hast brought forth for us the long-awaited Emmanuel. Thou art the holy city, founded by God himself, O Virgin worthy of all praise, who never hadst, nor ever wilt have, an equal. Truly art thou "blessed among women," who didst bring down from heaven the fruit of life. Thou art, O matchless Virgin, she whom God has laden with all the riches of the universe, the true tree of life, planted in the very midst of Paradise, from whose branches do not hang the fruit of sin, but the food of immortality.

Hail, Queen, clothed with the sun, for whose feet the moon is footstool, whose diadem is set with the stars of heaven! Hail, Mother, than all other mothers more fortunate, in that thou becamest for fallen man the gate of paradise! Hail, glory of heaven, splendor of the kingdom of God, ark of the eternal alliance, first fruit of our regeneration, fairest creature of the hand of God!

More beautiful than the rose art thou, purer than the lily's purity, more spotless than the fallen snow: thou dost shine with greater glory than the radiant sun. Thou art above all angels and all saints. Thou art the child of grace and blessing who hast given the children of Eve eternal life, in giving them thy Son.

O sweet, O loving Mother: to God, thy Son, do thou commend us, for by him thy every prayer is honorable. Obtain for us that while on earth we praise thee, we may by the innocence of our lives please thee, and thus merit to reach heaven, where, for all eternity, in thy glorification, we shall rejoice. Amen.

ST. VENANTIUS

—·—

An ancient hymn to Mary Immaculate

Tota pulchra es, Maria	Thou art all-lovely, O Mary,
Et macula originalis non est in te	and the stain of sin is not found in thee.
Tu gloria Jerusalem	You are the glory of Jerusalem,
Tu laetitia Israel.	
Tu honorificentia populi nostri.	You are the joy of Israel, You are, the greatest honor of our people.
Tu advocata peccatorum	You are the advocate of sinners.
O Maria	
O Maria	O Mary,
Virgo prudentissima	O Mary,
Mater clementissima	Virgin most prudent, Mother most merciful,
Ora pro nobis	Pray for us,
Intercede pro nobis ad Dominum Iesum Christum.	Intercede for us with our Lord Jesus Christ.

—·—

Ane Ballat of Our Lady

In this glorious sixteenth-century Scottish poem, Dunbar would seem to be inventing many of the words, many deriving directly from Latin. So I haven't provided a glossary. Try reading it aloud, if you have any diffculty understanding!

Hale, sterne superne! Hale, in etern,
    In Godis sicht to schyne!
Lucerne in derne for to discerne
    Be glory and grace devyne;
Hodiern, modern, sempitern, ·
    Angelicall regyne!
Our tern inferne for to dispern
    Helpe, rialest rosyne.
        Ave Maria, gracia plena!
    Haile, fresche floure femynyne!
Yerne us, guberne, virgin matern,
    Of reuth baith rute and ryne.

Haile, yhyng, benyng, fresche flurising!
    Haile, Alphais habitakle!
Thy dyng of spring maid us to syng
    Befor his tabernakle;
All thing maling we doune thring,
    Be sicht of his signakle;
Quhilk king us bring unto his ryng,
    Fro dethis dirk umbrakle.
        Ave Maria, gracia plena!
    Haile, moder and maide but makle!
Bricht syng, gladyng our languissing,
    Be micht of thi mirakle.

Haile, bricht be sicht in hevyn on hicht!
    Haile, day sterne orientale!
Our licht most richt, in clud of nycht,
    Our dirknes for to scale:

Hale, wicht in ficht, puttar to flicht
    Of fendis in battale!
Haile, plicht but sicht! Hale, mekle of mycht!
      Haile, glorius Virgin, haile!
          Ave Maria, gracia plena!
      Haile, gentill nychttingale!
Way stricht, cler dicht, to wilsome wicht,
    That irke bene in travale.

Hale, qwene serene! Hale, most amene!
    Haile, hevinlie hie emprys!
Haile, schene unseyne with carnale eyne!
    Haile, ros of paradys!
Haile, clene, bedene, ay till conteyne!
    Haile, fair fresche flour delyce!
Haile, grene daseyne! Haile, fro the splene,
    Of Jhesu genetrice!
          Ave Maria, gracia plena!
    Thow baire-the prince of prys;
Our teyne to meyne, and ga betweyne
    As humile oratrice.

Haile, more decore than of before,
    And swetar be sic sevyne,
Our glore forlore for to restore,
    Sen thow art qwene of hevyn!
Memore of sore, stern in Aurore,
    Lovit with angellis stevyne;
Implore, adore, thow indeflore,
    To mak our oddis evyne.
          Ave Maria, gracia plena!
    With lovingis lowde ellevyn.
Quhill store and hore my youth devore,
    thy name I sall ay nevyne.

Empryce of prys, imperatrice,
    Brycht polist precious stane;
Victrice of vyce, hie genetrice
    Of Jhesu, lord soverayne:
Our wys pavys fra enemys,
    Agane the feyndis trayne;
Oratrice, mediatrice, salvatrice,
    To God gret suffragane!
      Ave Maria, gracia plena!
    Haile, sterne meridiane!
Spyce, flour delice of paradys,
    That baire the gloryus grayne.

Imperiall wall, place palestrall,
    Of peirles pulcritud;
Tryumphale hall, hie trone regall
    Of Godis celsitud;
Hospitall riall, the lord of all
    Thy closet did include;
Bricht ball cristall, ros virginall,
    Fulfillit of angell fude.
      Ave Maria, gracia plena!
    Thy birth has with his blude
Fra fall mortall, originall,
    Us raunsound on the rude.

WILLIAM DUNBAR

O virgin full of all goodness, Mother of Mercy, I recommend to thee my body and my soul, my thoughts, my actions, my life and my death. Obtain for me the grace of loving thy Son my savior Jesus Christ with a true and perfect love, and after him of loving thee with my whole heart.

ST. THOMAS AQUINAS

In Honor of Saints and Angels

In honor of St. Peter

Glorious Saint Peter, in reward for your generous faith, your sincere humility and burning love, you were honored by Jesus Christ with the leadership of the other apostles and the primacy of the whole Church, of which you were made the foundation stone. Obtain for us the grace of lively faith that shall not fear to profess itself openly, fully, and in all its manifestations, even to the giving of blood and life should occasion demand it. May we sacrifice life itself rather than deny our faith. Obtain for us also a sincere attachment to our Holy Mother the Church.

Grant that we may ever keep sincerely and closely united to the Holy Father who is the heir of your authority, and the true, visible head of the Catholic Church. Grant that we may follow the teaching and counsels of the Church. May we be obedient to all her precepts so as to enjoy peace here on earth, and to attain one day eternal happiness in heaven.

TERENCE CARDINAL COOKE

In honor of St. Paul

Glorious St. Paul, from being a persecutor of the Christian name, you became its most zealous apostle. To make Jesus, our Divine Savior, known to the uttermost parts of the

591

earth, you suffered prison, scourging, stoning, shipwreck, and all manner of persecution, and shed the last drop of your blood. Obtain for us the grace to accept the infirmities, sufferings, and misfortunes of this life as favors of the divine mercy. So may we never grow weary of the trials of our exile, but rather show ourselves ever more faithful and fervent. Amen.

TERENCE CARDINAL COOKE

In honor of St. Joseph

St. Joseph, I humbly invoke you and commend myself and all who are dear to me to your intercession. By the love you have for Jesus and Mary do not abandon me during life and assist me at the hour of my death. Loving St. Joseph, faithful follower of Jesus Christ, I raise my heart to you to implore your powerful intercession in obtaining from the heart of Jesus all the graces necessary for my spiritual and temporal welfare, particularly the grace of a happy death. Be my guide, my father and my model through life, that I may merit to die as you did in the arms of Jesus and Mary. Amen.

ELIZABETH RUTH OBBARD

In honor of St. Thérèse of Lisieux

Eternal Father, whose infinite love watches in wisdom over each day of my life; grant me the light to see in sorrow as in joy in trial as in peace, in uncertainty as in confidence, the way your divine providence has marked for me. Give me that faith and trust in your care for me which was so pleasing to you in St. Thérèse of the Child Jesus, and I will walk in darkness as in light, holding your hand

and finding in all the blessings I receive from your loving
bounty that everything is a grace. Amen.

ELIZABETH RUTH OBBARD

Guardian Angels

O sweet angel, to me so dear,
that night and day standeth me near
full lovingly with mild mood,
Thanking, loving, love and praising
Offer for me to Jesu our King,
For his gifts great and good,
As thou goeth betwixt him and me
And knoweth my life in every degree,
Saying it in his presence.
Ask me grace to love him truly,
To serve my lord with heart duly,
With my daily diligence.
Keep me from vice and all perils,
Whilst thou with me daily travels
In this world of wickedness.
Set me my petitions granted,
By thy prayer daily haunted,
If it please thy holiness.

CALL: O sweet Angel that keepeth me,
RESPONSE: Bring me to bliss, I pray thee.

O my Lord Jesu Christ, as it hath pleased thee to assign an
Angel to wait on me daily and nightly with great atten-
dance and diligence, so I beseech thee through his going
betwixt us, that thou cleanse me from vices, clothe me
with virtues, grant me love and grace to come, see, and

have without end thy bliss before thy fair face that liveth and reigneth after thy glorious passion with the Father of heaven, and with the Holy Ghost one God and persons three, without end in bliss. Amen.

FIFTEENTH-CENTURY PROCESSIONAL
OF THE NUNS OF CHESTER

—·—

Angel of God, my guardian dear
To whom God's love commits me here,
Ever this day be at my side
To light and guard, to rule and guide. Amen.

—·—

To the archangel Michael

Holy Michael Archangel, defend us in the day of battle. Be our safeguard against the wickedness and snares of the devil. May God rebuke him, we humbly pray, and do thou, prince of the heavenly host, by the power of God, thrust down to hell Satan and all wicked spirits who wander through the world for the ruin of souls. Amen.

—·—

SUGGESTED SPIRITUAL READING

Writings of the great fathers of the Church (for example, Sts. Augustine, Ambrose, Gregory)

Writings of C. S. Lewis, Thomas Merton, and many others

Biographies of saints

The Cloud of Unknowing★

Crossing the Threshold of Hope (Pope John Paul II)

Dialogue of Comfort in Tribulation★ (St. Thomas More)

Eucharistic Meditations (St. John Vianney)

Holy Wisdom★ (Fr. Augustine Baker)

How to Pray (Fr. Jean-Nicolas Grou)

Imitation of Christ (Thomas à Kempis)

In Conversation with God (Francis Fernandez)

The Interior Castle (St. Teresa of Avila)

Introduction to the Devout Life (St. Francis de Sales)

Letters to Persons in the World (St. Francis de Sales)

The Life of Christ (Fulton Sheen)

Meditations for Layfolk (Bede Jarrett)

Mirror of Charity (St. Ælred of Rivaulx)

Opening to God (Thomas Green)

Revelations of Divine Love★ (Julian of Norwich)

The Sacrament of the Present Moment (Jean de Caussade)

The Scale of Perfection★ (Walter Hilton)

Spiritual Friendship (St. Ælred of Rivaulx)

Spiritual Letters (Dom John Chapman)

Union with God (Abbot Marmion)

★ Take a look inside the covers of these books before you buy them because you may find the language too archaic for your taste. In my opinion it's usually worth persevering, though in most cases you can find modernized versions.

ACKNOWLEDGMENTS

The compiler and publishers are most grateful to all those who have permitted their material to appear in this book. While all efforts have been made to trace copyright owners, apologies are offered to any whose material may have been inadvertently used without permission. Amendments will, of course, be made in future editions. In the references below, the arabic numerals refer to the page, and the roman numerals refer to the position on the page.

Quoted material has been made to conform to American spelling and usage.

From *St. Benedict's Prayer Book,* by permission of Ampleforth Abbey Trustees: 295ii, 296i, 296ii.

From assorted publications of Scepter Publishers: 289iii, 312i, 508i, 509ii, 517ii, 517iii.

From the *Essential Catholic Handbook,* published by Liguori Publications, Liguori, Missouri: 286ii, 287ii, 287v, 294iii, 351i, 380i, 397i, 574iii.

From the *Gold Book of Prayers* copyright © 1989 The Riehle Foundation; all world rights reserved; printed with permission; imprimatur: Most Rev. James H. Garland, auxiliary bishop of the Archdiocese of Cincinnati, February 24, 1989: 276ii, 280i, 337i, 340i.

Prayers from *St. Paul's Prayer Book* reproduced with kind permission of St. Paul's Publishers (U.K.): 259i, 266i, 298i, 344i, 345i, 345ii.

Prayers from *Prayers for Today* by Terence Cardinal Cooke, published by Alba House, with the permission of Society of St. Paul (U.S.): 379i, 379ii, 381i, 385i, 399i, 591i, 591ii.

From the *St. Vincent Prayer Book,* published by John S. Burns & Sons, Glasgow: 573i, 574i, 574ii, 575i, all prayers by Dom Hubert Van Zeller in the Stations of the Cross.

From *201 New Prayers* by Canon Francis Ripley, Print Origination (1989): 529ii.

The Pope's Prayer Book, published by E. J. Dwyer (Australia) Pty Ltd.: 303ii, 338ii, 341ii, 342i, 354i, 384ii, 384iii.

The following are reproduced with permission from *Enchiridion of Indulgences* copyright © 1969 Catholic Book Co., New York, N.Y. All rights reserved: all on pp. 308–11, 390ii.

The following are reproduced with permission from *Catholic Book of Prayers* copyright © 1990, 1982, Catholic Book Co., New York, N.Y. All rights reserved: 283iii, 509i, 524iii.

The following is reproduced with permission from *Treasury of Novenas* copyright © 1986 Catholic Book Co., New York, N.Y. All rights reserved: 285i.

A Walsingham Prayer Book by Elizabeth Ruth Obbard, published by Canterbury Press Norwich and used with permission: 576i, 592i, 592ii.

From *Hymns Ancient and Modern,* published by Canterbury Press Norwich and used with permission: 470ii.

From *The New English Hymnal,* published by Canterbury Press Norwich and used with permission: 267ii, 284i, 290iv, 329ii, 502i.

The following are sources of material believed to be in the public domain:

Traditional: 271ii, 273i, 294i, 297iv, all on pp. 299–300, all on pp. 304–5, 307i, 307ii, 307iii, 307iv, 315iii, O Antiphons on pp. 317–20, 327ii, 329ii, 339ii, 350i, 350ii, 357i, 357ii, all on p. 360, 361i, 361ii, 361iii, 377i, all on pp. 409–12, all on p. 444, 522i, 523i, all on pp. 545–54, all on pp. 577–82, 594i, 594ii.

In common use: all on pp. 445–48.

Manuscripts: 504iii.

Unknown: 348iii, 361iv, all on pp. 506–7, 516iii, 531ii.

The SPCK Book of Christian Prayer SPCK (1995): 278ii.

The Spirit of the Sacred Heart (1891): 259ii, 295i, 301iii, 321ii, 343ii, 511i.

The Poetical Works of St. Robert Southwell, Stewart (1876): 321iii.

Altar Servers' Manual, Burns & Oates (1907): 517i.

John Donne, *The Complete English Poems,* Penguin (1973): 351ii, 363iii.

The Crown of Jesus, Richardson (1862):281ii, 302ii, 303i, 341i, 341iii, 342ii, 343iii, 377i, 377ii, 378i, 378iii, 398i, 399ii, 507i, 520i, 520ii.

Simple Prayer Book, Catholic Truth Society (1891): 525ii.

A Catechism of Christian Doctrine, Catholic Truth Society (1889): 263i, 287i, 287iv.

The Way of Perfection, St. Teresa of Avila, Stanbrook ed. Baker (1925): 264i.

The Primer, Fr. Thurston, Burns, Oates & Washbourne (1923): all on pp. 560–72.

An English Primer of c. 1400, Longmans, Green & Co. (1891): 274i.

A Prayer Book, O'Connell and Martin, Catholic Press, Chicago: 266ii, 267ii, 268ii, 269i, 269ii, 397ii, 404iv, 575ii, 575iii, 584ii, 585i, 587i.

A Medieval Anthology, ed. Mary Segar, Longmans, Green & Co. (1915): 529i.

The Poems of William Dunbar, Faber & Faber (1932): 588i.

The Golden Manual, Burns & Oates (1850): 347i, 393 (alt), 524i, 524ii, 583ii, 584i, all prayers addressed to our Lord in the "Devotions for the Mysteries" section, the "Let us contemplate" introductions in the same section.

The Heart of Thomas More, Burns & Oates (1966): 267i, 343i, 343iii, 525i.

The Stripping of the Altars, Eamon Duffy, Yale University Press (1992): 531i.

These are reproduced from *The Sun Dances* by Alexander Carmichael, published by Floris Books and the Christian Community Press: 256ii, 258i, 306ii, 312iv.

Manual of Prayers, Burns, Oates & Washbourne (1886/1922): 400i, 401i, 401ii, 401iii, 402i, 403i, 403ii, 555i, 555ii, 556i, all prayers by St. Alphonsus in the Stations of the Cross.

Prayers, Verses and Devotions, Cardinal John Henry Newman, Ignatius Press (1989): 292i, 350iii, 352i.

The Raccolta, Burns, Oates & Co. (1873): 473i, 506iv, 507i.

Garden of the Soul, Bishop Challoner, Burns, Oates & Washbourne (c.1930): all prayers by Challoner in the Stations of the Cross, all prayers addressed to our Lady in the "Devotions for the Mysteries" section.

Devotions for Holy Communion, Alban Goodier, Burns & Oates (1909): 269ii, 270i, 487i.

The Rule of St. Benedict, Burns & Oates (c.1892): 289iii.

Gerard Manley Hopkins, Poems and Prose, Penguin (1953): 345iii.

INDEX OF SOURCES, TITLES, AND FIRST LINES

This index lists sources and better-known prayers by title or first line.

INDEX OF SUBJECTS